42.95

JUL 27 1992

✓ SO-ADE-385

NOTICE: Return or renew all Library Materials! The *Minimum* Fee for each Lost Book is $50.00.

The person charging this material is responsible for its return to the library from which it was withdrawn on or before the **Latest Date** stamped below.

Theft, mutilation, and underlining of books are reasons for disciplinary action and may result in dismissal from the University.
To renew call Telephone Center, 333-8400

UNIVERSITY OF ILLINOIS LIBRARY AT URBANA-CHAMPAIGN

JUL 2 9 1992

OCT 0 9 1992

MAY 2 3 1995

APR 2 8 REC'D

DEC 0 3 1998

JAN 0 3 2002

APR 1 2 2002

MAY 0 3 2002

WITHDRAWN
University of
Illinois Library
at Urbana-Champaign

L161—O-1096

POLITICAL MISCHIEF

Political Mischief

SMEAR, SABOTAGE, AND REFORM IN U.S. ELECTIONS

Bruce L. Felknor

New York
Westport, Connecticut
London

Library of Congress Cataloging-in-Publication Data

Felknor, Bruce L.
    Political mischief : smear, sabotage, and reform in U.S. elections /
Bruce L. Felknor.
        p.   cm.
    Includes bibliographical references (p.   ) and index.
    ISBN 0–275–94183–3 (alk. paper)
    1. Electioneering—United States—History.   2. Advertising,
Political—United States—History.   3. Political corruption—United
States—History.   4. Political ethics—United States—History.
5. Libel and slander—United States—History.   I. Title.
JK2281.F44   1992
324.7'0973—dc20   91–22105

British Library Cataloguing in Publication Data is available

Copyright © 1992 by Bruce L. Felknor

All rights reserved. No portion of this book may be
reproduced, by any process or technique, without the
express written consent of the publisher.

Library of Congress Catalog Card Number: 91–22105
ISBN: 0–275–94183–3

First published in 1992

Praeger Publishers, One Madison Avenue, New York, NY 10010
An imprint of Greenwood Publishing Group, Inc.

Printed in the United States of America

The paper used in this book complies with the
Permanent Paper Standard issued by the National
Information Standards Organization (Z39.48–1984).

10 9 8 7 6 5 4 3 2 1

Copyright Acknowledgment

The author and publisher acknowledge with thanks permission to quote from
"Impeachment of a President," by Bruce L. Felknor. Reprinted with
permission from the 1975 *Britannica Book of the Year*, copyright 1975,
Encyclopaedia Britannica, Inc., Chicago, Illinois.

324.70973
F335p
cop. 2

For Charles P. Taft (1903–82)

Contents

Tables

Acknowledgments

I am deeply indebted to many people—no few of them now dead—over many years for what is in this book, and I thank them all most heartily. They are found in several contexts.

First, that of the Fair Campaign Practices Committee (FCPC): Most important, Charles P. Taft, Harry Louis Selden, William Benton, and Anna Lord Strauss. For getting me involved in it (and out of it), and for a wealth of information, ideas, and support over many years, George E. Agree. For generous and underpaid staff support going well beyond the call of duty, Roslyn Hosenball (most especially), Woodruff M. Price, Fred Andrews, Sam Archibald, Rhoda Z. Bernstein, Barbara C. Brown, Leo Frome, Janet Kaufman, Joanna Mudrock, and many volunteers.

In the political science community: Herbert E. Alexander, Totton J. Anderson, Stephen K. Bailey, Hugh A. Bone, Paul David, Alexander Heard, Bernard C. Hennessy (especially), Donald G. Herzberg, Robert J. Huckshorn (especially), Frank H. Jonas, Charles O. Jones, Stanley Kelley, Jr., Evron Kirkpatrick, Arthur L. Peterson, Clinton L. Rossiter, John S. Saloma III, Richard M. Scammon, Paul Seabury, Rhoten A. Smith, Walter De Vries, Alan Westin, and many more.

Among members of Congress, variously for their support for the FCPC and for invaluable political insights and lore: Former Congressmen Thomas B. Curtis (especially), Hale Boggs, John Brademas, Gillis Long, William Steiger, and Charles A. Vanik; and former Senators Clifford Case, Hubert Humphrey, Jacob K. Javits, Thomas H. Kuchel, Herbert H. Lehman, Eugene McCarthy, Gale McGee, George McGovern, Charles E. Percy, Hugh Scott, Margaret Chase Smith, and several dozen others.

Political operatives of one sort or another: John M. Bailey, Sam Brightman (especially), Julius Cahn, James H. Duffy, Creekmore Fath, Meyer Feldman, Robert H. Finch, Ewing Hass, Russell Hemenway, Leonard W. Hall, Kenneth Harding, Albert B. (AB) Hermann, Emmet Hughes, Robert Humphreys, Libby Gatov, Mary Grimes, Howard Jewel, Max Kampelman, Roger Kent, Stewart McClure (especially), Wesley McCune, Sadi J. Mase, Stephen A. Mitchell, Philleo Nash, William R. Peer, Wayne Phillips, William B. Prendergast, George Reedy, Matt Reese, Maurice Rosenblatt (especially), Pierre Salinger, Hal Short, Frederick H. Sontag, Neil Staebler, John G. Stewart, Ted Van Dyk, F. Clifton White, and others for whose omission I apologize.

Journalists: Ben Bagdikian, Homer Bigart, Bruce Biossat, Douglass Cater, John Chancellor, H. L. Coppenbarger, Louis G. Cowan, Roscoe Drummond, George Dugan, Sheldon Engelmayer, Sid Goldberg, William Hill, Palmer Hoyt, Clayton Knowles, Peter Lisagor, Elmer Lower, Jack Mabley, Ralph McGill, Earl Mazo, Sig Mickelson, Arthur Morse, Templeton Peck, Neal R. Peirce, Robert Riggs, Paul Ringler, John Redden, Richard H. Rovere, Thomas N. Schroth, Jerald ter Horst, Paul Veblen, Teddy White, John Wicklein, James Russell Wiggins, and many more.

For assistance in research for this book: Joseph Michalak (early) and Terry Miller of Encyclopaedia Britannica; Martha Sloan of the Deerfield (Ill.) Public Library; William L. (Larry) Bird (especially), Keith Melder, and Wilcomb Washburn of the Smithsonian Institution; and the Donnelley Library of Lake Forest College. For "keyboarding" the text of *Dirty Politics*, from which I adapted perhaps a quarter of the present work, Jeanette McGee-Anyanele.

For the help of others too diverse to classify: Maureen Drummy, for unstinting support, assistance, suggestions, and insights over many years; William N. Cassella, Jr., Robert Coulson, Rev. Thurston Davis, S. J., Tilford (Ted) Dudley, S. Andhil Fineberg, Louis Harris, William J. Harrison, Carl F. H. Henry, Msgr. George G. Higgins, John Howe, Vann M. Kennedy, Dumont Kenny, Msgr. Francis J. Lally, Rita Libin, Isador Lubin, Alice Miller, Newton N. Minow, Noel E. Parmentel, Morton Puner, Alan Reitman, Joseph Roos (especially), Raymond S. Rubinow, Henry Edward Schultz, William C. Sullivan, Edward F. Thomas, Harold R. Tyler, Jr., Mildred (Mim) Vasan (for editorial encouragement, support, and great patience), Paul Felix Warburg, Alfred Willoughby, Paul Ylvisaker, Nick Zapple, and my candidate for Deep Throat, who figures importantly (and anonymously) behind the scenes in a non-Watergate chapter.

Finally, I thank my wife, Edith, who in our FCPC decade cheerfully shared significant economic uncertainty, and who, more recently, graciously put up with this project a lot longer than she bargained for.

Introduction

Great distress has been expressed by broadcast and print journalists, and by many of their listeners, viewers, and readers, over what is seen as a rash of unprecedentedly scurrilous and dishonest electioneering. Yet examination of the historical record demonstrates that the most substantial changes have been in the means of communicating electoral arguments, honest and dishonest alike. Since the essence of political argument is that freedom fundamental to all others, freedom of speech, calls for regulation must be issued with restraint and heard with skepticism. The citizen's most effective armor against smear and slander and distortion is what it has always been: critical analysis of what is said, and especially whether it is true and whether if true it has any reasonable bearing on the job to be filled.

U.S. critics seem most strident about political dirty work as an American phenomenon. But in fact there is nothing distinctively American about it. Contemporary political flim-flam as practiced in, among others, the United Kingdom, France, all of Latin America, Israel, and every other corner of the Middle East would make green with envy the most profligate and unregenerate old pol in North America. And since 1989 once-underground politicians throughout the recently Communist world make clear that newly free polities still in the process of self-creation confront all the same problems. Moreover, they do not blame those woes on U.S. imperialism.

And apart from particular imagery and technology, there is nothing new about the various strains of political mischief. Its elements of deception, demagoguery, and manipulation are amply chronicled in the Old Testament, the Greek and Latin classics, Shakespeare, and ancient as well as modern history.

Why, then, does *American* political chicanery and deceit get such a bad press? Perhaps because of idealism, inattention to history and world affairs, or some other failing so often attributed to American society and education.

But it cannot be improved by scolding the U.S. electorate, or licensing politicians, or raising expectations to U.S. freedom of speech or of the press.

In this connection it is well to remember that not voting may be a rational act for the citizen in any number of situations. A choice that the citizen considers immaterial need not be agonized about. "Either way," or "surprise me," or "oh, I don't know" are not necessarily abdications of responsibility when the subject is elections instead of what to have for dessert. Voters turn out when issues are of urgent importance to them. And they respond to rational political argument—or to argument they take to be rational.

This book focuses on two categories of political mischief. The larger is the attempt to subvert rational argument by deception or by hiding or disguising knowledge and information necessary for voters to make rational decisions. The other is the attempt to deny voters access to the electoral process by discouraging or preventing voting or by making a true count impossible.

A third kind of mischief is addressed only marginally here. That is corrupting the electoral process by the influence of money. Because the entire field of political finance in the United States is studied, analyzed, and reported so thoroughly in the work of the Citizens' Research Foundation, the interested reader is referred to its work, which I discuss only briefly. This book attempts no substantive treatment of the subject.

Here we are concerned primarily with the political arguments of election campaigns, their truth and relevance to the office or issue around which they revolve, and the means by which those arguments are offered to the voter. These are the real heart and substance of electoral politics. Ironically, they have received almost none of the careful observation and analysis lavished on raising and spending the money to pay for them. Underlying that irony, however, is a simple fact: All participants have long agreed on a standard of measurement for money. There is no dollar sign by which the truth and relevance of political argument can be counted.

Government has a role in regulating the process of voting and counting votes, and it can plausibly seek to prevent cheating in those categories. It can even claim some general success at doing so, interrupted sporadically by some of the rascally devices cited in these pages.

But as to the campaign itself, the communication and exchange of political ideas that will culminate in a vote, government cannot prevent dishonest electioneering. Only the intelligent voter with a healthy skepticism can accomplish that. The objective of this book is to supply a perspective on the U.S. political system and—money apart—the varieties of political mischief, and to put them in proportion, to help skeptical voters and other interested observers make sense out of a collection of phenomena that sometimes seem to make no sense at all.

Additional information about the political video materials discussed in this book can be located in note 2 for Chapter 3. Sources for these videos are cited in the text by identifying the subject and year in brackets (for example, [Benton of Connecticut 1950]). The "Political Television Ads" section of the Bibliography gives specific information for these references.

Many of the significant episodes of political mischief addressed herein are examined from different perspectives and at different locations in the book. To simplify tracking them down, I have included an Index of Mischief after the General Index. This will allow the reader to locate incidents by the various elements of mischief as well as by particular campaigns. The Index of Mischief is in sections devoted, respectively, to Invective and Accusations, Tactics, Special Media, Techniques, and Elections in Which Political Mischief Was Significant.

Part I

The Matrix of Political Mischief

In our concern with political mischief in American election campaigns, we need first to understand the universe in which the florid accusations and deceptions and chicanery go on. And, in order to realize that mischief in elections is as old as elections, we must know something of the history of both.

Suppose a time machine delivered John Adams, Thomas Jefferson, Andrew Jackson, Abraham Lincoln, and Teddy Roosevelt to your family room some October evening in an even-numbered year. Vitriolic campaign commercials are blaring from the TV.

Your visitors marvel at the black box, but all of them grasp instantly what is going on. Every one of them has been there before.

The substance of campaign propaganda—advocacy and attack—has not changed in centuries. Campaign advertising is among the artifacts that survived the extinction of Pompeii in A.D. 79. But the environment in which election campaigns are conducted—number of offices to be filled, qualifications for office, the process of selecting candidates, frequency of elections, scope of the franchise, mechanics of voting and counting, and so on—has changed more or less continuously throughout American history. Every such change necessarily affected various aspects of the electoral system, including the campaign itself. Meanwhile, the march of technology has worked its effects on each of these elements, most of all on the means of disseminating campaign arguments.

The three chapters of Part I will consider the origins and evolution of these principal elements of electioneering: the selection of candidates and the role of the party in it (Chapter 1); the development of the election campaign and campaign management and marketing (Chapter 2); and drawing attention to the deficiencies of opposition candidates, that is, negative campaigning (Chapter 3).

1

The Nominating Process: Finding Someone to Run

American colonists were electing delegates to various local and provincial offices long before the idea of independence from Britain gained any currency. Usually candidates for such offices were proposed by informal assemblies of local elders. At least by the 1720s, many of these candidate-selection sessions were called caucuses, or contemporary variations on what became that word.

CAUCUS: THE SMOKE-FILLED ROOM

However spelled, the caucus probably originated as the name of a Boston political club or clubs early in the eighteenth century. "Caucus" may or may not derive from an Algonquian word, *caucausu*, meaning an advisor, or from an obscure Latin borrowing from a Greek word for drinking vessel, *kaukos*. In 1763 John Adams wrote in Boston of learning

that the Caucas Clubb meets at certain Times in the Garret of Tom Daws [where] they smoke tobacco till you cannot see from one End of the Garrett to the other. There they drink Phlipp I suppose, and there...select Men, Assessors, Collectors, Wardens, Fire Wards, and Representatives are Regularly chosen before they are chosen in the Town. (Adams 1961, 1:238)

Elsewhere Adams spelled the word "caucass," but these versions were rendered as caucus in his grandson Charles Francis Adams's edition of the second president's papers. Other of John Adams's contemporaries wrote it as Caulkers, supposing the meetings to have occurred in a place where ship-related business went on. We know that there were several Boston caucuses, and in the 1740s one such meeting was known as the West-Corcus. However spelled, the term spread from Boston across the colonies, and if Americans did not know its origin they clearly understood its purpose.

By the time the Constitutional Convention established elections to the U.S. House of Representatives, the caucus was solidly established as a nominating procedure. Although there was discussion of various alternative ways of electing representatives, finally the choice was left to "the people of the several States." A means of pre-selecting candidates was neither discussed nor prescribed, but left, tacitly, to that long-standing informal institution on the American political scene, the caucus.

Unlike the parliamentary system, whose chief executive is first elected to Parliament and then elevated by that body, the American presidential system requires some regular means to select presidential candidates. Washington was an obvious and unanimous choice, and when he refused to seek a third term in 1796, he precipitated the first contested presidential election. The Federalists in Congress met in a caucus to pick a candidate, and a new group crystallizing against them, the embryonic Anti-Federalists, did so, too.

THE NOMINATING CONVENTION

This worked for a dozen years, but as the election of 1808 approached the waning Federalists had gone into their terminal decline. There were too few of them left in Congress to presume to speak for the Federalists in the country at large, so the party's leaders in and out of Congress got together on the outside to settle on candidates. This variation on the caucus amounted to a secret national convention, called outside the Congress expressly to pick a presidential candidate. The Federalists lost in 1808 with Charles Pinckney. They kept losing, and the party went under. But they had invented a presidential nominating convention outside the halls—and control—of Congress.

The Federalists disappeared because their focus and appeal was too narrow, like those of later short-lived quasi-parties whose bones litter the American political landscape. The Whigs, Anti-Masons, Abolitionists, Free-Soilers, Greenbackers, Populists, La Follette Progressives, Henry Wallace Progressives, Dixiecrats, a welter of left- and right-wing parties, a miscellany of bigots and maniacs posing as parties—all these and more were to greater or lesser degree one-idea, ideologically based parties, and they have not thrived as political parties in the American climate. They had more in common with modern single-issue reformist and advocacy groups than with any broad-based political party per se.

The First Durable Party: The Democrats

The first durable U.S. party emerged as a loose consensus group, the Anti-Federalists. They grew rapidly and, reflecting their admiration for the anti-monarchical ideals of the French Revolution, took up the name Republican.

They elected Jefferson in 1800, then Madison and Monroe. By the 1820s, they had become the Democratic Republican Party.

After the election of Andrew Jackson in 1828, the party, its base much broadened and its emphasis increasingly populist, pruned its name to simply the Democratic Party, which persists today as the oldest political party on Earth. But hostility to "King Andrew" stirred several currents in U.S. politics and spawned two short-lived parties that had important consequences.

The Anti-Masons: The Convention Goes Public

In the late 1820s, there was a flurry of agitation over the secret rites of the Masonic Order, to which Jackson belonged. Out of this grew the Anti-Mason Party, which spread across the country and elected many state and local officials in its short career. In 1831 it set out to run a presidential candidate.

Lacking a congressional presence, and given their built-in antagonism to secrecy and secret conventions, the Anti-Masons went the dead Federalists one better and called a public nominating convention in Baltimore in 1831. It selected William Wirt to oppose Jackson in 1832, but the effort was fruitless. The lasting legacy of the Anti-Masons was the public nominating convention, which immediately became the norm and which, much modified, functions to this day.

Other antagonisms to Jackson propelled such early nineteenth-century political leaders as John Quincy Adams and Henry Clay out of the Republican Party and into a new group styling itself National Republicans. This combination also attracted Daniel Webster and other ex-Federalists. With an eye to the British Whigs and their distaste for the trappings of royalty, they became the Whig Party, to which we owe what has been called the first modern campaign.

In the 1836 election the Whigs were not far enough advanced to manage a national convention. But they did nominate three candidates in sectional caucuses, hoping they might take enough votes from Jackson's vice president and designated successor, Martin Van Buren, to throw the election into the House of Representatives, where they were reasonably confident they could cut a deal.

Van Buren and Richard M. Johnson won decisively, but of the Whigs, William Henry Harrison did far better than the other two, Daniel Webster of New Hampshire and Hugh White of Tennessee. Thus Harrison was the logical Whig candidate for the next time around.

The Whigs and the First Modern Campaign

If the Democrats evolved into the first long-lived modern political party and the Anti-Masons pioneered the modern party convention, the Whig Party in 1840 managed the first modern election campaign.

What was modern about it was its emphasis on color, bombast, and excitement and the fact that a presidential candidate—Harrison—would make some stump speeches of his own instead of relying entirely on supporters to rally the faithful with their oratory.

There had been some parading and use of symbol in the 1832 campaign that reelected Andrew Jackson. Torchlight paraders carried and "planted" in the ground tall hickory poles marking their support of Old Hickory against the wealth and wishes of the Bank of the United States. But this kind of hoopla was vastly multiplied by the Whigs in 1840.

Harrison had led troops against rebellious Shawnee Indians in the Battle of Tippecanoe, where in 1811 he eked out a costly victory over a force led by Tenskwatawa, a brother of the great chief Tecumseh. He had been a general in the War of 1812, first governor of the Indiana Territory, and a U.S. senator and representative from Ohio. He had been touted as a military hero in his losing campaign of 1836, but now the Whigs pulled out all the stops for Old Tippecanoe.

In the remarkably rowdy 1840 campaign, the Whigs not only glorified Harrison's small-beer military record, they converted their aristocratic gentleman farmer into a simple rustic, and represented his home as a humble log cabin instead of his actual elegant manse.

In fairness to the Whigs, the idea was an unwitting gift from the Democrats. In December 1839 the *Baltimore Republican*, a Democratic paper, undertook to deflate Harrison's record of military and government service, and painted him as an aging and idle country dreamer. "Give him a barrel of hard cider and a pension of two thousand a year, and, our word for it, he will sit the remainder of his days in a log cabin by the side of a 'sea coal' fire and study moral philosophy" (Elliott 1883, 120).

Whig papers righteously denounced this slur on their gallant general, but a pair of imaginative Whig activists pounced on it as a theme to rally the multitudes to Harrison. In January an old Pennsylvania banker named Thomas Elder huddled with a young Harrisburg editor, Richard S. Elliott, and suggested commandeering the rustic image for their candidate. Elder proposed that they actually "build a cabin, or something of that kind." Over Elder's "excellent Madeira" Elliott fleshed out his idea as a design for a huge transparency showing

an imaginary log-cabin with a coon-skin tacked on it, an outside chimney of sticks and mud, a wood-pile consisting of a log with an ax stuck in it, and other accessories; and on taking leave I told him I would try to put his idea into operation. . . . Next day I had a carriage painter confidentially at work on a transparency.

This was previewed, to enthusiastic acclaim, at a mass meeting in Harrisburg on January 20, and two days later "a state mass convention assembled at Columbus, Ohio, at which log cabins on wheels appeared in the grand procession" (Elliott 1883, 121–25).

Political parades were the order of the day—and, by torchlight, of the night as well. The Whig managers went beyond mere transparencies and built log cabins large and small. Teams of husky marchers carried them on poles in the parades and set them up along roadsides, complete with barrels from which they dished out hard cider to the thirsty multitudes. Many were built on wagons. A Chicago contingent to a Whig assembly in Springfield hauled its log cabin behind thirty yoke of oxen. It was complete with a live hickory tree, with live raccoons climbing in it, and a barrel of hard cider (Sandburg 1926, 1:247). Interestingly, the Whigs' hickory tree evoked thoughts of Van Buren's predecessor and patron, the Democratic hero, "Old Hickory" Jackson, while the raccoons reminded some of the "sly old coon" of the Whigs, Henry Clay, whom Harrison defeated for the nomination.

Whether or not they are deemed silly, or even false, these were positive arguments, presenting Harrison as a man of the people, whom the people could trust. There was also room in the campaign for the negative.

The Democrats' candidate was "Van, Van, the used up man," as Harrison's Whig paraders chanted. If the Whig campaign had a theme besides Harrison as a backwoods war hero, it was deriding the opulent life of the effete Van Buren. Whig journals and legislators in sarcastic oratory painted the president as even more diminutive and elegant than he already was and labeled him an extravagant pretender after royalty, mocking his "pretty, tapering, soft, white, lily fingers" and his little "foreign Fanny Kemble green finger cups" in which to wash them. "Even his chamber pot cost two dollars."[1]

Horace Greeley, then a bright young editor on the eve of founding the *New York Tribune*, was an ardent Whig. He threw himself into the campaign, establishing and editing a pro-Harrison weekly, the *Log Cabin*. Its first issue described the candidate—utterly fraudulently—as "a rough, old farmer in homespun." Greeley said Van Buren was "a promoter of class war and an enemy of the Christian religion."

Each week the back page featured new Whig campaign songs, many of which Greeley wrote himself and set to popular tunes (Van Deusen 1953, 44). The songs were all the rage, and they helped build the illusions, both negative and positive.

> Let Van from his coolers of silver drink wine,
>   And lounge on his cushioned settee;
> Our man on his buckeye bench can recline,
>   Content with hard cider is he.
> Then a shout from each freeman, a shout from each state,
>   To the plain, honest husbandman true,

And this be our motto—the motto of Fate—
"Hurrah for Old Tippecanoe!" (McMaster 1906, 6:584n)

When Maine, voting early, picked a previously defeated Whig, Edward Kent, for governor, along with ten electors for Harrison and Tyler, a new verse was added to what was already the most famous campaign song, and the whole appeared on the back page of the *Log Cabin*:

Oh, have you heard the news from Maine, Maine, Maine
   All honest and true?
For Governor, Kent, and six thousand gain
   For Tippecanoe, and Tyler too.
And with them we'll beat little Van.
Van, Van, Van is a used up man,
And with them we'll beat little Van. (Greeley, September 26, 1840, 1:22)

The feckless President Van Buren and his supporters tried to retaliate as best they could, but to no avail. They sought vainly to point out that their vice-presidential candidate was a bona fide military hero, who had been hand-picked in 1836 by the great and genuine hero Andrew Jackson. Johnson had been a brilliant cavalry commander who did slay a Shawnee chief in battle, and it may or may not have been Tecumseh, who, in fact, was killed in that fight.

This the Democrats proclaimed in their own torchlight parades, chanting the inane ditty,

Rumpsey Dumpsey, Rumpsey Dumpsey,
Colonel Johnson killed Tecumseh!

But this and similar efforts were all to no avail. For "Tippecanoe and Tyler too" the Whigs had beguiled or bamboozled enough voters to beat Little Van and Colonel Johnson. The songs were important. James Schouler said Harrison was sung into office (1889–99, v. 4). "History has truthfully characterized the campaign as pure humbug," wrote a later critic (Stoddard 1946, 53).

Indeed, some of the participants acknowledged as much. The Harrisburg editor, Richard S. Elliott, who concocted Pennsylvania's Log Cabin campaign with Thomas Elder, said Elder's view was that "passion and prejudice, properly aroused and directed, would do about as well as principle and reason in a party contest" (Elliott 1883, 120–21).

But alas for the triumphant Whigs: Their conquering hero, Harrison, died a month after his inauguration. His successor, Vice President John Tyler, was a fallen-away Democrat who undid much of the Whig agenda. After electing one more president, Zachary Taylor in 1848, the Whigs' influence waned rapidly, and for all practical purposes they were dead when Taylor left the White House in 1853.

The Republicans Pick Up the Pieces

At once, on the eve of the Civil War, another coalition of interests arose to absorb the remnants of the Whigs. Along with some disaffected Democrats and Free-Soilers, the new group set up shop in 1854 as the Republican Party. Its appeal was broad, especially in the North, and immediate.

The first Republican presidential candidate, John C. Frémont, lost to the Democrat James C. Buchanan in 1856. But the new party won an Electoral College landslide for Abraham Lincoln in 1860, and the Republicans began a seventy-two-year reign interrupted only by Grover Cleveland and Woodrow Wilson. In other words, the Grand Old Party (GOP), as the Republicans came to be known in the Cleveland-Harrison campaign of 1888, won fourteen of the eighteen presidential elections between Buchanan and Franklin Roosevelt. They had fashioned an appeal broad enough to preempt parts of the national consensus that the Democrats had monopolized. But these inroads, particularly in the North, were not without price. Many Northern Democrats were sympathetic toward the seceding states, and their pejorative wartime labeling as Copperheads—by War Democrats as well as Republicans—poisoned American political waters for a generation or more.

REFORMING THE NOMINATING PROCESS

The Republican dominance of the national agenda ushered in a golden age of financial and political corruption as well as one-party rule and led inevitably to a welter of reform movements, even within the GOP. By the second decade of the twentieth century, Republican and Progressive reformers of the general stripe of Theodore Roosevelt, and populist supporters of Democrat William Jennings Bryan and others, were strongly influencing U.S. electoral politics.

One of their most far-reaching creations was the primary election. They hoped it would be a wholesome way to snatch politics away from corrupt politicians and get it into the hands of the whole electorate. It was a noble experiment, as well motivated as Prohibition, but hardier. Its success has contributed importantly to the decline and change of the two-party system in America.

The Primary Election

Primaries fall into two classes: *direct or indirect* and *open or closed.* In the direct primary voters select the party's nominees for a coming general election. The indirect primary selects delegates to a party convention or caucus, which will do the nominating. Depending on state or party rules, the delegates may be bound (required to vote for the candidate whom they espouse) or unbound (free to use their own judgment). The indirect primary also may elect members of the party's governing body.

The open primary, anathema to every politician of the old school, allows any registered voter to participate. A Republican may vote in a Democratic primary to pick that party's candidates, and vice versa. However, a voter may participate in only one party's primary in a given election year. The objectives of the open primary are to give unaligned voters a voice in selecting candidates for the coming general election and to protect them from manipulation and intimidation by party bosses. The closed primary requires the voter to prove (or declare) affiliation with that party. Its objectives are to give party voters a voice in the nominating process and to protect the process from meddling by members of the opposition.

The first primary election is believed to have been held in 1842 by the Democrats of Crawford County, in northwestern Pennsylvania. After sporadic use here and there, Wisconsin's reformist Governor Robert M. La Follette made it part of his Progressive movement in 1903. He easily persuaded his legislature to enact the first statewide primary law, and the idea swept the country.

Non-Partisan Elections. An ancillary reform, another legacy of the Progressive movement, was the adoption of nonpartisan local elections, which are proffered regularly under the guise of civic virtue in many American communities. A small caucus of concerned citizens usually picks a single qualified candidate for each office, operating completely outside party concerns or identification, and the candidate runs unopposed.

This scheme offers less actual choice than pre-1990 elections in the Soviet bloc, where a voter could pick "none of the above" by crossing out the name of the only candidate on the ballot, the Communist Party's choice. Xandra Kayden and Eddie Mahe, Jr., in *The Party Goes On* (1985, 41), point out that this nonpartisan election reform really is a massive attack on the political parties themselves, which the Progressives found so sinister.

Along with the Great Depression, Franklin Roosevelt and the New Deal wrecked the long suzerainty of the GOP, and by the time Republicans found their way back to the White House for longer than the Eisenhower interlude of 1953–61, the Democrats had become the more or less permanent congressional party, although after 1968 the Republicans again had a firm grip on the executive branch. What handed it to them was the self-destruct mode in which the Democrats addressed the Vietnam War and the revolutions of youth, sex, confidence, and drugs in the waning years of Lyndon Johnson's presidency. In terms of domestic U.S. politics, the dislocations accompanying World War II were trivial compared to those of the single election year of 1968.

The Furies of 1968: Reforming the Parties

"The furies in the street" is the epithet Theodore H. White applied to the implacable forces of militant youth that savaged the Democratic National Convention of 1968. Chicago "became the title of an episode," he wrote in *The Making of the President 1968*, "like Waterloo, or Versailles, or Munich. At Chicago, for the first time, the most delicate process of American politics was ruptured by violence, the selection of Presidents stained with blood" (White 1969, 257).

The disruption of the 1968 convention set in motion a monumental restructuring of the Democratic Party, a massive and completely unprecedented reform from within. After Hubert Humphrey's narrow defeat in November, the new national party chairman named Senator George McGovern to head a commission to study the debacle and propose changes. McGovern, a former political science teacher, had been instrumental in reviving the Democratic Party in South Dakota.

The guidelines eventually adopted were mandatory and stringent. Women, young people, and members of minority groups were to be represented in the party approximately as in the population. No party meeting could be convened without a quorum of 40 percent. Delegate selection rules had to be written and publicized. State party committees could select no more than 10 percent of total convention delegates, and there would be no ex-officio delegates. Power was stripped from the old pols and handed over to the people. Moreover, all—including the implementation of these Draconian measures—was to be done in the open, under the pitiless glare of the television lights.

It was a reformer's dream. It opened the 1972 convention to new voices and faces and closed it to many of the party's old pros. But it soon drove hosts of conservative and reactionary Democrats out of the party. (After the presidential defeats of 1972 and 1980, some of the more radical reforms were modified.)

The Republicans convened a review commission but proposed no dramatic changes. The party had already undergone some degree of renewal. In 1965 the GOP chairman, Ray Bliss, introduced a number of changes to integrate the 1964 flood of Goldwaterites into the party structure. Bliss, who had been Ohio's state party chairman, brought a new emphasis on professional staff, fund-raising by the national committee instead of state party committees, and a reorganization of local party structures. Before many years both parties' national committees were soliciting their own funds and, in a reversal of the traditional practice, supplying money to state committees instead of dunning them for national support.

Any presidential candidate, through his personal organization, calls the shots for his own campaign. But Richard Nixon's strategic control of his own reelection campaign for 1972 was historic. Indeed, he commented in a television interview the year before, "When I am the candidate, I run the campaign." In order to attract Democratic votes, he distanced the presidential campaign from the Republican Party. No party name or emblematic elephant appeared on campaign advertising. Furthermore, he insisted that the GOP not even campaign against thirty or more Democrats in Congress who had been friendly to his legislative initiatives.

However, when this downgrading of party combined with the eventual eruption of the Watergate Scandal (see Chapter 12), the net effect was a one-two punch for the Republicans' congressional delegation, which lost forty-seven members in the 1974 elections. This effect might have been even more drastic but for the existence of special committees in both parties that are concerned exclusively with congressional elections. These are the House and Senate campaign committees.

CONGRESSIONAL CAMPAIGN COMMITTEES

Whatever the ties of shared party label and political and socioeconomic outlook, the timetable and agenda for congressional candidates differ from those driving the presidential hopefuls of both parties. In 1866 these differences led Republican House members to establish what now is the National Republican Congressional Committee. The older party followed suit with its Democratic Congressional Campaign Committee in 1882. Both set up comparable bodies for the Senate in 1916, the National Republican Senatorial Committee and the Democratic Senatorial Campaign Committee.

These bodies are active in direct mail fund-raising for candidates. In varying degree, they help recruit and advise candidates. Both run training programs for inexperienced candidates. The Democratic Congressional Campaign Committee, for example, has pulled together sample reels of "generic" negative television commercials, demonstrating how to focus hard-hitting TV attacks on a chink in the opponent's armor. The Republican National Committee has prepared, for both House and Senate candidates, sample TV-spot responses to hard-hitting TV ads by Democrats.

In addition, to some extent, though not as much as in earlier years, the congressional campaign committees provide tactical assistance to their respective hopefuls. From time to time the campaign exploits of the professionals on these and national committee staffs have stirred great brouhahas in various campaigns, as may be seen in later chapters.

The Specter of Further Reform

Both parties were affected by the steadily increasing influence of primary elections at the expense of the traditional importance of the nominating conventions. Presidential preference primaries, which pick convention delegates, grew in their fascination for the news media after World War II. And as broadcast journalism developed, it began to give stellar attention to New Hampshire's February primary, which came to mark the start of a presidential election year.

Modern reformers have put forward many proposals for a nationwide presidential primary to nominate the candidates of both parties, but practitioners, scholars, and journalists of politics have been almost unanimous in rejecting the idea. The mix of primary results, associated opinion polling, and delegates' actions somehow add up to what the *Washington Post*'s David Broder has called a "web of influences at convention time which shape the ultimate choice of the nominee" (Broder 1972, 229).

Adjusting to the Computer Age

One result of the Republican Party's focus on professional staff was that when the computer arrived the Republicans were ready for it. Although the party was slow to adopt direct mail—even though its use in a national election campaign was pioneered by the Goldwater forces in 1964—the Republicans pounced on it when the computer revolutionized the handling of mailing lists.

The Democrats used direct mail in the 1972 campaign, but it was the GOP, later in the decade, that quickly harnessed it to the computer's ability to target specific audiences. Republican computers pinpoint voters by socioeconomic status, merging political geography and census data to synthesize lists of voters and contributors that can be motivated by a particular appeal.

These lists are coded so the computer can pull out individual names and addresses sorted by census tracts or other area groupings and reassemble them on the basis of political and economic conditions. Kayden and Mahe (1985) observe that

the California Republican party, for example, is able to send out a mailing to all the residents in precincts that voted over 60 percent for Reagan in 1984, with an average age of over forty-five, in houses costing over $100,000, who have lived there for more than five years. (P. 41)

It has become essential for every political organization to come to grips with the new age of the computer and digital communication. Although the Republicans were there first and developed a much larger staff, the Democrats also saw the computerized writing on the wall. Their headquarters corps is smaller but comparably sophisticated, and they farm out to specialists much of what the GOP does "in house." Both parties are staffed by men and women whose education and professional training would make a politician of the old days wince.

Gone are the days when instinct, long memory, favors, and friendship were the tools of the political pro. No more are volunteers needed to lick stamps and run errands as in the political apprenticeship of yore. In fact, some campaign organizations have staffers whose assignment is to find chores for what volunteers do show up just to keep them out of harm's way and out of mischief. The traditional grass roots are gone forever.

2

The Election Campaign: Marketing Politics

In the first days of the American republic, presidential politics was remarkably pure and simple: George Washington was the obvious and unanimous choice for the presidency of a grateful republic. In 1789 the new nation did not have a national anthem; however, the people improvised one to the tune of *God Save the King*: "God Save Great Washington."

Then, in the course of his two administrations, grumblings and suspicions arose, and even he was seen as pro-British, anti-French, and yearning for an American throne. So the first U.S. president, and the only one ever elected unanimously, also became the first victim of the envy-ridden lies, half-truths, and accusations that would traduce each of his successors.

Despite his later detractors, Washington had needed no advocates to plead his case in the thirteen states. But the instant he decided not to accept a third term, he precipitated his eight-year-old republic into the world's first open election campaign for the chief magistracy of a country that might one day span a continent.

THE FIRST PRESIDENTIAL CAMPAIGN

Two slates sought to succeed Washington in 1796. Vice President John Adams and the South Carolina Federalist Thomas Pinckney were pitted against the Democratic Republicans Thomas Jefferson and Aaron Burr. The country was sharply divided, and each slate had hosts of friends and enemies. The candidates were almost entirely silent, but their partisans were busy. Each side had its spokesmen and detractors.

The Selling of Adams and Jefferson 1796

In other words, both positive and negative campaigning were intrinsic elements of the first bona fide American presidential election campaign. In modern terms, the positive advocates "sold" or "marketed" their respective slates. James Madison was Jefferson's chief cheerleader, and Republican papers lauded to the skies his "unsullied integrity" and his enormous contributions to the nation. Adams's Federalist backers fulsomely praised his long service as patriot, diplomat, and Washington's vice president.

Antagonists pointed to the dangers or failings they saw in the other side— "negative campaigning." And although Chapter 3 of this book will focus on negative campaigning in general and Part II will review the elements of unfair campaigning, including the election of 1796, we will touch briefly here on the range of attacks employed in that first presidential campaign. On both sides some charges were true, some were false, and some were a little of both, with a liberal sprinkling of scabrous vilification.

Jefferson's Republican supporters denounced the well-born Adams and what they feared were his dynastic ambitions. Epithets for him included polar opposites: pro-British and pro-French. He was called vain and jealous, and tales were invented or magnified about his celebrated temper. A Boston paper, the *Independent Chronicle*, falsely accused Adams of a wartime plot to remove Washington from his command. In fact, he had persuaded the real schemer, his radical second cousin Sam, to scuttle the plot.

Federalist detractors, meanwhile, dubbed Jefferson a coward, a drunkard, an atheist, and the son of a half-breed squaw by a mulatto father. In a time when every packet ship brought news of the revolutionary terror in France, he was called a Jacobin. The Federalist press condemned his egalitarian leanings. In a fascinating foretaste of McCarthyism, he was accused of having, as secretary of state, presided over a State Department riddled with Jacobins.

Even the "dirty tricks" aspect of future political mischief was foreshadowed here, when Alexander Hamilton tried to rig the Electoral College to send the decision to the House of Representatives, where he was confident his allies could defeat Jefferson and Burr, elect Pinckney, and bury Adams in the vice presidency.

For several decades after the 1796 contest, presidential candidates themselves continued to take no active, public part in seeking election. But the tactics of their advocates became steadily more aggressive. The parties and party rivalry so dreaded by Washington had burst into existence, and the development of the American election campaign had begun.

Competition for political office is, of course, ancient. Its essence was pondered by Plato and Aristotle, who discussed elections in terms of political rhetoric, which Plato saw as dealing in the truths and values essential to a healthy society.

POLITICAL RHETORIC

That art, rhetoric, is neither dead nor irrelevant to contemporary political discourse, although as "mere rhetoric" it is often mistakenly thought of as sophistry in speech. Lloyd F. Bitzer, chairman of the Department of Communication Arts at the University of Wisconsin, has observed that political rhetoric actually is

far more than uses or misuses of language; it is the engagement of motives, principles, thoughts, arguments, and sentiments in communications—an engagement which functions pragmatically to form attitudes and assist judgments regarding the broad usage of civic affairs. Political rhetoric serves the art of politics at every turn, both as a mode of thought and as an instrument of expression and action. (Bitzer 1981, 225)

Aristotle identified three aspects of political rhetoric. *Deliberative* rhetoric discusses what is useful or beneficial; it examines issues in terms of the common good. In the setting of a campaign, in Bitzer's words, it "asks for a judgment by citizens regarding whether one or another candidate would best administer public affairs." *Forensic* treats of what is right or just. Forensic arguments often appear in negative campaign advertising and somewhat less frequently in general political discourse. "Occasionally," observes Bitzer, "forensic themes of guilt or innocence enter, as they did in 1980 regarding the candidacy of Edward Kennedy." *Epideictic* (from the Greek meaning to show or demonstrate) has to do with demonstrating the character of the candidate. Bitzer reminds us that

much campaign rhetoric, although mainly deliberative in function, works its way up by taking up the topics of epideictic: by celebrating the virtues of a candidate, citing his past good deeds, and showing that on selected issues he displays prudence. And, in opposing a candidate, speakers try to show that prudence, character, and intentions are suspect. Thus, discussion of issues (deliberative) tends to be subsumed under discussion of image (epideictic). (Bitzer 1981, 242–43)

It can be seen at once that all three elements admit negative as well as positive arguments.

The Inflammatory Harangues of 1840

Epideictic carried a heavy load in the rough-and-tumble campaign of 1840, described in Chapter 1. Not every contemporaneous observer found the spectacle enlightening. Former President John Quincy Adams, then serving in the House of Representatives, wrote that he saw the country

in a state of agitation upon the approaching Presidential election such as was never before witnessed.... Not a week has passed within the last four months without a convocation of thousands of people to hear inflammatory harangues against Martin Van Buren and all his Administration, by Henry Clay, Daniel Webster, and all the principal opposition orators in or out of Congress....
Here is a revolution in the habits and manners of the people. Where will it end?

These are party movements, and must in the natural progress of things become antagonistical. These meetings cannot be multiplied in numbers and frequency without resulting in yet deeper tragedies. Their manifest tendency is to civil war. (Adams 1874–77, 10:351–52)

The Enormous Voter Turnout of 1840

Though substantive issues were scarcely discussed, the agitation and high partisan feelings deplored by Adams obviously so stirred up the country that voters turned out in remarkable numbers. The combined Harrison–Van Buren popular vote increased by 83 percent over the 1836 election.

Only once since 1840 has such a surge in total vote even been approached. That was in 1920, when women were enfranchised and the combined popular vote rose by nearly 43 percent. Lowering the voting age to 18 in 1972 caused hardly a ripple (a 4.6 percent increase over 1968).

In percentage terms, the electoral surge of 1840 was exceeded by the increase of 1828 over 1824, the first presidential election for which popular vote records were preserved, but the 1828 campaign, too, was an acrimonious contest, in which Andrew Jackson won his first term by defeating President John Quincy Adams. The combined vote in 1828 was up 228 percent over 1824. The actual numbers, however, were much smaller (see table 2.1).

The objective of all the hoopla of the 1840 campaign was simple: to mobilize sentiment and get out the vote. One is forced to conclude that the marketers of 1840 succeeded.

POLITICAL MARKETING IN PERSPECTIVE

Joe McGinniss's book on Richard Nixon's 1968 presidential campaign, *The Selling of the President 1968*, and the eager shock with which its large audience received it so uncritically, popularized the notion that new and sinister craftsmen had perfected the marketing of presidents to a gullible

Table 2.1
Great Increases in Voter Turnout: A Comparison

Year	Combined Vote	Increase
1824	352,100	
1828	1,156,300	228%
1836	1,310,700	
1840	2,403,700	83.3%
1916	17,667,800	
1920	25,299,600	42.8%

Source: U.S. Bureau of Census, 1960.

populace. As an eminent scholar of campaigns and communication, Kathleen Hall Jamieson, dryly observes, "Had McGinniss been given access to the Republican campaign of 1952, the Democratic campaign of 1960, or either of the national campaigns of 1964, the undertone of astonishment that pervades *Selling* instead would have been one of ennui" (Jamieson 1984, 258).

In fact, the "marketers" of Eisenhower, Kennedy, Goldwater, and Johnson merely adapted the techniques of the real marketing pioneers going back through those of Teddy Roosevelt, McKinley, and all the way back to Harrison in 1840. In fairness, Van Buren's promoters should not be omitted. It was Little Van's misfortune that he simply wound up with a marginally smaller market share than Old Tippecanoe. That is, he came in second.

Fastidious observers often are dismayed by popular tastes and by efforts to reduce the noble concepts of self-government to the ken and savor of the masses. Fervent appeals to democracy always have been seen as demagogy by informed elites, and that goes for modern critics as well as Washington, Adams, and most of the other founders of the United States.

Even Theodore Roosevelt, who was to become perhaps the most bombastic and persuasive of self-promoters among American presidents, was appalled at the campaign process in 1896. Mark Hanna, the Republican boss and political marketer, was running William McKinley for his first term as president, and Roosevelt, who would be McKinley's running mate four years later, was police commissioner of New York City. Hanna's biographer Thomas Beer quotes Roosevelt's acid comment that Hanna had "advertised McKinley as if he were a patent medicine" (Beer 1929, 165).

Yet for all his disgust at the selling of the presidency 1896, a dozen years later, after he had been there himself, Teddy could read the tea leaves perfectly well. He told of coaching William Howard Taft, running as his anointed successor in 1908, against taking too lofty a plane in the campaign. "I told him that he must treat the political audience as one coming, not to see an etching, but a poster. He must, therefore, have streaks of blue, yellow, and red to catch the eye, and eliminate all fine lines and soft colors." He added, slyly, "I think Mr. Taft thought I was a barbarian and a mountebank at first, but I am pleased to say that he is at last catching the attention of the crowd" (Abbott 1924, 143–44).

Though Roosevelt was thinking in color, he was still thinking in print; in his day radio was hardly more than an audacious experiment in wireless telegraphy. But as soon as radio broadcasting of the human voice and other sounds began to arrive in America's living room the rules began to change. Harding was in the White House then, but it was not for another dozen years that a president—Franklin Roosevelt—would master the new medium.

Early radio was a curiosity but not an advertising medium, and it did not become an effective one until technical advances and widespread ownership of radio receivers generated the creation of regular programs to attract sizeable audiences. Radio advertising of politicians and political issues included both the paid broadcasting of set speeches by candidates themselves and broadcasts of other voices recommending them in commercial or spot announcements, as they were called. Radio drama techniques were adapted to produce spots that highlighted the candidate's noble or base qualities. Jingles and martial music added to the hoopla.

By 1928 radio advertising had grown so important that radio spending by both parties began to cut into newspaper ad budgets, and the increasing influence of political public relations people steadily eroded print media spending in favor of broadcasting. By 1952 radio spending by both parties exceeded $3 million. But already television was demanding nearly as much. In the next campaign, video expenditures doubled. This expansion never stopped.

There were differences in technique as well as cost. In dramatic representations narration was not needed to describe the setting. Moreover, because actors could actually *look* furtive or sinister, for example, they did not need script and time to make that point with their voices. A film clip from a video newscast needed less explanation than an audiotaped excerpt from radio news. It became simpler, if more expensive, to achieve quite devastating impact. Political TV absorbed these differences at once.

Political Television

Perhaps the first politician to take TV seriously was just ahead of the actual television revolution. That was an advertising genius, William Benton of Connecticut, whose former ad agency of Benton and Bowles played a major role in shaping the radio advertising and programming of the 1930s. In 1950 Benton was running (successfully) for the unexpired portion of a Senate seat to which he had been appointed.

He owned an educational movie company and had a short sound film produced to play on rear-projection devices mounted on trucks. The trucks would stop at street corners or wherever audiences could be found, and the show would go on. By modern standards the footage is pretty bland: shots of home and family, readings of newspaper endorsements, etc. However, it was an attention-getter and crowd-pleaser and clearly a precursor of political TV. Ironically, two years later when television was becoming a factor, Benton did not use it well, and he lost in the Eisenhower landslide [Benton of Connecticut 1950].[1]

Interestingly enough, an updated version of Benton's truck-mounted projector became a state-of-the-art campaign implement in India forty years later. At the end of the 1980s, an Indian pioneer in political media-consultancy, Ajai Sahni of New Delhi, found a way for parliamentary candidates to bypass the de facto blackout of political ads from government-controlled television and soon found substantial competition in catering to avid politicians. Messages that never could be broadcast are taken to the public under private auspices by means of Sahni's Video on Wheels.

A fairly elaborate video program, including a substantial entertainment component, is built around the candidate and projected via videocassette recorder on a large screen mounted in the side of a van, which is driven around the countryside precisely à la Benton's movie truck. Eager audiences cluster around the van to watch the show—including the candidate's message. Barbara Crossette reported in the *New York Times* that in 1991 the original producer alone operated more than one hundred of these video vans from eight regional centers around India, each van with its own generators to power the show in rural hamlets ("In India, the Star of Video is the Candidate," 1991).

But in the case of the Connecticut prototype of 1950, the star of the landslide that swept Benton away, the beloved General Dwight "Ike" Eisenhower, performed somewhat woodenly on television, and he only performed at all at the insistent counsel of his "marketers." In the still-experimental year of 1952, the Republicans mass-produced twenty-second spots featuring their hero-candidate. Each spot featured one question put to the general and one answer from him, both simplistic [Ike: Simple Answers 1952].

Loftier intellects on the other side—Adlai Stevenson and his fellow "eggheads"—were not so pliant, at first [Arm's Length TV 1952]. In 1952 the Democrats enjoyed making sardonic comments about Madison Avenue and the marketing of Republican politicians in that party's blizzard of commercials—exactly as the young Republican maverick Theodore Roosevelt had complained about Mark Hanna's merchandising of William McKinley fifty-six years earlier. Stevenson said he did not want to be marketed "like a breakfast food." His eloquent speeches of 1952 and 1956 galvanized the liberal elite, and deeply stirred a generation of them to get involved in politics. But Ike was being marketed to the hoi polloi, who had the votes.

In 1956, both parties used television in a longer format than mere spots. They bought five-minute segments to "hitch-hike" on entertainment shows with established audiences, paying both air time and preemption fees to take over the last five minutes of the regular programs. Both parties also used occasional short commercials in the intervals between programs. But it was not until 1964, under the tutelage of their advertising agency, Doyle Dane Bernbach, that the Democrats finally abandoned the five-minute segment completely in favor of the shorter spots.

But with all the political ads of the television era, from Eisenhower's simple questions and answers to the most celebrated or notorious spot of any future campaign, only the medium of dissemination is new. Their rhetorical function is ancient. Their lineage as political communication is traced succinctly by Kathleen Hall Jamieson.

In many ways televised political advertising is the direct descendant of the advertised messages carried in song and on banners, torches, bandannas, and broadsides. Ads continue to ally the candidate with the people, only now that takes the form of showing the candidates pressing the flesh or answering questions from groups of citizens. Candidates continue to overstate their accomplishments and understate their failures. (Jamieson 1984, 448–49)

THE RISE OF THE CAMPAIGN CONSULTANT

It was to enable candidates to negotiate the tricky waters of modern election campaigns that the craft of professional political consultants proliferated, especially during the 1980s. The entire phenomenon of the campaign consultant is often thought to be that recent, but in fact the practice is quite ancient. In the first century B.C., Quintus Tullius Cicero laid out a campaign plan for his brother, Marcus Tullius Cicero, to use in seeking the consulship at Rome.

Quintus reminded his older brother to keep the rhetorical skill for which he was famous "always ready and available" and counseled him on displaying the number and high stature of his friends. He enumerated the extravagant failings of the competition: "both assassins from their childhood, both men of lascivious character."

He had advice on gaining "the zeal of your friends. . . . Make friends of every sort;—friends for show, men illustrious from their rank and reputation, who, even if they are not very effective as voters or canvassers, nevertheless add some dignity to the candidate."

Quintus suggested approaches to remind some friends of past favors and to promise new favors to others: "solicit them, make them promises; take care that they canvass for you in their neighborhoods." He prescribed a virtual parade for the candidate: "the company of saluters, who come to your house; another, of those who escort you home again; a third, of those who accompany you in your walks through the city."

Be wary, he wrote, "on the topic of rumour." And "Lastly, take care that your whole canvass is splendid, illustrious, and full of pomp, pleasing to the people, set off with the greatest beauty and dignity, so that if possible your competitors may derive no advantage from the infamy of their wickedness."

But this was no mere family connection; Quintus obviously saw other clients in prospect, for he concluded his tract with a request for a critique: "If you think any point requires to be changed, or altogether omitted, or if you consider that anything has been passed over, I should be glad if you would tell me; for I wish to make this little manual for canvassers entirely perfect" (Cicero 1853, 485–503).[2]

The rise of Quintus Cicero's successor, the modern professional campaign consultant, is often blamed for the decline of the American political parties. But many party professionals, Eddie Mahe, for instance, argue that the effect has been to change the party's nature and focus, not to diminish it (Kayden and Mahe 1985).

Some consultants manage every aspect of a campaign, from pre-primary maneuvering to the general election. Others specialize in certain aspects of campaign management, such as gathering signatures for nominating petitions or creating television and radio advertising (some also including print ads). Media specialists place such advertising. Other specialists handle direct mail. "Pollsters" or survey research specialists and public relations advisors or other "image-makers" are part of the mix.

Modern Origins: Political Public Relations

This new craft or calling grew out of the business of political public relations. Public relations, or PR, is itself a relatively new phenomenon, with roots in the publicity agents of the very early twentieth century and before that in "free publicity" that newspaper publishers often allotted, a hundred years earlier, to encourage advertisers.

It did not take long for the political benefits of PR to become evident. Within a decade after 1900, various government agencies in the United States and Great Britain had engaged publicity agents, and by 1913 the U.S. Congress was already trying to regulate (i.e., control) it. Like later efforts in Britain, this proved vain. In America euphemistic substitute titles such as "public information" outstripped congressional efforts to define PR. Hardly a government agency anywhere in the world struggles along without a public relations directorate and staff, under whatever name. And the once-apprehensive U.S. Congress? No member or committee of the U.S. House or Senate lacks a press secretary.

The earliest political PR campaign specialists appeared in California, as a direct outgrowth of the reforms that Hiram Johnson introduced there early in the twentieth century to wrest political control from the railroad interests. Key among the Progressive-era reforms was the ancient democratic device of referendum and initiative.

In election years the perennially overburdened California ballot puts to the voters a dozen or more initiative or referendum propositions. Thus the hapless voter is challenged to exercise wisdom about public policy questions on water, health, oil, taxes, housing, beach erosion, and the like, plus the occasional recall of some elected official—all this in addition to electing a governor, lieutenant governor, numerous other state officers, and state and U.S. legislators.

Only a rare ballot initiative really captures the ardent and immediate interest of the electorate, as did the famous Proposition 13 of 1978, a tax-limitation measure that won in a landslide and set off a national storm of tax-cutting demands. But ordinarily not more than a few thousand people in the state will have a firm opinion on any ballot proposal. With perhaps two dozen propositions on every ballot, confusion reigns—and is compounded by the rootlessness for which California's mushrooming and restless population has long been notorious.

The situation in California, then, was primordial soup for the precursor of the modern campaign management firm. And, sure enough, there it arose, a few months after Franklin D. Roosevelt's first inauguration in 1933: the pioneering political public relations firm of Whitaker and Baxter. Clem Whitaker was an ex-newspaperman and publicity agent, and Leone Baxter, also a former journalist, was a widowed chamber of commerce manager who became Whitaker's partner in 1933 and his wife five years later.

The Pioneer Consultants: Whitaker and Baxter

A referendum campaign was the flash of lightning that brought Whitaker and Baxter to life. Pacific Gas & Electric, the mighty PG&E of California politics, had managed to get a referendum measure on the ballot that would disable the Central Valley Project Act. The project was selling hydroelectric power directly to public agencies and undercutting PG&E and other utilities. Most California politicians of both parties supported the act, and one of them brought Clem Whitaker into the campaign as a publicity agent to help defeat the proposition. Leone Baxter's Redding Chamber of Commerce was already working against the measure, and by the time the campaign ended in victory (defeating PG&E by 33,000 votes), Whitaker and Baxter were a team, under the name Campaigns, Inc.

The firm was busy and successful at once, for many years winning nine-tenths of their fights, even when they were handling several different issues in the same election. They also worked for a long list of governors and other major officials. All the individuals were Republicans, and the ballot issue causes they took on were generally, but by no means only, conservative. Nearly all, however, were victorious. As Theodore White described them, this pair was "to California politics what Tammany had once been to New York politics" (White 1975, 54).

What Whitaker and Baxter did, as did all the other political PR specialists who came quickly after them and thrived similarly in the fertile California soil, was to take control of all aspects of communication in a campaign: the written and spoken word, images and recordings, brochures and billboards; and making and placing their own ads in movies, radio, and later, television commercials.

The team was brilliant in its framing of issues and devising symbols to move voters. They beat a famous recall campaign for San Francisco Mayor Roger Lapham in 1946 by inventing an opponent. Lapham's foes only mounted a recall drive; logically enough, they did not offer a successor—who could only be chosen if the recall succeeded. Whitaker and Baxter named this putative successor the "faceless man," and made him Lapham's sinister enemy. They persuaded San Franciscans that he was their enemy, too.

Campaigns, Inc. (later Whitaker and Baxter Campaigns) also quickly mastered the gathering of signatures to get an initiative measure on the ballot, and that is no mean thing. California requires legally correct petitions signed by registered voters equalling 5 percent of the total vote in the last previous election. In Hiram Johnson's era (circa 1915) that was peanuts: 25,000 or 30,000 signers. In 1990, it was half a million.

The practice they invented spread rapidly, first in California, then beyond. In the process its name changed as the role expanded beyond political PR to campaign consulting, or campaign management consulting. In the heady days of the 1960s, anything was possible. One of the second-generation practitioners promised clients they could be elected to any office of their choice so long as they would (1) pay bills promptly, (2) follow orders exactly, and (3) say nothing, absolutely nothing that was not on the script, to anybody. This counsel scandalized reformers when it became known in the early 1960s. However, it is an ancient bit of campaign wisdom, echoing precisely what a biographer of Horace Greeley said of that editor's 1840 presidential candidate, William Henry Harrison. He strictly "obeyed instructions to say nothing, write nothing, deny nothing, affirm nothing" (Stoddard 1946, 53). This may be seen as slightly hyperbolic, since Harrison did make stump speeches. However, there is a good deal of testimony that in them he actually did say nothing.

Campaign management firms have long since become essential, a central ingredient in virtually every important election campaign. "Important" in this instance means a campaign that is hotly contested in any jurisdiction larger than a small town or state assembly district. The use of campaign consultants—and especially their skillful and effective use of all the means of gathering and disseminating information and their fully commercialized mastery of gathering petition signatures—is what has driven the incessant increases in the cost of electioneering.

Fears and Realities

An early fear of many observers of this phenomenon was that it would spawn a new race of adventurers whose only constraint would be winning, hired guns who would elect anyone regardless of party or ideology. As the business has developed, it generally has followed the pioneers with respect to party orientation. As Whitaker and Baxter worked only for Republican candidates, so most of their successors adhere to the party of their own inclination. Indeed the ranks of party campaign organizations have been perhaps the richest training ground for big-league campaign management firms.

There have been occasional brash tyros who entered the field with exaggerated cynicism and no sense of commitment to the political system, and who would do anything to win and Devil take the hindmost. This is not a concern to be dismissed lightly. Walter De Vries, who is both a political scientist and a veteran campaign consultant, observes that consultants "used to be drawn principally from government, journalism and advertising careers, but now they come from just about anywhere.... Many ... are very young; many are inexperienced." Lacking the restraints of both tradition and seasoned judgment, they may pose some risk to the integrity of the field ("American Campaign Consulting: Trends and Concerns," 1989).

Perhaps more consultants occasionally will play either side, and still more, when economic needs dictate, will, as one put it, "hold my nose and take on a guy I really don't like very much." Very few, however, would support a candidate whose positions were really antithetical to their own. Few, in fact, are asked to do so.

When it comes to issues, flexibility is more general than with candidates, and most consultants will take on any cause that comes along that does not do violence to their deeply held personal convictions.

By the 1980s the sages and pundits of print and broadcast journalism were bewailing the continuing proliferation of campaign consultants on the ground that their evil ministrations had brought campaign ethics to an all-time low. Hosts of reformers and simply concerned citizens joined these lamentations.[3]

The most casual reader of this book or any other examination of campaign tactics since the 1790s will quickly see how hyperbolic such tragic assessments are. Still, there is plenty of room for criticism of modern campaigning and campaign management. One may hope, and indeed expect, that the industry will develop a system for self-examination and correction of its own excesses. Any prospect for strict regulation by law or government regulatory agency, however, is sure to founder on the First Amendment to the U.S. Constitution, for the coin these firms deal with is nothing less than freedom of speech.

Fear and loathing of this political phenomenon cannot help the individual citizen who is sufficiently interested in politics to stay informed and vote regularly. What is needed is a realistic understanding of it and its very large role in the American polity.

A nice irony in this connection is that in the closing months of 1989, while scholars and journalists in the United States were pondering ways to restrict the communication techniques of campaign consultants without quite abridging freedom of speech, new heralds of freedom in the crumbling Communist domains of Eastern Europe were seeking the counsel of those very consultants.

In 1981 Larry J. Sabato counted at least thirty-two other countries where U.S. political consultants had been called in by one party or another, including most of the democracies of Western Europe, Australia, Canada, Israel, and Japan (Sabato 1981, 57–60).

The Berlin Wall and the rest of Churchill's Iron Curtain were demolished not by tanks and bulldozers but by television, radio, and an underground press offering fragmentary glimpses of freedom that escaped jamming and confiscation. How to use these media to win crucial elections in a new climate of legitimacy? Whom to ask but the campaign consultant?

3

Criticizing Opponents: Negative Campaigning

However appealing the prospect may appear on a theoretical level, election campaigns in the United States are unlikely to return to a golden age that never was, in which discourse is substantive and seemly and the voter's passions are stirred only by beauty of phrase and logic. Since Washington every president has been sold to the populace in some degree. That—along with rational debate whenever it crops up—is positive campaigning.

UNDERSTANDING NEGATIVE CAMPAIGNING

The modern American name for public examination of the other candidate's relevant defects is negative campaigning. In its absence, any knave or mountebank in the land may lie and steal his or her way into the White House or any other elective office. Negative campaigning has been practiced since 1796, and it is likely to occur with some frequency as long as the United States holds free elections.

Depending, of course, on the way it is done, there is much more to negative campaigning than smear and slander. The advantages of incumbency in any modern, highly valued, elective office pose great obstacles to the challenger. This subject is explored in Chapter 13, but suffice it to say here that without attention-grabbing, cogent, memorable, negative campaigning, almost no challenger can hope to win unless the incumbent has just been found guilty of a heinous crime.

And what of a campaign between two non-incumbents? Must they, in order to avoid the onus of negative campaigning, refrain from pointing to each other's pertinent shortcomings? The idea is preposterous. But it is ardently advocated by many modern reformers.

Ironically, one of the lasting heroes of U.S. reformers, Theodore Roosevelt, advanced negative campaigning as both tactic and strategy. After choosing William Howard Taft to be his successor in 1908, he counseled negative campaigning again and again: "I want us to choose our ground and make the fight aggressively" (August 29). "Do not *answer* Bryan; attack him! Don't let *him* make the issues" (September 1). "Hit them hard, old man! Why not call attention to Bryan's insincerity.... Now hit at them; challenge Bryan on his record. Ask that you be judged on your record, and dare Bryan to stand on his!" (September 11). No half-way measures for Teddy (Roosevelt 1952, 6:1202–31).

But the great reformer's emphasis on the attack is ironic only because modern reformers (in and out of the news media) are thrown off the track by the red herring of negativity as naughty.

The Critical Issue: Truth and Relevance

Popular anxiety over negative campaigning is entirely beside the point. In distinguishing between fair and unfair campaigning, the critical issue is not positive versus negative but the dual issue of truth and relevance. Negative campaigning based on lies or inflammatory truths that are irrelevant is disreputable not because it is negative but because it is false or irrelevant, or both.

Why does such opprobrium attach to negative campaigning instead of the crucial questions of truth and relevance? Probably because negative campaigning, which need not be but often is the carrier of false or irrelevant charges, is easy to identify, whereas clever distortions and inflammatory irrelevancies are painfully hard to pin down and evaluate.

"Everyone knows" that rumors sometimes turn out to be true. Where there is smoke there is fire. And so on. Truth can be difficult to prove in any circumstance, let alone in the heat and bustle of an election campaign. Moreover, what is germane and extremely important to one observer may be completely inconsequential to another. What is important, especially in negative campaigning, is the emotional voltage of the charge, whether it is utterly false or completely true, utterly germane or completely immaterial.

This became apparent in the presidential election of 1796, which broke new ground in many ways. It was the first actual presidential campaign, the first negative campaign, and, as demonstrated by the spectacular mudslinging directed at both John Adams and Thomas Jefferson (mentioned in passing in Chapter 2), the first dirty campaign. It also cast a sinister shadow on the electioneering of the future.

TROUBLESOME SUBSPECIES: THE PROFESSIONAL SMEAR ARTIST

The 1796 campaign introduced a troublesome subspecies of negative campaigner: the great American smear artist. The métier of this kind of political operative is the gray area between truth and falsehood. The pioneer was a turbulent, resourceful, and facile researcher and writer named James Thomson Callender. Callender was a Scotsman who had fled England under charges of sedition, settled in Philadelphia, and found work as a reporter of congressional debates for the *Philadelphia Gazette*. In 1796 he began publishing a series of lurid political pamphlets. One of them embellished rumors that Alexander Hamilton, Washington's Secretary of the Treasury and an arch-Federalist, had defrauded the U.S. Treasury. Another painted him as the villain in a sordid affair with a prostitute named Maria Reynolds and her blackmailing husband and depicted Maria as Hamilton's innocent victim.

This brought the virulent pamphleteer to the attention of Jefferson, who despised Hamilton. But Jefferson was not only a Republican and anti-Federalist, he was also a longtime colleague and friend, though a political rival, of the Federalist John Adams. Adams shared Jefferson's distaste for Hamilton, whom he called "a bastard Bratt of a Scotch pedlar" (Adams to Jefferson, 12 July 1813, *The Adams–Jefferson Letters*, 2:354).

Jefferson bought several copies of a new Callender work, *History of the United States for the Year 1796*, and covertly gave the author a stipend as well as information of the sort we call leads for his next undertaking.

Adams won the 1796 election, and Jefferson was elected vice president. After the passage of Adams's Sedition Act in 1798, Jefferson arranged for his friend Meriwether Jones to hire Callender away from the national capital of Philadelphia for Jones's newspaper, the *Richmond Examiner*. This was thought to be a relatively safe haven for the seditious scrivener, for the Virginia legislature strongly opposed the Alien and Sedition Acts. Before long Callender also was writing for a number of other Jeffersonian Republican papers.

His next book, *The Prospect Before Us*, appeared early in the election year of 1800, in which Jefferson would unseat Adams. In it Callender traduced Adams at length, not only as a traitor who had stolen the election of 1796 but also as a "hideous hermaphroditical character which has neither the force and firmness of a man, nor the gentleness and sensibility of a woman." Adams represented "war, and beggary, and Jefferson, peace and competency." He even ridiculed Washington as "the grand lama of Federal adoration, the immaculate divinity of Mt. Vernon."[1]

This tract helped set the tone for the election, launching a wave of campaign calumny that enmeshed Federalists and Republicans alike. Although Adams's Sedition Act was widely unpopular, and very much so in Virginia, Federalists were outraged, and Callender in June became one of a handful of pamphleteers convicted, fined, and jailed under the act.

In contrast to Adams, Callender's book had painted Jefferson as a hero and the hope of the nation. Moreover, apart from the constitutionality of the Alien and Sedition Acts, which Federalists supported and Republicans denied, Callender's trial was a mockery, with a patently biased judge and jury. This was evident in the trial record, which Republican journals trumpeted up and down the land, and it helped rout Adams and the Federalists in 1800.

Callender Changes Sides

Early in Jefferson's first term, the new president pardoned the pamphleteer and arranged for the private reimbursement of his $200 fine, a charity he quickly came to regret. For the scoundrel had changed sides— after being denied a postmastership and further financial assistance by President Jefferson, who was belatedly growing concerned about the man's rabidity.

In the summer of 1802 Callender tossed his first anti-Republican bombshell, laying bare the details of Jefferson's encouragement and even subvention of his earlier anti-Federalist diatribes. Of course the Federalist press pounced on this disclosure and trumpeted it everywhere. Now it was the turn of betrayed Republican editors to denounce Callender, which they did at once and in high dudgeon. When Jefferson's connection with the slanderer of Adams was revealed, the once-cordial Adams–Jefferson relationship froze instantly (although it recovered later).

In his six-year career, Callender won substantial notoriety, which is exactly what more contemporary smear artists try assiduously to avoid. Moreover, they do not think of themselves as smear artists. One of the busiest and most effective of Callender's successors, operating just over a century later, styled himself a "political dynamiter."

Walter Quigley, Political Dynamiter

Walter Eli Quigley was born into a family of frontier Democrats in North Dakota in 1890, and he grew up passing out literature and running political errands. Like Callender, he became a facile writer early and was a quick, deft researcher. Unlike Jefferson's nemesis, Quigley had one strong ideological orientation. He was a devoted anti-Communist. Otherwise, once he fell into political dynamiting, he was an all-purpose, itinerant smear artist, for sale anywhere and, as several satisfied clients testified, he stayed bought for the rest of the campaign.

Quigley was a Roman Catholic, a twice-disbarred lawyer, and a consummate pamphleteer who had no qualms about traducing for hire even a candidate whom he personally liked. Only once is he known to have said he enjoyed savaging a candidate whom he genuinely disliked. He was no anti-Semite, but he never scrupled at evoking by slur or innuendo the anti-Semitism that was widespread in the plains states in Quigley's golden age, which extended from around 1915 to the late 1950s, a few years before his death.

Quigley was a quintessential professional. He claimed a win ratio of four to one, and certainly he won most of his campaigns. He would do whatever was necessary to win. And although his personal preference was for a hot-and-heavy campaign—"He would have preferred to axe my opponent," said one satisfied client—he was willing if required to play it straight. "He was a bit unhappy doing a positive job for me, but did it very well." In his own words, "Old Eli [Quigley] has to eat, and where the money comes from is unimportant" (Jonas 1970, 27, 33).

The Campaign Tabloid

Quigley pioneered the idea of a campaign tabloid that seemed to be well-established and accurate but was actually ad hoc and ad hominem. His "dynamiting" technique was to find issues or areas in which the opposition candidate was or could be made to appear vulnerable. Then he would fashion his special "newspaper" around them, selecting bits and pieces out of context to "make the most respected individual appear a downright scallawag, but there never is anything upon which a libel pleading can be based" (Jonas 1970, 39). He was adept at one of the oldest smear tactics, the whispering campaign, and persisted in its use long after it had become infrequent elsewhere. But his real trademark was delivering plausible disinformation via the campaign tabloid.

One such tabloid helped bring down the onetime wild man of Montana politics, Senator Burton K. Wheeler, in 1946. The senator was an ardent and prickly advocate of the common man against "the interests" and an advocate of the populist Non-Partisan League, a plains states phenomenon around the end of World War I. When the league ran him for governor in 1920, opponents called him "Bolshevik Burt." As a wartime U.S. attorney in Montana, he had been startled by the depth of hostility to German Americans and spoke out strongly against patriotism of that stripe. His political hegira took him from Republican to Progressive (he was Robert La Follette's vice-presidential candidate on that ticket in 1924) to Democrat. But on the eve of World War II he found himself in the isolationist camp and was described as a fascist and a Nazi.

In 1946 A. F. Whitney, president of the Brotherhood of Railroad Trainmen, hired Quigley to help the union beat Wheeler in the Democratic primary. He did so by harnessing the accumulated resentments from two world wars, lifting comments and quotes from numerous sources to depict Wheeler's isolationism as thoroughly un-American.

In the tabloid, *Montana News*, Wheeler's opponent, Leif Erickson, was a "Distinguished Montanan" while Wheeler was heartless, greedy, pro-Nazi, and anti-American. Partial quotations from his enemies made him out to be a fascist, and his own pre-war isolationist statements were mined for bits suggesting he wanted Germany to win both world wars. All quotations predated December 7, 1941, when the United States entered World War II. Quigley's own interpretations filled any gaps. Wheeler lost.

NEGATIVE CAMPAIGNING IN THE ERA OF NEW TECHNOLOGY

To dig out gems from a candidate's past utterances that will be embarrassing today, Walter Quigley, like other researchers, had to pore over old news clippings in a friendly newspaper morgue or some other library and copy down useful excerpts by hand. In just such fashion the Democrats in 1952 laboriously compiled an "Ike-lopedia" of nearly 600 pages, crossindexing every utterance of the Republican candidate, "Ike" Eisenhower, on every subject from *Acheson, Dean [see also Secretary of State]* to *Yugoslavia*. Thereafter, any idea for an embarrassing old Eisenhower quote out of context could be documented at once.

Then the computer arrived to simplify storage and retrieval of such information and, together with audio and video recording, changed the technical milieu of negative campaigning. Technology took the drudgery out of negative campaigning. The work got easier and faster—and its effects more devastating.

The Electronic Smear

As expert practitioners turned to the new medium, radio spots proved to have high potential for distortion, and this was exploited with great imagination. A well executed radio commercial could have devastating effect and was persuasive to a degree difficult for a child of the television era to comprehend.

To understand, in a video age, the power of radio political ads in the previous era, one must recall how the radio drama of that day worked. It relied, for the profound impact it had on its listeners, entirely on the combination of script (including background narration), vocal characterization (i.e., acting skill), and sound effects and background music. From the 1930s well into the 1950s, weeknight and Sunday afternoon and evening radio audiences for dramatic and comedy broadcasts in the United States numbered in the many millions. Scenery, color, and the visual appearance of actors had to be supplied by the listeners' imagination, and listeners entered fully into this tacit compact.

This was the period in which Orson Welles's radio classic, a vivid adaptation of H. G. Wells's *War of the Worlds*, despite repeated disclaimers, convinced millions of American listeners that the United States had been invaded by a space armada from Mars.

An excellent illustration of how this willing audience could be exploited in an election campaign is a classic radio smear that came from the National Republican Congressional Committee in 1954. The spot begins with a sound effect. Printing presses roar in the background, and over them is heard the voice of the ubiquitous professional neutral, the announcer: "Those are the printing presses of the Communist Party. Listen to them!" The presses roar louder, then fade under the announcer's voice as he sets the scene: "The date is April, 1954. Those printing presses are turning out the official Communist Party line."

A Russian-accented voice is heard over the sound of the presses. "Defeat the Republican Congressional candidates in 1954! That is our order from Moscow. Return America to a New Deal type administration! Moscow orders that!"

After some further business from the announcer about the Red blueprint for America, he concludes with the voice of authority: "Don't take orders from Moscow! Vote for a Republican Congress."

By this time the radio era was giving way to the new wave, television. The dramatic techniques of entertainment television were not only simpler but substantively different from those of radio. Sound effects were less important. No announcer needed to describe settings, visual props, or actors' appearances or actions, for they could be seen.

A classic video smear from the 1970 congressional campaign was a worthy successor to radio's Communist presses of 1954. It appeared during the height of the Vietnam War and featured a figure representing Democratic U.S. Senator Vance Hartke of Indiana handing an AK-47 assault rifle to a Vietcong soldier. It carried its message in a fraction of the time, and it left nothing to the imagination [Rifle 1970].

THE ARRIVAL OF ATTACK VIDEO

But it was the Democrats who fired the first gun in the video era of negative campaigning.[2] In the 1960 campaign against Richard Nixon, they mined newsreel archives and put together a television spot featuring the Republican President of the United States putting down his own vice president, Nixon. A reporter at a news conference asked Eisenhower for an idea of Nixon's that he had adopted. Ike's response: "If you give me a week I might think of one. I don't remember." The president joined in general laughter [Ike on Nixon 1960].

The Democrats in 1960 also scored heavily in positive advertising addressing their candidate's Roman Catholic faith, and this is considered at some length in Chapter 6.

Again in 1964 the Democrats were first off the mark with an ad campaign designed to savage their opponent. In those days it was customary for the two national party chairmen to open the fall campaign by endorsing the

Code of Fair Campaign Practices at a Washington press conference. When the first of these biennial rituals took place in 1954, the party leaders, then Republican Leonard W. Hall and Democrat Stephen A. Mitchell, had at one another while the ink was still wet on their newly signed code. Most of their successors did so, too, as in 1964.

At the end of summer a *Wall Street Journal* story had detailed the Democrats' 1964 TV plans and described a vivid commercial featuring a nuclear explosion and suggesting that only the election of Lyndon Johnson could save the world from destruction—which it obviously would face if Barry Goldwater were elected president.

At the code-signing session, Republican Chairman Dean Burch cried foul at the plans. Burch bitterly criticized the Democrats' portrayal of Goldwater as a trigger-happy militarist who would set off bombs heedlessly. John Bailey, the Democratic chairman, rejoined that the image of Goldwater had been created by the senator himself and that the Democrats could hardly be blamed for exploiting it.

The Little Girl and the Daisy

When the bomb spot appeared, it bore out Burch's fears. A winsome little girl in a sunny meadow is wholly absorbed in picking the petals off a daisy. Her childish voice counts: "one, two, three, four, five, seven, six, six, eight, nine . . . " At "ten," a portentous male voice overrides the girlish tones, counting backward, louder and louder: " . . . four, three, two, one, zero." The child is obliterated as the screen goes black and then fills with the stunning, fiery umbrella of a nuclear explosion. The shape distends into the dread mushroom cloud, and shock waves ray out and off the screen. Now the somber voice of Lyndon Johnson: "These are the stakes. To make a world in which all of God's children can live, or go into the dark. We must either love each other, or we must die." The screen goes into the dark. One line of type appears, white on the black void: "VOTE FOR PRESIDENT JOHNSON ON NOVEMBER 3." The voice of doom urges the point: "The stakes are too high for you to stay home" [Daisy 1964].

The advertising agency that created it, Doyle Dane Bernbach, Inc., defended the spot as an entirely proper presentation of the central theme of the 1964 campaign: nuclear responsibility. Larry Sabato quotes Tony Schwartz, who actually made the ad, as saying the Democrats' rationale for it was Goldwater's earlier justification of tactical nuclear weapons (Sabato 1981, 169–70). But this spot, taking mankind "into the dark," obviously represented the use of a high-yield strategic weapon, no mere battlefield nuclear shell. The argument recalls Quigley laboriously snipping out a word here and a word there to reverse the meaning of a statement.

Other observers believed the issue was central to the campaign. For several years Theodore H. White and I carried on an intermittent argument over its legitimacy and propriety, in which he never retreated from his belief that the bomb spot was both germane and fair. Yet he found a companion commercial—another little girl, with a strontium-laden ice cream cone, discussed in Chapter 7—to be "as cruel a political film as has ever been shown" (White 1965, 323).

Protests from Both Parties. The minute the girl with the daisy appeared, Republican protests mushroomed almost like the bomb cloud in the commercial. Hosts of Democrats also disapproved, including the vice-presidential candidate, Hubert Humphrey, who privately told me and many others that he considered it "unfortunate." Hundreds of Democrats complained to local television stations and wrote bitter letters about it to the Democratic National Committee and the Fair Campaign Practices Committee.

Attack Video as News/Ad

The daisy spot was only broadcast once—by the Democrats. Erik Barnouw, a historian of television, says Doyle Dane was *not* ordered to withdraw it but ran it only once because the "attention won at the first showing was so overwhelming that re-use seemed redundant" (Barnouw 1975, 361). However, Democratic National Chairman John Bailey, although he defended the development and use of the spot as justified by Goldwater's own past statements, told Fair Campaign Practices Committee Chairman Charles P. Taft and me that its withdrawal had been ordered. ABC and NBC television replayed the spot in covering the resulting sensation on their network news shows.

The *New York Times* and other papers covered it as news stories. It became an early example of what Kathleen Hall Jamieson has identified as the "News/Ad," an ad intended by its content to make news, "blurring... the boundaries between news and ads."[3]

Another Doyle Dane spot in the 1964 campaign was at once closer to the mark, hilarious, and extremely effective in citing Goldwater past against Goldwater present. Earlier, the Arizona senator, celebrating the conservative values of the Southwest, had made the pungent observation that it would be just as well if the eastern seaboard of the United States were sawed off and allowed to float out to sea. With script-writing of this caliber, Doyle Dane hardly needed writers. They filmed a plywood map of America with the eastern seaboard being cut off with a carpenter's hand saw and floating off into the Atlantic [Eastern Seaboard 1964]. This spot, lacking the desperate overtones of the bomb commercials, brought the Democrats huge merriment, no complaints, and certainly some votes.[4]

The Nixon Weather Vane. Another Democratic commercial in 1968 used a theme that Lyndon Johnson employed against Goldwater in 1964 and that became a staple of negative campaigners, a weather vane to represent inconstancy. The 1968 weather vane was a caricature sculpture of a bust of Nixon. It flipped and whirled back and forth, while the unseen announcer asked, "Ever notice what happens to Nixon when the political winds blow?" As the voice-over ticked off the issues of the day, the Nixon vane swung mindlessly to right and left, round and round. "Which way will he blow next?" the voice asked [Nixon Weather Vane 1968].

Larry Sabato says Nixon was so offended by the caricature of him in this 1968 ad that he telephoned Humphrey demanding its withdrawal, and that Humphrey did kill it (Sabato 1981, 172). For all Nixon's distaste when his own ox was being gored, his 1972 campaign against George McGovern employed the same device.

Two decades after Nixon's protest about the weather vane ad, the media elite wanted the 1988 presidential candidates, Democrat Michael Dukakis and Republican George Bush, to tell voters how they would handle the great issues: the breakup of Soviet Europe (which was starting to accelerate as the U.S. campaign ended); the U.S. budget and trade deficits; and the complicated financial debacle of the American savings and loan industry. These were themes that greatly concerned the media elite and that loomed before the next president, but there was little evidence that the general electorate wanted to hear about them.

Knowing What Will Work

More ordinary voters were concerned with more prosaic issues: a return to family values; punish the criminal, not the victim; and clean up pollution. How do modern-day winners know what concerns the electorate? Precisely the way modern marketers know what will sell before the product even exists: market research. "Focus groups" with the right demographic mix discuss issues with a moderator while the client—in this case key campaign decision-makers—watches and listens attentively from behind a one-way mirror in the next room, observing facial expressions and listening for oral inflections. This kind of market research guides the creation of the campaign's game plan, as it is frequently styled, or flight plan.

Every politician regards "going negative" as a dangerous tactic, susceptible of calamitous backfiring if it goes wrong, that is, if it is perceived as overkill, untrue, unfair, too cruel, or gratuitous. The clever ones chart their course in these treacherous waters with great care and, usually, no little anxiety. The compass that successful political managers—whatever their party—use to navigate modern campaigns, positive and negative, comes, like focus groups, from marketing: the tracking poll, a small but highly representative polling sample, meticulously selected with "the right demographics" to reflect the whole electorate. Thus the campaigners know from day to day how a campaign theme is being received.

Candidates who disdain these applications of long-proven market research methodology may sleep better at night, and they have a lot of good company—all in the losers' column with other politicians who told the people what they ought to hear: Horace Greeley, William Jennings Bryan, Charles Evans Hughes, Al Smith, Thomas E. Dewey, Adlai Stevenson, Barry Goldwater, George McGovern, Walter Mondale.

"In 1988 George Bush communicated an attitude, not issues, through powerful images—his grandchildren, Willie Horton, Boston Bay." So wrote a thirty-six-year-old media executive in the *New York Times*, explaining how Republicans reached the "generations who grew up with TV" and who "communicate differently than previous generations" ("We're Talking the Wrong Language to 'TV Babies,'" 1990).

Communicating Crime and Punishment

The Republican Bush campaign was heavily criticized for its emphasis on prison furloughs in one widely aired spot, which attacked Democratic Governor Dukakis's commitment to fighting crime. "As Governor, Michael Dukakis vetoed the sentences for drug dealers," it began. "He vetoed the death penalty. His revolving door prison policy gave weekend furloughs . . ."

The principal visual feature now appeared, a barred revolving door in a prison wall. Actors in prison garb—whites and blacks intermingled—filed into the revolving door and right back out again. The voice-over continued: ". . . to first degree murderers not eligible for parole. While out, many committed other crimes like kidnapping and rape. And many are still at large."

Then the finale: "Mike Dukakis says he wants to do for America what he's done for Massachusetts. America can't afford that risk" [Revolving Door 1988].

This spot distorted by overemphasizing first-degree murderers and by falsely implying that there were many of them in the program. There weren't many, but there were several. One of them, a first-degree knife-murderer on his *tenth* weekend furlough, had kidnapped a Maryland couple, repeatedly raping the young woman and stabbing her fiancé. The commercial turned this individual nightmare into the specter of a virtual plague of rape, all the scarier because many of the furloughed Massachusetts prisoners were in fact still at large.

The implication was that Dukakis had invented the furlough program. Actually, enlightened penology has employed furlough programs for decades—though not for murderers ineligible for parole—and Dukakis had inherited the Massachusetts program from a predecessor, and a Republican at that.

Here were two misleading implications, but the central facts were true. And the program, which Dukakis strongly supported, had obviously been managed ineptly. The symbolism was powerful, and the Bush campaign broadcast the ad extensively on network TV. The case of this particular escape and its consequences had been explored with focus groups months earlier, and the Bush campaign knew it would be an effective weapon if Dukakis were the Democratic nominee.

Outsiders Inject Race. But the official ad was given an extra dimension and new life by an independent commercial that came out of left—or right— field with a potent and unambiguous pro-Bush spot that its independent sponsor scheduled for four weeks on cable TV. It identified the Massachusetts murderer-escapee and Maryland rapist by name and photograph, a police mug shot of a black convict named Willie Horton [Weekend Passes 1988].

The ad was made by an independent group, the National Security Political Action Committee, operating under the aegis of a Washington organization calling itself Americans for Bush. The Bush campaign complained later that fund-raisers for the rump group misrepresented it as part of the Bush campaign. Once the ad appeared, the Bush people urged the sponsors to drop it, which they eventually did a few days ahead of their original schedule.

As an ad, in terms of total viewer impressions, by which TV advertising is measured, this spot did not reach a large audience. But its impact was so blunt and so brutal that it became the very essence of the News/Ad, in Kathleen Hall Jamieson's words, an ad so hard-hitting that it is covered as news and, as in this case, replayed on television news and reported in print from coast to coast, reaching many times more viewers than the original schedule could have.

Bush's campaign organization had made the decision in the spring that they would not use Horton's name, race, or photograph and that the campaign would concentrate on the symbolic facts using an entirely anonymous group of actors, by far most of them white but with a sprinkling of blacks. Now, however, the National Security PAC had explicitly introduced race into the campaign.

This stirred a great furor in all the media, and the reverberations of the Willie Horton News/Ad drew ever more attention to the central message of the color-blind Bush ad: murderer in badly run Massachusetts furlough program rapes and stabs couple. It added the fact that the criminal was black.[5]

The net impact was a steady increase in negative ratings for Dukakis in the electorate and increasing hostility toward the Bush campaign among the media elite for not having prevented the Horton ad or stopped it sooner. Indeed, the independent provenance of the ad with Horton's name and picture was mentioned only sporadically in critical news accounts, and the two ads quickly merged in the public mind.

Other authentic Bush commercials, meanwhile, were endeavoring to depict the Massachusetts governor as a liberal far to the left of the moderately conservative American mainstream, and Dukakis's response to the crescendo of attacks was to abandon at last his early and quixotic decision not to counterattack even if subjected to heavy negative campaigning.

Several early spots sponsored by the Democratic National Committee had cited Dukakis for what they said to be his effective attacks on crime, jailing drug dealers and putting more cops on the street. One showed him in a sea of massed U.S. flags. But the candidate had no stomach for pursuing these conservative and patriotic themes. Meanwhile, the Bush people hit the same points effectively and with verve and stole his own game away with far more potent spots that just devastated the Dukakis image.

Belated Retaliation. At last Dukakis struck back with a series of wry ads showing a confab of political packagers figuring out how to make Bush and his vice-presidential candidate, Dan Quayle, look good [Packaging Bush and Quayle 1988]. However, essentially these were complicated inside political jokes, and quite amusing as such, but they never caught fire.

Next the Democrat addressed the Bush campaign's distortions of his record directly and bitterly: "I'm fed up with it. Never seen anything like it in 25 years of public life—George Bush's negative TV ads. Distorting my record. It's full of lies and he knows it" [Fed Up 1988]. Dukakis's media people virtually duplicated the Bush revolving door ad, identifying an escapee from a *federal* prison furlough program who raped and murdered a pregnant mother of three [Furlough from Truth 1988].

But it was too little, too late, and on ground long since preempted by the Bush campaign. The new president-elect had started his campaign remarkably far behind Dukakis in popularity polls. From its keynote address to the closing gavel the Democratic convention that nominated Dukakis had been turned into a circus mocking Bush as a feckless "wimp" who was never in the right place at the right time, a corporate gesture of contempt never really precedented in a century and a half of presidential nominating conventions.

Those few nights of self-indulgence, trumpeted on live television and throughout the press, not only made the Democrats feel good but also cemented the "wimp factor" in the public mind as an issue, which a couple of months of aggressive negative campaigning turned around for George Bush. He took the advice of his "handlers" that the best defense was a good offense.

NEGATIVE CAMPAIGNING FOR CONGRESS

As any American with a television receiver knows, attack video is not restricted to presidential elections. Indeed, the tactic has become so important to modern House and Senate elections that the national or congressional campaign committees of both parties go to considerable lengths to school their inexperienced candidates in how to employ it effectively and safely when needed.

For instance, in 1986 the Democratic Congressional Campaign Committee (DCCC) prepared a sample of a proper approach to cutting an incumbent opponent down to size. The screen shows fat envelopes being dropped on an in-box that is heaping full and overflowing. The voice-over enumerates congressional problems, as notebooks and more fat envelopes plop onto the swelling pile on the overloaded in-box.

Unemployment [plop]. Pollution [plop]. Deficits [plop]. The problems before Congress keep piling up [plop] [plop] [plop]. So where is Congressman Borman? [The camera pans slowly to our left as the voice continues.] Well, he's visited thirteen countries this term. Played lots of golf. Appeared [the voice rises in wonderment] in a fashion show. But for sixty-eight votes in the House of Representatives, Congressman Borman has been absent. [The camera stops and holds on a congressional chair with an OUT sign on desk before it.] So you could say John Borman is already out. It's time to send in Pat Michaels. [The scene cuts to a photo of the challenger.] (John Franzen Multimedia for DCCC; author's descriptions in brackets; [In-Box 1986])

As Chapter 7, which deals with distortion, makes clear, missing sixty-eight votes in a two-year congressional term may well be a matter of little moment, and no one knows it better than the party organizations (both parties) that coach their hopefuls on how to win a seat in the House or Senate. But these same party functionaries know equally well that it is almost impossible to dislodge an incumbent, so this is one of those areas where (almost) anything goes.

Using the Other Side's Footage

When Harriett Woods, a Missouri state senator and a former reporter and television news producer, ran for the U.S. Senate seat occupied by Republican John Danforth in 1982, she set out to show that Danforth's TV ads misrepresented him as a liberal on social issues. Her campaign consultant, Joe Slade White, learned that the incumbent's commercials had not been copyrighted (as is often the case) and obtained and used excerpts from Danforth's actual footage to undermine his credibility.

The resulting Woods commercials used Danforth's opening shot, and so, as the consultant later boasted, "when voters saw the Danforth ads, they were never quite sure whether they would turn out to be *Danforth's* Danforth ads, or *Harriett Woods's* Danforth ads."[6] Moreover, after the Woods spots had been on the air for a time, whenever genuine Danforth commercials were aired viewers were reminded of Harriett Woods [Woods/Danforth 1982].

The hybrid ads opened on Danforth, with his name running across the screen and his own voice proclaiming, for example, "Social Security is the most important program we've ever developed in the United States." Here Woods's announcer would take over: "That's what Senator John Danforth says, but what are the facts? Facts: Republican John Danforth has voted time after time to cut Social Security and other programs." A video "crawl" reiterates the point in print, and the voice-over now states, "The choice: Senator Harriett Woods..."

Danforth responded more or less in kind, as State Senator Woods surged in late polling, and she ultimately came within 2 points of overtaking him, no doubt failing in part because she ran out of money and had to stay off the air for the last week.

Instant Attention Is Mandatory

An arresting visual element is absolutely essential at the opening of any attack commercial, or indeed of any commercial. For example, the spot may open on an image of the rival candidate or some mechanical device making erratic flip-flops or gyrations. The reason is the television remote-control switch in the hand of the viewer. Longtime Republican political and media consultant Douglas Bailey has called the remote control "the biggest technological breakthrough in political TV advertising. If you don't have their attention *instantly*, they're gone."[7]

A wildly fluctuating polygraph needle did the trick for a Texas Democrat seeking to keep his House seat in 1980. Jim Mattox, the incumbent, attacked the credibility of his Republican opponent, Tom Pauken. As the needle darted back and forth, the voice-over began: "Testing Tom Pauken's qualifications isn't a job for the voter, it's a task for a lie detector" ([Lie Detector 1980]; Mattox won and later ran successfully for attorney general in Texas. In 1990 he sought the Democratic nomination for governor in a vicious campaign against State Treasurer Ann Richards, using negative TV profusely to smoke out Ms. Richards on whether she, an acknowledged recovering alcoholic, had ever used cocaine. This time the negative approach was too much for the voters, who chose Ms. Richards.)

The Chickens Come Home

"Opposition research" is the contemporary term for the digging that Walter Quigley and James Callender did into the personal histories of their targets. A prudent candidate must assume that any potentially embarrassing past misstep or gaucherie will come back to haunt his or her next campaign. Henry Wallace, a left-wing icon of the 1940s, once noted sourly that if you read far enough back in the *New York Times* you could find everything that anybody ever said.

Jack Loudsma, a Michigan Republican seeking to unseat Democratic

Senator Carl Levin in 1986, found out you could get it played back to you on your own television screen. A Levin commercial opened on a *Detroit News* headline: "Auto Jobs Disappear Despite Recovery." The voice-over intoned, "In October 1983, 133,000 auto workers were unemployed. Senator Carl Levin [now shown in a Senate committee session] was in Washington fighting to strengthen the American auto industry. Jack Loudsma was in Japan, giving a public speech. In Toyota Hall." [The scene shifts to Loudsma before a Japanese audience; the scene is labeled "Toyota Hall, October 1983."] Now Loudsma speaks: "As a matter of fact, I have a small investment in this hall. Because, you see, back home in the United States I do have a Toyota automobile." [Now the camera is back on the hardworking Levin.] The voice concludes: "We deserve a senator who understands our problems and who will fight for Michigan. We have one. In Carl Levin." Loudsma lost [Toyota Hall 1984].

Defense: Milking NCPAC for Laughs

In some situations humor can be a most effective defense weapon. The widely feared National Conservative Political Action Fund (NCPAC, usually pronounced Nickpack) took aim at Montana's Democratic Senator John Melcher in 1982. NCPAC's campaign theme was that Melcher was too liberal for Montana. Various of his Senate votes were cited, and each time a rubber stamp would bang down on a picture of the senator's face, labeling it, in stamp-pad red, "TOO LIBERAL" [Too Liberal 1982].

Melcher was an Iowa native who moved to Montana fresh out of college and set up a veterinary practice. He had been a Montanan thirty years and a country boy all his life. He responded to the heavy-handed NCPAC attacks with one of the funniest political commercials in history, and it made his dreaded assailants look like utter nincompoops.

The scene was a parked airliner. Down the boarding steps we see descending the legs and feet of Important Executives. Their black briefcases are also in the shot, labeled "NCPAC." The narration is in an authentic Montana drawl:

VIDEO	AUDIO
Legs descending, NCPAC briefcases swinging beside them.	NARRATOR: For over a year now a pack o' East Coast politicos've been scurryin' to Montana with brief cases full of money, tryin' to convince us that our Senator Melcher is out of step.
A briefcase opens. Money blows around. Cut to several cattle at feed trough.	Montana isn't buying it. Especially those who know bull when they hear it.

CLOSEUP: cow, chewing cud. She speaks.

Mellow, relaxed, female voice synchronized with her contented chomping. SHOT WIDENS and calf noses under talking cow to seize a teat on her full udder.

CUT to broad shot of pasture where Melcher and rancher walk past a cow or two.

CUT back to cow.

CUT back to Melcher and rancher. ZOOM on their legs striding along in step.

COW: Did y' hear about those city slickers out here, bad-mouthin' Doc Melcher? One of 'em was steppin' in what they been tryin' t' sell. He kept callin' me a steer. That'll come as some surprise to Junior there.

NARRATOR: John Melcher has been solvin' Montana problems most of his life; as a veterinarian, a legislator, a congressman, and as our U.S. senator. He loves this land. And he knows its people. He works long and hard to make sure our needs are met.

COW: Now tell me. Does that look like a man who's out of step with Montana?

NARRATOR: Those outsiders who say Melcher's out o' step with Montana ju-u-ust don't know Montana. Experience we can trust. Montana's John Melcher.[8]
[Talking Cow 1982]

Part II

The Elements of Unfair
Campaigning

The six chapters that follow examine the campaign aspects of political mischief, the fundamental elements of defamation and deception as practiced in American election campaigns. These include efforts to turn voters against a candidate: by sheer vituperation (Chapter 4); by the attribution of gross moral or mental defects (Chapter 5); by appeals to religious or other biases and prejudice (Chapter 6); by distorting the truth (Chapter 7); by outright falsehood and other fabrications (Chapter 8); and by spurious appeals to patriotism or the imputation of treason (Chapter 9).

The reader will note that those who employ these tactics of deception and disaffection span a broad range, including rival candidates, campaign or other political organizations, citizens or organizations with a particular axe to grind, some elements of the news media, religious bodies, individuals bearing some grudge against a candidate, and people or groups that see the candidate as a threat to society.

It is also noteworthy that motivations for using these methods of disrupting the political dialog of election campaigns range from a merely tactical willingness to cheat a bit for a few more votes to a deeply sincere conviction—which may be either rational or quite demented—that the candidate under attack is profoundly dangerous to public safety or morals.

All of the tactics described here are ancient. Only the means by which they are employed have changed with the continuing technological revolution, which was under way when the country was young. From this it may be seen that the exploitation of new ways to perpetrate old tricks is one of the oldest political traditions.

4

Personal Vilification: The Classic Smear

Vilification, name-calling, mudslinging, vituperation, personal abuse, con-tumely—whatever you call it—has been part of political life since office-seekers first competed for votes. It has precipitated canings, beatings, lawsuits, and duels, given apoplexy to some of the Founding Fathers (and their successors), and driven others out of politics. And it long has brought color and brio to the practice of politics in the halls of state as on the hustings.

But of late, colorful political invective has fallen on evil days. There was a certain magisterial eloquence, even grandeur, to the better rhetorical barbs of the nineteenth century. Gone is the time when a John Randolph could proclaim to the whole House of Representatives that Edward Livingston was "a man of splendid abilities but utterly corrupt. He shines and stinks like rotten mackerel by moonlight." No longer is there a Henry Clay to harpoon a long-winded speaker addressing "posterity" with the comment that the speaker is determined to await the arrival of his audience. In the modern rhetorical desert drab and unimaginative slurs are thought to be historic slanders.

Not that all the language was high-flown in days of yore. Eighteenth- and nineteenth-century politics also had a large quotient of harsh and insulting vituperation of a sort almost never heard today—except perhaps in the bitter invective of a hard-fought British election or in the florid abuse of parliamentary discourse in the House of Commons where, whether in re-sponse to contemptuous Tory sneers or to deride conservative proposals, Labour members of the Militant Tendency have not infrequently interrupted an opposition speaker with a rousing rendition of the Communist anthem "Red Flag." The Tories, of course, are just as abusive, though most strive to make their sneers more elegant.

NINETEENTH-CENTURY VITUPERATION

Political slurs of the first few elections under the Constitution have been mentioned in passing in Part I, but for a dozen years or so after the War of 1812, American politics was so serene that its rowdier antecedents were almost forgotten. Historians borrowed a phrase of the time to describe that span as the Era of Good Feelings.

However, all this sweetness and light ground to a halt as competition grew intense in the abusive election campaign of 1824. There were four presidential candidates, all supported and attacked by friends and foes, including the press. One observer protested that if the "calumnies of the most abandoned newspapers [were taken] for the moral standard of this nation [one would suppose] that our Presidents, Secretaries, Senators, and Representatives, are all traitors and pirates, and the government of this people, had been committed to the hands of public robbers" (Mooney 1974, 287).

In the 1824 campaign William H. Crawford was charged with malfeasance as Secretary of the Treasury; Andrew Jackson was labeled a multiple murderer; the Speaker of the House of Representatives, Henry Clay, was the subject of a pamphlet titled "Twenty-one Reasons Why Clay Should Not Be Elected," one of which was that he "spends his days at a gaming table and his nights in a brothel."

Although Jackson had ninety-nine electoral votes to John Quincy Adams's eighty-four, Clay and Crawford had won enough votes to deprive either Jackson or Adams of the required majority. Thus the choice of the president fell to the House. The Speaker, Henry Clay, persuaded his colleagues to elect Adams, and the new president made Clay secretary of state. The charge of "bargain and sale," the presidency for a cabinet post, rose at once and dogged both men to the end of their careers.

The Bitter Campaign of 1828

In a rematch in 1828, Adams himself refrained from personal attacks on Jackson, but few of his advocates were at temperate. Jackson was depicted as a dangerous roughneck, a wild man of the frontier, a bloodthirsty, trigger-happy knave and brawler.

Jackson's roistering adherents mocked Adams for his patrician bearing and demeanor and spread word along the frontier that he despised the common folk. Paradoxically, puritans among the Jacksonians denounced the "gambling furniture" in Adams's White House—a billiard table and a chess set. There were lurid claims that while Minister to Russia Adams had arranged for an American maidservant to be turned over to the Czar. Some said she was sold, others that Adams was a pimp. Adams was so offended at the way he was savaged by the Jacksonians that he refused to attend the inauguration of his successor (Remini 1988, 177–78).

Jackson easily won reelection in 1832, and at the end of his second term he designated his vice president, Martin Van Buren of New York, to succeed him. The Whigs, with regional candidates in the North, South, and West, put on a roistering if uncoordinated campaign that was a fitting precursor of 1840 (see below). Whig papers in New York, the *American*, the *Courier*, and the *Enquirer*, lambasted the Democrat Van Buren, the political "magician" of the Albany Regency. He was a fox prowling near the barn, illiterate, Jackson's sycophant, politically corrupt.

Davy Crockett, the quick-witted Tennessee frontiersman and anti-Jackson congressman, may have been the actual author of this popular thrust at Van Buren that was published for the Whigs: "He struts and swaggers like a crow in the gutter." The line appeared in a biography of Van Buren under Crockett's name, *The Life of Martin Van Buren*; it is somewhat more likely that the book was one of a great many ghost-written works to which the flamboyant westerner (i.e., Tennesseean) freely lent his name.

The book also touched on the much-used theme of Van Buren's slight stature and his delicate mannerisms. Crockett, or his ghost, described Little Van "laced up in corsets" and found it "difficult to say, from his personal appearance, whether he was a man or woman, but for his . . . whiskers." Ironically, this "Crockett" work was published posthumously. The fearless Tennesseean, characteristically, had dashed off to the Mexican War and was killed at the Alamo.

Whigs called the Democrats of 1836, among many other names that were quite scurrilous at the time, revolters, renegades, brawlers, infidels, unclean birds, scum, knaves, cheats, and swindlers. "Van Buren and Ruin," they said, was the alternative to "Harrison and Prosperity." The voters chose Van Buren. (It is worth noting in passing that the Democrats borrowed the theme in 1924, urging the election of John W. Davis as the alternative to the "RepUblIcaN" Coolidge. "FDR and Ruin" was a theme of Republican campaigners in 1932, 1936, and 1940. Ruin won every time.)

Horse Thieves and Mileage Elongators

One of the Whig managers in the madhouse campaign of 1840, Horace Greeley, said that although not every Democrat was a horse thief, every horse thief was a Democrat (Van Deusen 1953). When Abraham Lincoln ran for Congress as a Whig in 1848, his Democratic opponent was a tough old tub-thumping, circuit-riding preacher named Peter Cartwright, whose supporters spread rumors throughout the district that

Lincoln's wife was a high-toned Episcopalian, that Lincoln in a temperance speech in Springfield had said that drunkards are as good as Christians and church members, that Lincoln was a "deist" who believed in God but did not accept Christ and the doctrines of atonement and punishment, that Lincoln said, "Christ was a bastard." (Sandburg 1926, 1:336)

Near the end of Lincoln's only term in the House, Horace Greeley, a Whig and future Republican like Lincoln, was elected to a vacancy in New York's House delegation. He became acquainted with the Illinoisan, for whom he developed a strong dislike. In his brief tenure Greeley, ever the reformer and ever pure of heart, was startled to discover numerous irregularities in the conduct of members, including, no doubt to his keen pleasure, Abraham Lincoln. Greeley launched a crusade in his *New York Tribune* against what we would call the padding of expense accounts. Then the padders were known as "mileage elongators."

Congressmen were reimbursed for travel between Washington and their home districts on the basis of the route they usually took. Many, including young Lincoln, filed mileage claims on the basis of the longest and most circuitous route they could figure out. In the *Tribune* Greeley published a table comparing the mileage actually received by each member, along with what he would have received based on the most direct route.

The table showed that House members received for one session an excess of $47,223.80 because of the circuitous routes they had taken or claimed to have taken, while the upper chamber was in pocket a total of $14,881.40 for the same reason. Old Bullion Benton had profited to the extent of $689.60. Abraham Lincoln's excess mileage was $676.80. (Van Deusen 1953, 127)

In a time when $1.50 could get you board for a week and $5 an acre of land, this was important pelf.

By 1852 the Whigs were falling apart, and although they managed a respectable popular vote for their candidate, the Mexican War hero Winfield Scott, they lost lopsidedly in the Electoral College. They did succeed in somewhat muddying the reputation of the victorious Democratic candidate. Franklin Pierce, a senator from New Hampshire and a heavy drinker. The Whigs called him a drunkard and the "hero of many a well-fought bottle." He was falsely branded an anti-Catholic and, separately, a coward—twisting the fact that he had fainted in battle in the Mexican War and had to be carried from the field (Lorant 1968, 210).

IN THE SHADOW OF CIVIL WAR

The 1856 campaign was shadowed by violent conflicts over the future of slavery. There were murders, lootings, and press-smashings in the "Bleeding Kansas" territory. A Massachusetts Abolitionist, Charles Sumner, was clubbed unconscious in his Senate seat after bitterly denouncing an elder absent colleague, South Carolina's Senator Andrew P. Butler. The beating was administered by a young kinsman of Butler, a member of the House.

Republicans nominated John C. Frémont for president and ran a campaign that subtly reminded everyone of Sumner's near-fatal beating. The Democrats nominated Pennsylvania's James Buchanan on a compromise platform aimed at placating slavers and abolitionists. The campaign echoed all the bloody themes of the day. Republicans carried most of the North and lost to the Democrats, who picked up most of the West and all the slave states but Maryland, which went to the Know-Nothings.

Before the 1860 presidential campaign Lincoln was not generally known outside the Northwest, but his fame was starting to spread. Democrats in the border states said he supported Negro suffrage, which he did not. He won, and when the Republicans convened in 1864 under a National Union banner, they renominated the president and chose as his running mate a pro-war Democrat from Tennessee, Andrew Johnson. The Northern Democrats named that arrogant, highly political and often insubordinate soldier, General George B. McClellan. Strongly influenced by their Copperhead, or anti-war wing, they drew up a platform calling for immediate cessation of hostilities, which McClellan repudiated. But he and the Democrats sedulously courted the substantial defeatist vote in the North.

Slandering Lincoln

The campaign was bitter. A month before election day one Ohio editor viewed the verbal carnage with distaste:

The vulgar language of Republicans and Democrats is disgusting. Stump orators vie in scurrility and obscene allusions. Surely the friends of Mr. Lincoln do not expect to gain votes by calling all the friends and supporters of General McClellan traitors and Copperheads; and we know that the course [*sic*] epithets applied to Mr. Lincoln are hurting the cause of Gen. McClellan a great deal. (Felknor 1966, 26)

The coarse epithets applied to Mr. Lincoln were remarkable both in volume and in viciousness. Those excesses have been extensively chronicled. The quickest summary is a negative one: Lincoln was not called a ladies' man. And none of the smear words spread throughout the Union began with the letters Q, X, Y, or Z.

Otherwise, every letter of the alphabet was the initial of at least one harsh epithet for the wartime president. A fragmentary but representative list includes: ape, buffoon, coward, drunkard, execrable, fiend, ghoul, hopeless, ignoramus, jokester (in the face of war tragedies), knave, lunatic, murderer, Negro, outlaw, perjurer, robber, savage, traitor, usurper, vulgar, and weakling.

Radical Republicans already were turning on Lincoln for his resistance to their demands for a repressive Reconstruction of the postwar South, and Greeley's *New York Tribune* opposed him and published a Radical anti-Lincoln manifesto. There was an aborted Radical conspiracy to remove his name from the Republican ticket.

Lincoln won reelection, with a bare 55 percent of the popular vote and an electoral landslide, although he carried New York's thirty-three electors by less than 1 percent of that state's 750,000 votes. The returns focused attention on the vice president-elect, who had received only incidental mention during the campaign. Copperheads, perhaps exhausted by their maligning of Lincoln, and also possibly more comfortable with a known devil than a strange one, now voiced their dread "that only one frail life stands between this insolent, clownish drunk and the presidency." The reference was to Johnson—although the same phrase had been used to describe Lincoln.

On Good Friday, forty days after his second inauguration, Lincoln was shot. The next day the "insolent, clownish drunk" was president, and then by the very grace of the Demon Rum. Vice President Johnson's assassin-designate in the Lincoln plot had consumed too much bottled courage the night before and slept a drunken sleep past the appointed hour—a few yards away from Andrew Johnson's hotel room.

President Johnson, shortly to be maligned as "King Andy I," inherited the calumny as well as the office from Lincoln. Immediately on taking the presidential oath, Johnson began to implement Lincoln's conciliatory Reconstruction policies, with some changes. The Radical Republicans in Congress resisted and hampered him at every turn, demanding their own Radical formula for Reconstruction.

Johnson's reaction was contentious, and in 1866 he took to the hustings in a negative campaign aimed at electing moderates to displace the Radical Republicans in Congress. His tour became a series of harangues, and it failed completely. The Radicals won control of both House and Senate and proceeded virtually to seize the reins of the executive and dominate the Reconstruction effort. The tide continued to run their way, and the Republicans elected the war hero General Ulysses Grant over the Democrats' Horatio Seymour in 1868, though with a popular vote plurality of only 300,000.

THE SLURS OF THE GILDED AGE

In 1872, the Republicans divided over Radical Reconstruction and the growing corruption of the Grant administration. The Radicals, now regulars, stuck with Grant. The new reform faction, the Liberals, nominated Horace Greeley, who was then somewhat uneasily endorsed by the Democrats and more happily by the Colored Republicans. Greeley was a strange combination of fuzzy idealist, fighting reformer, and crusading journalist.

He was despised by the regular Republicans, and they joyously assailed him in a vicious campaign.

Old Chappaquack and Free Love

Much of the campaign rhetoric they hurled against him was true. He was accused of favoring free love and Fourierism, a brand of utopian socialism which he did promote. To support the free love charge, his name was linked with that of the notorious Victoria Woodhull, who actually ran for president against him, and her sister, Tennessee Claflin.

These two were American originals and a pair of women utterly astonishing for their time. They were spiritualists, publishers of a women's rights magazine, ardent advocates of free love, enemies of prostitution and abortion, and successful stockbrokers, bankrolled by Cornelius Vanderbilt. Victoria was the first woman ever nominated for president, by the new Equal Rights Party. Greeley, a genuine radical in so many ways, opposed women's suffrage.

The derisive epithet "Old Chappaquack" was derived from his home town of Chappaqua, New York; to alienate his black supporters he was called a "Negro trader"; whispers among Catholics and the foreign-born made him out to be a Know-Nothing; and because in a typical burst of Greeleyan inspiration and charity he had made bond for the defeated Confederate President Jefferson Davis after the war, he was called a secessionist. Finally, and not without plausibility, he was labeled a madman (see Chapter 5). Poor Greeley died after the election but before the Electoral College met, and his meager forty-two votes were scattered to the winds.

The most notable unsavory attribute of the next election had more to do with election fraud than with vilification, and accordingly it is treated in Chapter 11. But important groundwork for the next really dirty campaign, that of 1884, was laid in the Republican convention of 1876 and again in 1880, where there was more fancy footwork than what went on in the fall campaigns.

Plumed Knight, Continental Liar

For a time in 1876, James G. Blaine, chairman of the House Rules Committee and former Speaker, seemed to be a logical favorite for the Republican nomination. Then word leaked out that as Speaker he had done a very valuable favor for a railroad, the Little Rock & Fort Smith, by quietly scuttling a piece of threatening legislation. The grateful railroad made Blaine some $100,000 richer. But a rumor about the transaction began to spread around Washington, compromising his presidential hopes. A House committee launched an investigation.

At this point Blaine came across a bookkeeper named James Mulligan, who had worked for the railroad lawyer, Warren Fisher, who essentially was the railroad's bagman in the affair. Mulligan not only knew about Blaine's role but had letters proving it. Incredibly, he loaned the letters to Blaine, who brandished them before the committee and read selected excerpts from them to demonstrate his innocence.

Blaine's famous rhetorical skills and his glib quotations out of context bamboozled the committee, just as he had bamboozled the gullible Mulligan out of the letters, and his name was cleared—for the nonce. At the Republican convention the opportunistic congressman from Maine was nominated by Robert G. Ingersoll, a famous orator of the day. He delivered a stem-winding paean to Blaine, who, he cried, had marched gallantly down the halls of Congress "like an armed warrior, like a plumed knight," to defend his fair name. But for all Ingersoll's effulgent oratory, Blaine lost the nomination to Rutherford B. Hayes, and his reputation never fully recovered.

After trying again in 1880, when one of his unsuccessful rivals was Grant angling for a third term, Blaine managed to beat the president, Chester A. Arthur, out of the nomination in 1884. In doing so, he alienated one faction of Reform Republicans, who supported the Democratic nominee and shortly came to be called Mugwumps.

The Democrat the Mugwumps turned to was a vigorous reformer, governor of New York and former mayor of Buffalo, Grover Cleveland. But this reformer, so attractive at first to the fallen-away Republicans, had clay feet, too. He was a bachelor and was accused of fathering the illegitimate child of an attractive Buffalo widow named Maria "Bunny" Halpin, with whom he was known to be friendly.

Cleveland admitted that he had been intimate with Mrs. Halpin and that he had contributed to the child's support. However, he denied that the child was actually his. The denial was not widely believed. But it was not really material because he admitted the hanky-panky, and it made for a ribald campaign.

There were two other colorful candidates. The Greenback Party had nominated a flamboyant old pol and Civil War general, Benjamin Franklin Butler. He had been a Democrat, then a Radical Republican congressman, and the original waver of the bloody shirt in the House to demonstrate Rebel brutality. Butler's bleak countenance led Mark Twain to say that "when he smiles it is like the breaking up of a hard winter."

The other added starter was Victoria Woodhull's successor, Belva Ann Lockwood (née Bennett), the candidate of the Equal Rights Party (as she was to be again in 1888). Mrs. Lockwood also was a remarkable woman, far ahead of her time, who in her forties studied law, was admitted to the bar, and became the first woman admitted to practice before the Supreme Court. A feminist, a suffragist, a highly competent lawyer, and an influential advocate, she left her mark on several areas of the law.

But in 1884 her candidacy occasioned considerable merriment among the male chauvinists of that day, who could not have imagined that within a single generation women would have the vote. She was the object of jokes and campaign gadgets, one of which was circulated so widely in Ben Butler's campaign that many copies are still extant and much traded by collectors. On a sheet of stiff paper is the slogan, "OUR NEXT PRESIDENT." Below it appears a drawing of Mrs. Lockwood, wearing a full, floor-length skirt of paper, which may be lifted to reveal the Greenbacker candidate hiding beneath it, grinning and thumbing his nose.

Meanwhile, Blaine's hardy loyalists did not waver either in their admiration of the "Plumed Knight" from Maine or their contempt for the Democrats' tarnished reformer. Cleveland's supporters knew that at least their man was honest and the Plumed Knight was not. The campaign quickly degenerated into a sea of mud.

Cleveland was described as a drunken saloon lounger and the epitome of immorality. Republicans chortled over cartoons showing Bunny Halpin cradling an infant labeled "one more vote for Cleveland." Their torchlight paraders took to chanting, "Ma, ma, where's my pa?" Democrats rejoined, "Gone to the White House, ha, ha, ha!"

But Blaine could not enjoy the taunts at Cleveland, for the bookkeeper, Mulligan, had reappeared on the scene with, worse luck, more letters. Like the others, he had filched these out of the files of his former employer, the railroad attorney Warren Fisher. Mulligan turned the new set of letters over to a newspaper, the *Boston Journal*. Two in particular were devastating.

One was a draft Blaine had prepared for Fisher to sign, in effect a false affidavit that would exonerate Blaine completely. The other was a covering letter from Blaine to Fisher entreating him to sign and to keep the exchange in strictest confidence. It concluded, "Kind regards to Mrs. Fisher. Burn this letter!"

Unluckily for the perfidious Blaine, Fisher neither signed the exoneration nor burned the letter, and once it appeared in the *Boston Journal* Democrats flaunted it far and wide. Their torchlight paraders and the faithful at rallies set up chants: "Burn this letter! Burn this letter! Burn, burn, O burn this letter!" and "Blaine, Blaine, James G. Blaine! Continental liar from the State of Maine! Burn this letter!"

OLD-FASHIONED SMEAR IN THE MODERN ERA

Like the Democrat Cleveland, the Republican Theodore Roosevelt was a tough and scrupulous reform governor of New York when he was injected into national politics. The corrupt GOP old guard in New York sidetracked him into the vice presidency under McKinley to get him out of Albany. To their dismay he succeeded the murdered McKinley less than six months after his inauguration. By the time the Rough Rider's inherited term in the White

House ended in 1904, American big business was viewing this wild man with alarm and distaste.

Roosevelt easily won nomination and reelection in 1904, but throughout the campaign and afterward he was vilified extensively. He was described as ruthless, cowardly, a bluff, a braggart, a trigger-happy maniac, a traitor to his class, the enemy of business and of freedom, obsequious to Negroes, and arrogant to well-born whites. He was cartooned as a militarist, as a windbag, and—no doubt because of his liberal attitude toward other ethnic groups—as a stereotypic Jewish merchant.

Although Roosevelt stepped aside in 1908 in favor of William Howard Taft, Teddy changed his mind in 1912 and ran what turned to be a spoiler campaign on the Progressive or "Bull Moose" ticket against Republican President Taft and the Democratic nominee, Woodrow Wilson. Republican conservatives despised Roosevelt and continued to disparage him with zeal.

But they also saw Wilson, a teacher, lawyer, college president, and reform-minded governor of New Jersey, as too much the puritan and taunted him as a visionary and an intellectual snob. The GOP–Bull Moose split elected Wilson. When he sought a second term in 1916, World War I was raging in Europe, and the president's campaigners boasted, "He kept us out of war!" But an interventionist temper was rising in America, and a jingoistic press caricatured him as spineless. The *New York Herald* ran a cartoon of a human spine in an anatomy lab labeled "BACKBONE," beside the legend, "LOST! (Somewhere in Washington)" (Coyle 1960).

If Wilson was seen as puritanical and too much the scholar and intellectual, exactly the opposite attributes were ascribed to the Democratic presidential nominee a dozen years later, Governor Alfred E. Smith of New York. Although religion is the most remembered element of the 1928 campaign against Smith, the Demon Rum and snobbery were probably as important.

The governor, universally known as Al Smith, was a Roman Catholic, and the substantial role of anti-Catholicism in his defeat is treated in Chapter 6. But he also was a foe of the Prohibition Amendment, which had been in force but scarcely enforced since 1920, and he was the child of Irish immigrants and a New Yorker with an East Side accent. His nasal pronunciation of "raddio" brought sneers and snickers from snobs everywhere. He was a pushy newcomer, an Irishman in the day when the epithet "donkey" was still heard in the Middle West to describe the Irish railroad laborers of the previous generation. A rhetorical question swept women's clubs: "My dear, can you imagine a president named *Al*?"

After a long wrangle, the framers of the Democratic platform of 1928 had agreed to declare that Prohibition should be enforced; Al Smith had argued for its repeal. The slogan raised against Cleveland in 1884—rum, Romanism, and rebellion—was revived among Americans who had learned to live with Prohibition and bootleggers. The Demon Run, Ten Nights in a Barroom, the Face on the Barroom Floor—these were the images Al Smith conjured up among the self-righteous. They helped keep him out of the White House and helped put Herbert Hoover in.

It was Hoover's bad luck to see his presidency defined by the stock market crash of 1929 and the Great Depression. Any dream of a second term was destroyed in the campaign of 1932, when the Democrats made his name a synonym for depression, misery, and blind reaction. Political smear in that election consisted almost solely of defamation of Hoover as callous, indifferent, and heedlessly helpless against the ravages of the depression. Poor Hoover did not even get off a good negative sound bite until the end of the campaign, when he warned of what a victory by Franklin D. Roosevelt would bring: "The grass will grow in the streets of a hundred cities, a thousand towns; the weeds will overrun the fields of a million farms."

Baiting the Other Roosevelt

By 1936 Roosevelt, to Republicans, was the enemy of the people. The GOP named Alf M. Landon of Kansas to topple the new monarch. He started out on a high plane, but many of his spokesmen left it quickly. His vice-presidential candidate, the Chicago publisher Frank Knox, warned, "Today no life insurance policy is secure; no savings account is safe." He compared FDR to George III (Schlesinger 1960). By September it was becoming fashionable to call Roosevelt a Communist, among other epithets.

Landon carried Maine and Vermont. In those days, Maine was a bellwether state, since it voted—usually "right"—in September, two months early. "As Maine goes, so goes the nation," went the adage. James A. Farley, the Democratic national chairman, did it in: "As Maine goes, so goes Vermont."

The attacks on Roosevelt went on year in and year out, not just in election campaigns. He saw early supporters turn into implacable enemies. The "radio priest," Father Coughlin, in 1932 said it was Roosevelt or ruin; in 1936, FDR was anti-God and a liar. FDR was a Bolshevik, doing fiendish surgery on all that was fine in the economy and the nation.

Roosevelt also saw fanaticism among his supporters, particularly in the 1940 campaign. To be sure, there was some light-hearted and deft harpooning, too. His Interior Secretary, the irrepressible Harold Ickes, whose occupational disease was said to be hyperbole, deflated Republican challenger Wendell Willkie's carefully cultivated homespun image by describing him as "the barefoot boy from Wall Street." But more obscure and less responsible Roosevelt partisans made Willkie out as pro-German, and some even called him a Nazi, on the eve of American involvement in World War II.

Harry S Truman, the Missouri Democrat who was Roosevelt's last vice president, inherited all but three months of FDR's fourth term, long enough to make plenty of his own enemies. When he decided to seek a full term he was immediately outflanked on the left by Henry Wallace, his predecessor as vice president, and a new Progressive Party with all the left-wing sweepings.

On the right, militant Southerners bolted the Democratic convention over the strong civil rights plank in its platform. This Southern rump became the States Rights Party, or the Dixiecrats, who ran Senator Strom Thurmond of South Carolina. The Republicans renominated Thomas E. Dewey, who in 1944 had held Roosevelt to the narrowest victory of his career.

The contest between Truman and Dewey was a lot tamer than the malicious attacks on Truman from the Wallace and Thurmond camps. One of the less malign barbs from the right was a two-inch campaign button proclaiming:

> Washington Could Not Tell A Lie
> Roosevelt Could Not Tell The Truth
> Truman Does Not Know the Difference (Friz 1988, 149)

The major candidates were well matched in hyperbole and invective and pithiness of speech. They offered a bitter, old-style, give-em-hell campaign that made diverting, often exciting, listening and reading. Truman played the hard-fighting underdog role. He often was more abrasive than Dewey. Occasionally, he would mime a small mustache, which was a trademark of Dewey as well as of Adolph Hitler, then dead for only three years. This was a deliberate maneuver to imply that his opponent might be Hitler instead of Dewey. Truman even joked about this to his oral biographer, Merle Miller (1973, 188). James Reston dourly remembers the campaign as "one of the dirtiest of the century" and Truman as "comparing Thomas E. Dewey to Hitler and Mussolini" (Reston 1988). My own judgment is somewhat less severe; the century has seen some vile campaigns.

Johnson–Goldwater and Nixon–McGovern

One of the most vicious was that of 1964. The political year opened with a Republican primary campaign that was so fratricidal that its winner, Barry Goldwater, later said that he wouldn't vote for anyone of whom all the things said about him were true. Like Horace Greeley in the murderous campaign of 1872, the candidate often couldn't tell whether he was running for president or the penitentiary.

The significant smears of the 1964 presidential election are treated elsewhere. However, except for the elements of the Watergate scandal, which is the subject of Chapter 12, the Nixon–McGovern election of 1972 was a kind of fun-house-mirror image of the 1964 Johnson–Goldwater campaign.

In both years the eventual losers ran their party conventions like sardonic parodies of a group therapy session. It was obvious that the presidential candidates had actually been chosen in the primaries. The real function of each convention was the public humiliation of ideological enemies within the party—the liberals Rockefeller and Scranton in 1964 and the nonliberals Hubert Humphrey and Richard Daley (Chicago's powerful mayor) in 1972. As black comedy, however, the Democratic circus of 1972 was better slapstick than the Republican bloodletting of 1964 because of such Punch and Judy touches as throwing out elected delegates and bowing in unelected ones.

And the winners: instead of nominating conventions the 1964 Democrats and the 1972 Republicans staged stately coronation pageants glorifying not-very-popular incumbents who were extravagantly despised by most in the other party and very many in their own. The result in each case was a landslide in favor of a flawed and disliked figure somewhere in the mainstream, a landslide which, in each case, buried a highly moral and ideologically pure prophet.

Although the Democrats in 1972 elected Nixon when they nominated McGovern, they went on to squander what scanty political capital they had left by conducting a campaign of increasingly shrill and bitter vituperation. McGovern repeatedly likened Nixon to Hitler and depicted him as cynically manipulating the Vietnam War on and off as needed to garner votes. The most creditable aspect of the Democrats' 1972 campaign was the fact that the vilification was coming straight from the candidate's mouth and not from what purported to be the invisible mouth of God, as with the Johnson Democrats' television spots of 1964, which suggested that Goldwater wanted to blow up the world and poison little girls (see Chapter 3). The McGovern Democrats were perfectly ready to suggest that Nixon was willing to napalm little girls, but at least the candidate said it himself.

Mudslinging Close to Home

Personal abuse on state and local levels often reveals no pattern. It may be sardonic, irrelevant, somebody's idea of humor, or merely scatological. Bumper stickers are a favorite vehicle. Three from the 1966 campaign for governor of California, in which the actor Ronald Reagan defeated the incumbent Edmund G. "Pat" Brown, will illustrate:

An Actor Killed Lincoln.
Ronald Reagan is a Lesbian.
If It's Brown, Flush It.

In 1974, Democrats everywhere used the revelations of the Watergate scandal to oust Republican legislators. Ramsey Clark, a transplant to New York from Texas who had been Lyndon Johnson's attorney general, seized this occasion to try for the U.S. Senate seat of the Republican Jacob K. Javits. Clark, humble in mismatched suits and $100 contribution limits, repeatedly alluded to Javits as "one of Nixon's [Watergate] thugs."

That GOP senator, a liberal hero for decades, finally was goaded into referring to Clark as "Hanoi Ramsey" to remind voters of his wartime pilgrimage to North Vietnam in 1972. He borrowed the epithet from Clark's opponent in the primary campaign, on whom it had backfired. It did not hurt Javits, who won by 300,000 votes while his Republican colleague, Governor Malcolm Wilson, was losing by 800,000.

ATTACKING FAMILY AND HEALTH

Attacking a politician through his family is so old that Caesar was well aware of the practice. Determined to avoid that risk, he divorced Pompeia because she was no longer above suspicion, so Plutarch tells us. Family relationships were the focus of domestic scandals that ruined many reputations in the early days of the American republic, and somewhat tarnished even the most exalted, from the Founding Fathers on.

Taunts of adultery and slurs and whispers about the validity of his wife's prior divorce during the scurrilous campaign of 1828 deeply scarred the personal life of Andrew Jackson and, most serious biographers agree, drove his modest and pious wife, Rachel, to her death. Others traduced Jackson's mother, who they said had been a prostitute and had married a Negro, who had then sired the president. They said Jackson's older brother had been sold as a slave.

One of the most searing episodes of American history revolved around Abraham Lincoln's wife and groundless but persistent rumors during the Civil War that she harbored Confederate sympathies. Midway in his first term, and midway in the war, these stories were embroidered further to make her a Confederate agent. The Senate members of the Joint Committee on Conduct of the War, set up at the end of 1861 under Radical Republican pressure, met secretly one morning to consider these spreading reports. They had barely come to order when the guard at the door rushed in with a stunned expression, followed immediately by President Lincoln.

Towering above the committee table and the astonished senators, hat in hand, he paused for a long moment, then spoke slowly and quietly: "I, Abraham Lincoln, President of the United States, appear of my own volition before this Committee of the Senate to say that I, of my own knowledge, know that it is untrue that any of my family hold treasonable communication with the enemy" (Sandburg 1939, 2:199–200).[1]

Much of the abuse Franklin Roosevelt took after his first term was really directed at his wife. Eleanor Roosevelt's visibility, her activity on behalf of many social and humanitarian causes, and her wide range of interests irritated many of the rich and powerful, who found her a meddlesome busybody who would do better to stay at home. FDR also was accused of quietly arranging favored treatment for his sons.

Even the First Dog, a scotty named Fala, was not immune. Whispers and printed rumors arose during the 1944 campaign that FDR had diverted a Navy ship to bring Fala home from Alaska, where he had been inadvertently left behind on a presidential trip. The president laid this to rest with a classic public squelch. "The Republican leaders have not been content to make personal attacks upon me, or my wife, or my sons," he told a cheering partisan audience. "They now include my little dog, Fala. Unlike members of my family, Fala resents this.... I am accustomed to hearing malicious falsehoods about myself, but I think I have a right to object to libelous statements about my dog" (Felknor 1966, 37).

Richard Nixon, a young Navy officer at the time, was so struck by the effectiveness of FDR's riposte that he consciously borrowed from it for the famous "Checkers" speech on television that saved his vice-presidential candidacy in 1952 (Nixon 1978, 99; see also Chapter 11).

Spreading Tales of Disease

Publicity about the physical health of politicians has followed a curiously checkered career. Much has been made at various times of alcohol problems and real or imagined venereal diseases suffered by political leaders, but at other times they have been all but ignored. Franklin Roosevelt's paralysis was not talked of much, but several absurd rumors told of various dread maladies he "suffered." What turned out to be his terminal illness fed rumors in the 1944 campaign—encouraged by many Republicans.

False rumors circulated by a New Hampshire whispering campaign helped cost a Democrat, John Shaw, the governorship in 1956. The story was launched that he was a drunk. Actually, he was a teetotaler. By an ironic coincidence in the same year, a moderate drinker nearly was defeated for governor by a rumor that he was a secret temperance worker. The tale was spread about the candidate, Republican Vernon Thompson, by a pair of professionals who toured resort country taverns in Wisconsin revealing Thompson's "secret plan" to dry up the state.

A Nebraska representative named Glenn Cunningham suffered from a disease that affected his balance. In 1964 a local Democratic chairman noticed that Cunningham always had to be helped to the platform on any speaking engagement. He leaped to the assumption that this was because the congressman was always drunk, and he launched a puritanical attack on Cunningham, a conservative Republican who was somewhat puritanical himself—and who was a teetotaler.

John F. Kennedy also had a serious ailment that impaired his freedom. It was Addison's disease, which he and his staff as a policy matter always euphemized as a "partial mild insufficiency of the adrenal gland" rather than its more frightening name (Sorensen 1965, 38–39). In the course of their general background research on John Kennedy in preparation for the 1960 elections, the Republicans had looked carefully into the state of his health, as also had some journalists. They were aware that he was being medicated for an adrenal insufficiency, which already had become fairly well known.

Near the end of the campaign, a California surgeon, acting for himself, wrote a letter that he circulated widely, noting "that Kennedy takes cortisone to support his adrenal needs." The doctor went on to equate taking cortisone with addiction to marijuana, cocaine, and heroin. In 1960, for the general public, these drugs were not commonplace, but the idea of addiction to them represented a kind of shocking depravity. "Such an unreliable, sick man," the good doctor concluded, "should not be allowed to assume the responsibility of our national leadership" (Felknor 1966, 65).

5

The Ghoul Gambit: Putting the Other Side Beyond the Pale

Since before the fifteenth century, "the pale" has meant the stockade enclosing human settlement, shutting out the barbarians and wild beasts beyond. For almost as long as there have been elections, one way of winning them has been to describe the opponent as beyond the pale: subhuman, alien, dangerous.

What if Thomas Jefferson is elected president? "Murder, robbery, rape, adultery, and incest will all be openly taught and practiced,...the soil will be soaked with blood, and the nation black with crimes" (Editorial, *Connecticut Courant* (Hartford), September 15, 1800).

Horace Greeley, running against Grant in 1872, is caricatured by Thomas Nast reaching across the grave of Abraham Lincoln to shake the hand of his assassin, John Wilkes Booth ("The next in Order—Any Thing! Oh, Any Thing!" 1872).

Guns and swords form the facial features of Theodore Roosevelt: his teeth are bullets; his neckerchief a tattered U.S. Constitution. So the *Atlanta Constitution* saw the president, seeking reelection in 1904, in an editorial cartoon by L. C. Gregg (Coyle 1960).

And as for Franklin Roosevelt, that "paranoiac in the White House is destroying the nation, [and] a couple of well-placed bullets would be the best thing for the country" (Coyle 1960, 372; as much has been said of at least a dozen other presidents).

WAR DEATH TOLL POLITICS

Think of Andrew Jackson as a serial murderer. That was the point of the notorious "Coffin Hand Bill" of 1828, a flier illustrated with drawings of eighteen coffins, each with a mournful caption and each representing a supposedly innocent victim of Old Hickory's wanton cruelty. Most of the decedents were soldiers under Jackson's command who had been court-martialed and executed for mutiny or desertion. One was a man he had slain in self-defense, for whose death he was tried. But, in the loaded language of the handbill, "finding means to convince the petit jury that he committed the act in self-defense, he was acquitted" (Coyle 1960, 124–25).[1]

The Coffin Hand Bill was the work of John Binns, editor of Philadelphia's *Democratic Press*. Binns was convinced that Jackson was a madman of tyrannical bent. His handbill enraged Jackson partisans, who attacked Binns's home. His paper went out of business.

Another anti-Jackson handbill, possibly the first overt forgery in a U.S. presidential campaign, doctored excerpts from court-martial records to make the Coffin Hand Bill executions seem useless and arbitrary as well as brutal. Its title, "Official Record from the War Department," and imprimatur, "Ordered to be printed by the Congress," were completely false.

After the United States entered World War II, it dawned on some Republicans that Democratic presidents—Woodrow Wilson and Franklin Roosevelt—had gotten the country into the two most devastating wars in history. From that moment until 1969, when the Vietnam War carried over into the Republican administration of Richard Nixon, the War Death Toll gambit was a GOP campaign staple. The Democrats became the party of war and death.

The pioneer in this field may have been a widely circulated handbill created by a Pennsylvania woman calling for the impeachment of Roosevelt and Vice President Wallace during the "undeclared war" period of 1941. At that time the third Roosevelt administration was asking American families to contribute food staples and clothing as "Bundles for Britain" to succor America's staunchest ally. Mrs. Catharine Brown secured a photograph of a roomful of flag-draped coffins and made it the centerpiece of her flier. The headline asked, "Will one of these Bundles FROM Britain be your son?"

A Vietnam variation on this theme appeared in 1964: a tabulation of the death tolls of all the Democratic wars, with a battlefield photo of an American GI cradling in his arms the head of a dead buddy.

After being on the receiving end for so long, the Democrats got into this game with a memorable bang in 1964 with their nuclear explosion TV commercial against Barry Goldwater (see Chapter 3).

But Republicans had the last laugh in 1968 with a television commercial for Richard Nixon. It was a series of quick intercuts alternating the beaming face of Hubert Humphrey with scene after scene of riot, violence, and warfare. With classic last-minute timing, it was aired on a popular, satiric, Sunday evening show on NBC—Rowan and Martin's "Laugh-In"—just before election day. A highly placed ad executive in the Republican campaign conceded to Sam Archibald, director of the Fair Campaign Practices Committee, that it was a deliberate smear. [Humphrey Laughing 1968].[2]

SEXUAL INNUENDO

Attributing depraved sexual habits and appetites to political candidates is a familiar approach to putting the candidate beyond the pale of civilization. It has been a popular category; the real and imagined sexual proclivities of leading political figures have always intrigued and often scandalized Americans. Even George Washington, hero president in his own time, was subjected to some of the whispers and rumors that have dogged so many of his successors. There was talk that while he was in New York, then the capital, he kept a woman named Mary Gibbon in a lodging there. It is known that he always had a keen eye for the ladies. If, in his younger days at home in Virginia, there were raised eyebrows about his appreciation for his old neighbor's young wife, Sally Fairfax, later discoveries confirm that there was considerable fire beneath the smoke (Flexner 1969, 19–20).

Much attention and controversy attached to Thomas Jefferson's sexual activities, but because it focused on his putative relations with his Negro slave Sally Hemings, this affair is treated with matters of race in Chapter 6. Jefferson was the implacable enemy of Alexander Hamilton, and he surely took comfort from the embarrassments that the younger man's sexual activity brought upon him.

Hamilton's peccadilloes were debated in the public prints, in pamphlets, and on the hustings. This brilliant young politician was only thirty-two when killed in his duel with Burr. He already had been Washington's aide-de-camp in the Revolution, a delegate to the Continental Congress and the Constitutional Convention, and the first Secretary of the Treasury when he retired to practice law in New York City. He was the leading Federalist and a lightning rod for all anti-Federalists and indeed many more sedate members of his own party such as John Adams.

Hamilton's public reputation was effectively destroyed (for the two years remaining of his life) by his amorous adventures in the Maria Reynolds affair as detailed by the scurrilous pamphleteer, Callender (see Chapter 3). Before that scandal, his sexual adventures, if any, had been tacitly accepted by his peers.[3] Indeed, Adams sourly attributed Hamilton's unslaked political ambitions to "a superabundance of secretions" that he "could not find whores enough to draw off" (Miller 1959, 523).

The Peggy Eaton Affair

A sexual scandal involving his cabinet created a serious crisis that came close to ruining Andrew Jackson's first term as president. When in Washington, Tennessee's Senator John Eaton, a young friend and protégé of the president, roomed at a Georgetown tavern, where the landlord's daughter was a beautiful and witty young woman named Peggy O'Neale. She was married to a navy purser, and while he was at sea, she became the mistress of Eaton—"and eleven dozen others," one of his colleagues snorted.[4]

Jackson made Eaton his secretary of war—which enabled him to lengthen the voyages of Peggy's husband, John Timberlake. When the luckless sailor died, Eaton married the notorious Peggy and utterly scandalized Washington society, especially the wives of Eaton's cabinet colleagues. Jackson, whose own wife had been the victim of scandalmongers, dismissed the outrage of the cabinet wives and insistently proclaimed the virtue of the profligate Peggy. This blind gallantry made him the laughing stock of the capital and inspired Henry Clay's immortal Shakespearean paraphrase: "Age cannot wither her, nor custom stale her infinite virginity."[5]

Martin Van Buren, "the little magician," who was secretary of state, recognized the gravity of the problem and precipitated the resignation of the entire cabinet, including Eaton and himself, and both the derisive laughter and the resultant crisis subsided. Van Buren's deft defusing of the crisis endeared him to the president, who designated him to be vice president in his second term and president four years later.

Grover Cleveland remained a bachelor until his second year in the White House, when he was almost fifty. His courtship and marriage were strikingly romantic and utterly charming. Frances Folsom, the daughter of his late law partner, was virtually Cleveland's ward for years. They fell in love, and he courted her secretly while he was governor of New York and she was at the point of graduating from college. Their marriage was long, happy, and fruitful. Nevertheless, in his second and third campaigns for the presidency, whispering campaigns insisted that he was a wife-beater.

The scrupulously moral and abstemious Woodrow Wilson was frequently said to be oversexed. In his second term he was widely rumored to suffer from a venereal disease contracted during a Paris fling while he was negotiating the Versailles Treaty. His presidential physician and friend, Cary Grayson, was so disturbed at the ubiquity of these reports that he had blood tests made to prove for posterity the falsity of the whispers (Smith 1964, 96).

Closeted with the President: Harding

Wilson's successor, Warren G. Harding, initiated a longtime love affair with Carrie Phillips while he was still lieutenant-governor of Ohio and eagerly launched into another with Nan Britton while a U.S. senator. With the cooperation of a trustworthy Secret Service man, Jim Sloan, he and Nan pursued their amour wherever fate suggested, often in a capacious White House closet. Once when the suspicious first lady, "the Duchess," nearly barged in on them, two resourceful aides alerted the president and the "first mistress" and spirited Nan out of sight. This affair with Nan Britton was known to all Washington cognoscenti, but it was almost never alluded to in print (Russell 1968, 467).

Franklin Roosevelt was long dead before any knowledge of his extra-marital liaison got into the public domain. And although Eisenhower was the subject of much gossip and speculation, he, too, was dead before his paramour and onetime Women's Army Corps aide, Kay Summersby, published the story of their affair (Morgan 1976). Rumors of affairs swirled around Lyndon Johnson, but without documentation. John F. Kennedy, however, was another matter.

Encyclopedists sometimes group together in a family entry notable participants in public affairs who share the same name. When it comes to sexual affairs both accurately and speculatively attributed to President Kennedy and his two presidentially inclined brothers, Robert (Bobby) and Edward (Teddy), such a grouping is appropriate.

Some of his journalistic detractors have been awed by John Kennedy's amatory exploits. Victor Lasky, for instance, called JFK "an activist President beyond Warren G. Harding's wildest hopes and dreams" (Lasky 1977, 7). During his candidacy and presidency, diligent and remarkably effective staff work kept his amours in the realm of speculation. After his assassination two affairs with political overtones came to light. One was a liaison lasting nearly two years until his death with the ex-wife, herself murdered a year after JFK, of a high CIA official, Cord Meyer, Jr. ("JFK Had Affair With D. C. Artist, Smoked 'Grass,' Paper Alleges," 1976).[6]

The other was with Judith Campbell, later Exner, who also had relationships with two Mafiosi, both of whom were later murdered. When J. Edgar Hoover, chief of the FBI, learned of Kennedy's Campbell connection he immediately and successfully urged the president to abandon it (Exner 1977; Lasky 1977). John and Bobby Kennedy, more frequently the latter, were both implicated by gossip and rumor in affairs with Marilyn Monroe not long before her death.

Teddy Kennedy's major contribution to the family sex saga grows out of his misadventure on the night of July 18–19, 1969, when his car veered off a bridge on Chappaquiddick Island beside Martha's Vineyard in Nantucket Sound. Ostensibly, Teddy was driving a young woman named Mary Jo Kopechne to the Edgartown ferry. Miss Kopechne had been a legislative secretary on the Senate staff of the late Robert Kennedy. She and Teddy had left a late house party on the island, a reunion of a dozen of their fellow-workers in Bobby's 1968 presidential campaign.

The car sailed off the bridge and submerged in a tidal pond. Kennedy, an expert swimmer, got out of the car safely but did not rescue Miss Kopechne, swam to shore, and disappeared overnight. The details of the whole affair have never been assembled completely and coherently despite a grand jury inquiry, a nationally televised and somewhat disjointed explanation by Senator Kennedy, and court proceedings in which he pleaded guilty to leaving the scene of an accident. (He was given a suspended sentence of two months in jail and a year's probation.)

It is generally acknowledged that Kennedy's overnight disappearance and evident inability to deal with the difficult circumstances immediately and resourcefully ended any likelihood of his being elected president. The fact or prospect of exposure even in less tragic circumstances has ruined many a politico, although some—Harding and John Kennedy come to mind— have handled presidential profligacy with great élan. One former senator in the 1980s dealt with a persistently rumored peccadillo with an insouciance that bordered on the suicidal.

After managing George McGovern's successful campaign for the Democratic presidential nomination and his unsuccessful general election campaign in 1972, Gary Hart went on to the U.S. Senate from Colorado, one of the "Watergate Babies" of 1974. He did well there and became a plausible candidate for the Democrats' presidential nomination in 1984 and again in 1988. During the pre-primary maneuvering in the spring of 1987, rumors persisted about his extramarital sexual activity.

To lay these allegations to rest, Hart virtually challenged questioning *New York Times* reporters to follow his every move, assuring them that they would find no evidence of marital infidelity.

Instead of the *Times*, the *Miami Herald* picked up the gauntlet, placed him under round-the-clock surveillance, and reported on page one his overnight tryst with a model while his wife was out of town. A week later, after the *Washington Post* revealed that it had evidence of another extramarital affair of several years' standing, Hart withdrew from his "crusade" to move the country forward.

Congress, Sexual

Perhaps sexual adventures at the congressional level have less earth-shaking consequences than among presidential contenders. But in the spring of 1881 one much-observed episode of hanky-panky frustrated a power play by New York's junior Senator, Thomas C. Platt. President Garfield, a reform or Half-Breed Republican, was bypassing the advice of Platt and his senior Senate colleague, Roscoe Conkling, in dispensing federal appointments in New York. Platt persuaded Boss Conkling that they, both Stalwarts, or old-line Republicans, should resign their Senate seats and be immediately re-elected by the legislature to demonstrate their clout and get a little more respect from the president.

Having set the plot in motion, Platt, who cultivated an image of piety and rectitude, allowed himself to unbend with some female companionship overnight in Albany's Delavan Hotel. A Half-Breed legislator discovered the assignation, alerted his colleagues, and silently set up a stepladder by the door to Platt's room. A succession of assemblymen in stocking feet silently mounted the ladder, peered through the transom for a moment, and left, chortling silently, to spread the word of this unseemly encounter between the Sage of Tioga County and what the next day's papers described as "an unspeakable female." Platt's night out made him an object of snickers instead of awe, and the New York Assembly elected two others to the Senate (Josephson 1938, 315).

Many other mighty men of Congress, otherwise unbeatable at the polls, have been toppled by indulging their libido. In 1974 it happened to the powerful Wilbur Mills, chairman of the House Ways and Means Committee. His escapades with a sometime strip dancer, Fanne Fox, laid him low. First the nineteen-term congressman and the exotic dancer were stopped by D.C. police for irregular driving in Washington. Next, they were identified at a Boston burlesque house. Mills was forced by publicity over his increasingly erratic behavior to step down as chairman of Ways and Means after sixteen years. Shortly thereafter, he decided not to seek reelection in 1976.

The same year Wayne Hays, the powerful and autocratic chairman of both the Committee on House Administration and the Democratic Congressional Campaign Committee, gave up both his chairmanships under increasing pressure from other party leaders. Hays then announced he would not run for reelection and resigned from the House a few days later. What brought him down was negative publicity about his sex life with a secretary on his Administration Committee staff.

Elizabeth Ray, thirty-three, said she was paid $14,000 a year for semiweekly sex with the chairman. Hays insisted that she had been hired as a secretary, that she actually did work, and that the sex was incidental. Her own assessment was, "I can't type, I can't file, I can't even answer the phone."

Two other sex scandals the same year involved lawmakers who had been unlucky or imprudent enough to solicit policewomen for sexual favors. One was a Louisiana representative, Joe D. Waggoner, Jr., who was reelected. The other, from Utah, Allan Howe, was defeated.

Sexual Imagery on the Campaign Trail

Also in 1976, an independent candidate for the U.S. Senate from Maine charged that sexual sabotage was ruining his campaign. Hayes E. Gahagan, a former Republican state senator who was seeking the vote of "Christian patriots," said his supporters had been disturbed by what they claimed was subliminal advertising directed against him. For example, one of his adherents cited a restaurant menu ostensibly illustrating a plate of fried clams, in which the critic could make out an orgy involving seven women and a donkey.

To the candidate's dismay, his photograph on one of his own campaign brochures appeared to have been doctored so the word "sex" appeared beneath his eyebrow, and an image of female genitalia could be seen in his hair. The candidate took the dirty trick with the utmost gravity. The electorate did not—some of whom, like a number of campaign reporters, were preoccupied with inventing ribald epithets for the feckless candidate.

A modest but much-publicized sex scandal unseated an Ohio Republican congressman, Donald E. Lukens, who was beaten in the 1990 Republican primary after receiving a jail sentence for sexual activity with a girl of more mature appearance than her age, which was sixteen.

In the bitter 1974 Texas contest for the U.S. Senate, the Republican incumbent, John Tower, was depicted as a womanizer disdained by "nice women, who would avoid getting on Senate elevators with him." When Tower protested, his Democratic challenger said he did not approve of the flier but that it was distributed by aides.

Tower had been the subject of such charges and whispers for years, and they were resurrected again in 1989 during bitter confirmation hearings for his appointment as President George Bush's secretary of defense. The charge, which in earlier times probably would not even have been raised, helped deny him confirmation by his former Senate colleagues, although they would have been truly relevant only for a job as an elevator operator, or perhaps counselor at a girls' camp.

In a rare display of symmetry, the House Ethics Committee in 1983 voted overwhelmingly to reprimand two representatives, a Republican and a Democrat, for engaging in sexual activities with seventeen-year-old House pages. Daniel B. Crane, a conservative Republican dentist and a three-term congressman from Danville, Illinois, was involved with a girl page. He was defeated in the next election.

Gerry E. Studds, a Democrat from Cohasset, Massachusetts, in his sixth term, had a homosexual affair with a boy page. He was reelected easily after the reprimand. Congress is often criticized for exempting itself from wages and hours and other requirements it imposes on business, but in these cases the House demonstrated that in terms of sexual misbehavior, it was an equal-opportunity employer.

Innuendoes about homosexuality figured in several 1976 races. In Nebraska's Second Congressional District and in the Oklahoma campaign for the U.S. Senate, these whispers were denied by their targets and ignored by the voters, who elected both of the accused. In New York, Brooklyn voters reelected Congressman Frederick W. Richmond despite his acknowledgement of sexual approaches to two boys. A misdemeanor charge stemming from the episode was dropped when Richmond agreed to submit to psychiatric counseling. After other charges arose, he resigned before the 1982 election.

Another 1980 case involving a Maryland congressman and a teenage boy contributed to the defeat in 1982 of the Maryland representative, Robert E. Bauman. However, his opponent, Democrat Roy Dyson, refused to make a campaign issue of the case. When Bauman tried for a comeback in 1984, he was defeated in the Republican primary.

MADMEN IN THE WHITE HOUSE

"If I wanted to go crazy, I would do it in Washington, because it would not be noticed." This line, attributed to Irvin S. Cobb, an early twentieth-century humorist, reflects the more or less gently sardonic attitude Americans hold toward their national capital and those who govern from it. Sometimes a politician is dubbed "crazy," or a "madman" or "madwoman" out of a sort of admiration for daring or persistence. But perhaps more often it is intended to characterize its object as truly insane—enough so to be quite beyond the pale. Many presidents and presidential contenders have been called madmen, but usually the charge has been merely a matter of invective expressing anger and disapproval but not accompanied by any effort to prove insanity in clinical terms. Efforts to vest such an accusation with scientific trappings have been few.

Long-Range Analysis: The Sanity of Barry Goldwater

The craziest imputation of insanity to a major American political candidate may well have been a mass excursion into irresponsibility involving hundreds of psychiatrists in 1964. The September-October issue of a magazine named *Fact* featured a "poll" of psychiatrists about Barry Goldwater's mental fitness to be president of the United States.

That summer *Fact*'s publisher, Ralph Ginzburg, mailed a question to more than 12,000 names on a rented list of psychiatrist members of the American Medical Association: "Is Barry Goldwater psychologically fit to be President of the United States?"

More than 15 percent responded, two-thirds (1,139) of whom said he was unfit. *Fact* published a wide selection of their diagnoses:

Never forgiven his father for being a Jew.... Behavior which has a schizophrenic quality.... Adolescent desire to attract attention by provocative or belligerent statements.... Paranoid traits.... Sensitivity to questions about his honesty and integrity—obvious unconscious substitutes for masculinity.... Any psychiatrist who does not agree with the above is himself psychologically unfit to be a psychiatrist.

Slightly more than half as many of the long-range observers (675 of them) found Goldwater fit, and in more restrained language. "Opportunity for the public to choose between conservatism and moderate socialism ... he is a sane man." "Statements, when not distorted or misinterpreted, indicate him to be a thoughtful, capable person."

In defense of the psychiatric profession, 10,000 practitioners did not respond. And of the 571 who were charitable enough to answer Ginzburg and responsible enough not to diagnose by mail, none put it better than Dr. Hubert Miller of Detroit: "If you will send me written authorization from Sen. Goldwater and arrange for an appointment, I shall be happy to send you a report concerning his mental status. The same goes for you" ("What Psychiatrists Have to Say About Goldwater," 1964).

This mad undertaking was denounced in the October bulletin of the Fair Campaign Practices Committee, *Fair Comment*, by Democratic Chairman John Bailey, the AMA, and the American Psychiatric and American Psychological associations. The psychological group had been protesting the whole affair since the questionnaire went out and told its members that any of them responding to the questionnaire would be brought up on ethical charges.

Goldwater was irritated enough to sue Ginzburg in Federal Court for "deliberate character assassination." The curtain finally fell on this nutty business in May 1968, with a jury award to Goldwater of $75,000 ("Goldwater Awarded $75,000 in Damages in His Suit for Libel," 1968).

The sheer number of psychiatrists willing to diagnose Barry Goldwater by mail was unprecedented, but allegations of insanity have an ancient lineage. In 1864 Lincoln was said to have been driven insane by melancholy over the Civil War. Horace Greeley was repeatedly described as insane in his ill-starred presidential campaign of 1872. This may have been the truest of all the maledictions heaped on that unfortunate fellow. It hounded him to his grave.

From the middle of November onward, Greeley's mental condition grew steadily worse. Put under medical care, he was removed to the private sanatorium of Dr. George S. Choate at Pleasantville, New York. There he lingered a few days, increasingly incoherent, until his death released him from his suffering. (Van Deusen 1953, 424)

William Jennings Bryan was the Populist and Democratic presidential nominee opposing the Republican William McKinley in 1896, and the youthful Democrat, with his formidable rhetorical arsenal and his single-minded silverite attack on the gold standard, struck terror to conservative hearts.

His oratorical thunderings invoked "all the wars of the past ... from the time that Cain killed Abel" and "all the pestilences that have visited the earth" to characterize the "infinite disasters that a gold standard means to the human race." It "carries the mask of the burglar and the knife of the assassin." He couched the issue as "between the idle holders of idle money and the struggling masses." To wealth he laid the loss of jobs, and resultant crime, finding that thereby it menaced "the safety of every citizen of the land" ("Mr. Bryan as Revealed by his Speeches," 1896).

This torrent of denunciation won Bryan an enormous following among workers and farmers, especially in the South and West, and that November he polled more than 6,000,000 votes, more than any previous winning candidate. He came within 600,000 votes of outpolling McKinley. Not idly did Republicans and all good conservatives "walk in fear and dread" of Bryan. They pulled out all the stops.

Long-Range Analysis: Bryan as Mattoid

Adolph S. Ochs had just bought the *New York Times*, which he announced in an editorial on August 19, 1896, that hinted, in passing, at his position on Bryan. He promised not to depart from the paper's stance on public questions "unless it be, if possible, to intensify its devotion to the cause of sound money" ("Business Announcement," 1896). He joined the drumfire being poured on Bryan by the establishment. On September 27 the *Times*'s Sunday editorial page carried, under a pseudonym, the long-range "diagnosis" of a psychoanalyst that Bryan was insane and "developing into what Italian alienists call a political mattoid, or what German writers would call paranoia reformatoria." The author signed himself, "Alienist."[7]

He presented "the reasons why, as an alienist, it has gradually seemed to me that the mind of Bryan is becoming unhinged." This evidence included the fact that his father was a judge in southern Illinois who prayed for divine guidance before rendering a decision. Bryan's "restless and 'errabund' tendency" indicated "the insane taint." He suffered "megalomania." His speeches were a "continual series of fault-findings, scoldings, and defensive criticism" adding up to "paranoia querulenta" and "querulent logorrhoea."[8]

"Alienist" went on for some 1,800 more learned and ominous words. A lengthy editorial across the page answered the question of its headline: "Is Bryan Crazy?" A qualified yes: "is it not plain that the man's mind is not sound, and that its unsoundness is increasing?" ("Bryan's Mental Condition," 1896; "Is Bryan Crazy?" 1896).

Two days later the *Times* ran a long news story as a followup. The reporter showed the Sunday diagnosis to "seven of the leading alienists in the city." Two refused to talk. One believed Bryan sane and was quoted briefly. One thought the candidate probably sane but still dangerous: "[H]e appears to be both ignorant and sincere." The devastating conclusions of the other two constituted the bulk of the article, reinforcing "Alienist's" long-range diagnosis. The fifth expert, Dr. Joseph Collins, stated his antipathy for Bryan and his support for McKinley, but he said of the glib "Alienist," "I have no sympathy with the person who is so intolerant of another human being's honest opinions that he brands him with the horrible stigma of insanity because his views are different" ("Is Mr. Bryan a Mattoid," 1896).

Teddy Roosevelt: "The Peril of an Insane Administration"

McKinley's modest triumph over Bryan was repeated on a larger scale in 1900, this time carrying in with him Theodore Roosevelt—the wild man New York GOP bosses had decided to sidetrack in the vice presidency. But McKinley's assassin put "that damned cowboy... in the White House," in Mark Hanna's disgusted phrase. By the time he left it in 1908, most regular Republicans thought he was crazy, too. They were sure of it when, after a term of uneasy retirement, Roosevelt decided in 1912 to oppose the president, once his hand-picked successor, William Howard Taft, in a three-way race with the Democrat Woodrow Wilson. Once again, the *New York Times* picked up the cudgel. On Saturday, March 23, a *Times* editorial-page feature boasted that on the morrow it would "for the first time, so far as we know," subject "a public man of Colonel Roosevelt's rank" to examination

> by what with entire accuracy is called the new psychology—the psychology which is a science as exact as chemistry, or even as mathematics, and entirely different from the psychology which was so little more than rash assumption, misleading analogy, and confusing metaphor.
>
> The new psychology is as practical as the old was unpractical, and it deals no less confidently with the mental operations of a statesman than with those of a newsboy. ("Topics of the Times," 1912)

Brave new world! And *pace*, poor William Jennings Bryan, formerly maligned so unscientifically! The next day the Sunday *Times* gave over the first page and one-half of its (full-newspaper-sized) magazine section to the promised long-range "psycho-analysis" under a seven-column headline, "ROOSEVELT AS ANALYZED BY THE NEW PSYCHOLOGY." The author, Dr. Morton Prince, it had already described as an acknowledged master of "the new or laboratory psychology."

After dismissing earlier similar undertakings as superficial and unsatisfactory, the good doctor deduced that Teddy loved being president and that when he left the White House voluntarily in 1908, "he went away with a lurking liking to be President again," and this eventually unhinged the poor fellow. The wish "was intolerable... so he put it out of his mind and it went into his subconscious."

"I think it safe to say that Mr. Roosevelt will go down in history as one of the most illustrious psychological examples of the distortion of conscious mental processes through the force of subconscious wishes" ("Roosevelt as Analyzed by the New Psychology," 1912).

Seven weeks later the *Times* struck again with its lead Sunday editorial, sternly reproving the "very large proportion of American citizens" who had been "at fault in paying too little heed to the dangerous influences working for the overturn of our social and political systems." It sounded a call to arms: "But the time has come for the serious men of this Republic to join hands against its psychopathic enemies." With a weak sop at last to the fading Bryan, the editorial continued:

For a time the Nebraska orator who contested for the Presidency was the only very conspicuous demagogue in our politics, but though still conspicuous he is no longer foremost. The danger has increased. As Dr. Hamilton [see below] says, both political parties now have among their candidates men whose "instability, temperamentally or through disease," unfits them for high office. The paranoid type, of which Robespierre and Marat were examples, is too much in evidence in our politics, State and National.

The male citizens of the country of voting age have only to do their duty, to take up their share of political work honestly, to remove the danger.... The majority is sane and of clear vision, but the sober-minded, well-balanced citizens have been neglecting their duty. ("Psychopathology and Politics," 1912)

The noted alienist this time was Dr. Allan McLane Hamilton, a grandson of Alexander Hamilton. He had been a professor of mental diseases and was engaged in writing his memoirs. He, too, occupied the front page of the Sunday magazine section, under the lurid, seven-column headline, "THE PERIL OF AN INSANE ADMINISTRATION." Until the death of Mc-Kinley, he began, the people chose as their highest representatives "calm and well-balanced men about whose mental integrity there was never the slightest doubt, ... all sane and conservative" except for Jackson, all "willing to be absolutely guided by the Constitution, despising clap-trap and trickery."

The previous day's editorial saluting the Hamilton article was an excellent précis of the piece itself, which without so much as mentioning Roosevelt by name left no room for doubt that he was a psychopath who might

advance ideas of the loftiest kind, but they are often impracticable, and if adopted and enforced lead to untold misfortune because of their crazy radicalism.... The querulent lunatic who may quarrel or find fault with everything and everybody is really a psychopathic individual, who should be looked upon with pity, or properly protected....

It therefore becomes the great American public to exercise the greatest care in the selection of a President, for if men are accepted at their own estimate, or hysterical suggestion takes the place of good common sense, there is nothing but ruin and dissension ahead. ("The Peril of an Insane Administration," 1912)

But it was a three-way race, and the third man won. Unfortunately, he was crazy, too, though this was not proven by the new science for some time. Mad Teddy and his Bull Moosers split away enough votes from the sound President Taft to elect mad Woodrow Wilson. His particular dementia was confirmed in a posthumous and trans-Atlantic diagnosis—by no less than Sigmund Freud! The story forms a curious and ironic coda to this account of mad presidents and pretenders.

Long-Range Analysis: Wilson and Freud

The onset of Wilson's ultimately fatal illness was described by the president's own physician as "a complete nervous breakdown." This led to rumors that he was insane. His biographer Gene Smith observes that people suddenly noticed bars on a White House window and took that as confirmation. Actually, President Roosevelt had been sane enough to have them installed, to keep his rambunctious children from falling out of their room.

Freud's involvement began in the 1920s, when William C. Bullitt, who knew both Wilson and Freud, approached him about a book on Wilson's sanity. They agreed to collaborate. The project was completed a decade later, and not published until 1966, after the death of Edith Bolling Wilson, the president's widow.

Freud acknowledged a longstanding and growing aversion toward Wilson. Bullitt was a twenty-eight-year-old diplomatic prodigy when he led a mission to newly Bolshevik Russia to evaluate its role in the peace after World War I. He resigned from the State Department in protest when President Wilson (no doubt unwisely) rejected his recommendations. In a passionate letter reporting his resignation, young Bullitt told Wilson he had made "effective labor for a 'new world order' possible no longer" ("Clearing the Air," 1919). One reason for his pique, Bullitt's letter made clear, was the president's failure to understand Russia. Bullitt's view, later drastically revised, was reflected in his famous observation after visiting Lenin: "We have seen the future and it works!" The line is usually credited to Lincoln Steffens, who accompanied Bullitt on the mission and revised it as his own for his autobiography.[9]

The Freud–Bullitt critique made much of what it saw as Wilson's need for a mother figure: his "full-bosomed" second wife brought him "a mother's breast on which to rest." Every few pages found that Wilson considered himself

God's anointed....
In his unconscious [he] was God and Christ....
Woodrow Wilson as the Prince of Peace: Arbiter Mundi.... his unconscious identification with Christ.... he was again able to speak freely as Christ....
The Only Begotten Son of God....
He was rapidly nearing that psychic land from which no travelers return, the land in which facts are the product of wishes, in which friends betray and in which an asylum chair may be the throne of God. (Freud 1967)[10]

And the long-distance analyst's couch?

6

Appeals to Bigotry: Religion, Race, Ethnic Background

All but four of the framers of the U.S. Constitution were Protestants, and many of them were conspicuously devout.[1] Yet every one of them had given much thought to civil disabilities based on religion. They had seen mischief in the established religions of the Old World, and nearly all were determined to avoid it in the New. But it was not unanimous. As Luther Martin of Maryland put it, some members were

so unfashionable as to think, that a *belief of the existence of a Deity*, and of a *state of future rewards and punishments* would be some security for the good conduct of our rulers, and that, in a Christian country, it would be *at least decent* to hold out some distinction between the professors of Christianity and downright infidelity or paganism. (Farrand 1966, 3:227; Martin's emphasis)

Martin's view was shared by others and was considered. However, the Constitution the framers drew up concluded, "but no religious test shall ever be required as a qualification to any office or public trust under the United States."

The ratification debates revealed popular demand for a Bill of Rights, and the First Congress proposed one in the form of twelve amendments.[2] Ten were promptly ratified, the first of which began, "Congress shall make no law respecting an establishment of religion, or prohibiting the free exercise thereof." In and out of the great Convention of 1787, the United States was founded in freedom from domination by any religion and freedom to practice any religion.

BIAS AGAINST THE UNORTHODOX

The reluctance of some of the Founders to countenance infidels or pagans in high public office did not disappear with them. Only their Constitution stands between the unwashed and the wrath of the righteous. Many orthodox Christians consider the Unitarian denial of the Christian Trinity and the divinity of Christ to be heresy. This view accounts for charges that Jefferson was an atheist. William Howard Taft was a Unitarian when he ran for president in 1908 against the fundamentalist Christian William Jennings Bryan. Many of the devout were appalled. "Think of the United States with a *President* who does not believe that Jesus Christ was the Son of God, but looks upon our immaculate Savior as a common bastard and low, cunning impostor!" So the editor of the *Pentecostal Herald* fulminated on July 15, 1908 (Pringle 1939, 1:374; italics in original).

In the Bible Belt South the Good Fight goes on. Candidates are assailed for supporting the Supreme Court on the "prayer issue." In 1982 the National Republican Senatorial Committee ran a TV spot with this voice-over against a Democratic senator from Tennessee:

James Sasser claims to be in favor of voluntary school prayer. You wouldn't have known it last November 16. On that day Senator Helms had proposed a very important amendment that would have helped to restore the right to voluntary prayer in our schools. Sasser voted with the Northeastern liberals. Against the right to voluntary school prayer. Defeat James Sasser. He'd rather vote with his liberal colleagues than stand for what he says he believes in. [Sasser Against Prayer 1982]

These controversies muddy the political waters in several ways, and they raise uncertainties about the religious rights and responsibilities of believing politicians and of religious authorities. The secular outlook of much of the news media has stirred confusion about the constitutional protection *of* religion as well as *from* religion. But under the U.S. Constitution, just as no church may force its dogma or doctrinal position on anyone by civil law, neither can a church be compelled to change or abandon its dogma or doctrinal position. Nor can a minister, priest, or rabbi be forced by the state either to flout or to follow any particular stricture of his or her religion. By the same token, of course, no public official may impose the strictures of his or her religion on political constituents.

ANTI-SEMITISM

Appeals to anti-Semitism as an election campaign tactic are relatively new in American politics, not appearing in any number or significance until around the time of World War II, when the subject was spotlighted by the plans and depredations of Hitler. However, the civil liberties of the few Jews in the colonies at the time of the Revolution were seriously, sometimes inadvertently, restricted, and this continued in the United States of the Federal Period.

Jonas Phillips and the Constitutional Convention

It is not much remembered that a Jew brought this topic to the attention of the Constitutional Convention. Over date of "24th Ellul 5547 or Sepr 7th 1787," Jonas Phillips of Philadelphia wrote to "the president and the Honourable Members of the Convention assembled." His subject was an oath specified in the Constitution of Pennsylvania to which any public officeholder was required to swear, an explicitly Christian statement of faith that included acknowledging the New Testament "to be given by divine inspiration."

Phillips pointed out that this language deprived any Jew of holding any public office, and he respectfully urged the Convention to create "a government where all Relegious societys are on an Eaquel footing" (Farrand 1966, 3:78–79). When Phillips wrote, the subject had been discussed repeatedly, and the Committee of Style at that very time was at work on a late draft containing the prohibition of a religious test, exactly as he had prayed they might do.

NAZI INFLUENCES

In the mid-1930s Hitler had explored the possibility of intruding into American domestic politics, and by the close of the decade his regime was financing the German-American Bund and related activities. These augmented the discords sounded by native fascist types, such as William Dudley Pelley and his Silvershirts, and Reverend Gerald B. Winrod and his Defenders of the Christian Faith, and a variety of others. Some of these were longtime anti-Semites; others found it an easy jump from white to Northern European supremacy.

Third Reich philosophies echoed in the 1940 presidential campaign. Roosevelt was constantly portrayed as a Jew, as also, occasionally, was Willkie. Both were called members of the "international Jewish conspiracy" seen at every hand by the paranoids of the day. Some anti-Semites described the president as Franklin Rosenfeld, President of the Jewnited states, and former governor of Jew York. The Roosevelt slanders sickened the Republican nominee. When he was offered the endorsement of Father Coughlin,[3] who by this time was a high priest of the hate-Roosevelt sect, Willkie rebuffed the anti-Semite in what was and remains a classic repudiation of vicious unsolicited support:

I have no place in my philosophy for such beliefs. I don't have to be President of the United States, but I do have to make my beliefs clear . . . to live with myself. I am not interested in being President of the United States to compromise with my fundamental beliefs.

In 1944 Willkie was dead and the GOP nominee was New York's Thomas E. Dewey. Anti-Semitic innuendo of the kind Willkie had repudiated (but could not stop) continued. At the Democratic convention Roosevelt reluctantly agreed to dump his vice president, Henry Wallace, whose increasing leftward tilt had made him a lightning rod to the Democrats' right wing. When FDR settled on Senator Harry S Truman of Missouri, Wallace supporters on the convention floor grumbled. Arthur Krock of the *New York Times* quoted the president as sending the national chairman to nominate Truman "before there's any more trouble. Clear everything with Sidney" ("In the Nation: The Inflammatory Use of a National Chairman," 1944). Sidney was Sidney Hillman, an important Roosevelt advisor, a labor leader, and a Jew.

"Clear everything with Sidney" spread like a blob of mercury on a linoleum floor, usually recited with a leer and a wink and a fancied Jewish accent. In a multiple guilt-by-association ploy, some Republicans circulated cards reading, "Browder, Hillman and the Communists will vote. Will you?"

Anti-Semitism in presidential campaigns has been neither a prominent nor a frequent distraction, in part of course because no major party candidates have been Jews. Barry Goldwater's father was Jewish, but the candidate's sunny good humor about his background disarmed all but the most rabid Jew-haters. He told an apocryphal story about being turned away from a restricted country club, quoting himself as protesting, "But I'm only half-Jewish. Can't I play nine holes?" A Jewish humorist of the time observed, "I might have known the first Jew to have a chance at the White House would be an Episcopalian."

Anti-Semitism in Local Campaigns

The most pernicious exploitation of anti-Semitism in American political campaigns occurs at congressional and local levels and at the hands of such established anti-Semites as neo-Nazis, members of the Ku Klux Klan, and the like, plus individual bigots found in any large and many small communities. Responsible political party professionals and organizations are uniformly quick to repudiate such tactics.

Independent candidates, outside any party influence, occasionally inject an anti-Semitic pitch into a campaign. A typical instance cropped up in 1978 in South Carolina's Bible Belt Fourth Congressional District. An independent candidate named Don Sprouse said the Democrat, a Jew, should not be elected because he would be unable "to turn to Jesus when the going got tough" ("Dirty Campaigns 1978: '76's Record Low Equalled," 1978). The Republican contender, who ran a straightforward campaign, won. Mr. Sprouse was raising precisely the kind of concern voiced by Luther Martin in 1787, but he was apparently unwilling to abide by the answer supplied in the completed Constitution.

There are occasional instances of what appear to be a classic anti-Semitic appeal but whose author insists it is not. In a California congressional campaign in 1958, a Republican incumbent named Craig Hosmer freely claimed full responsibility for a leaflet that had all the earmarks of standard anti-Semitism. Hosmer was using the ever-popular approach of a comparative biography. The sponsor of the leaflet is described in heroic terms and the rival is depicted as trivial and incompetent.

Hosmer listed his own patriotic background in the U.S. Navy and in Congress, citing *Who's Who in America* as the source of the information. In the opposite column he dealt with his opponent, a Jewish businessman who had been educated for the rabbinate. Hosmer listed every Jewish and Jewish-sounding affiliation he could find, identifying the source for the opponent's biography as *Who's Who in World Jewry.*

In addition, Hosmer translated the opponent's business from "President, Metal Products Corp., South Bend, Indiana," as it read in *Who's Who in World Jewry*, to "Scrap Metal Business." Ergo! Jewish junk dealer.

Hosmer said he merely wanted to show that his experience was relevant to the office he held and the opponent's was not. Some politicians wondered why he did it. One observed that the district was so anti-Semitic that the Virgin Mary would be too Jewish for the electorate. When Democrats began gathering copies of the leaflet for fund-raising in nearby Jewish communities, Hosmer destroyed the remaining half of his print order of 100,000 copies.

ANTI-CATHOLICISM

In a United States where Jew-baiting had long been viewed with opprobrium, anti-Catholicism has sometimes been called the anti-Semitism of the intellectuals. Members of "the Romanish religion" were denied civil rights by all the early colonies except Maryland. It was not until 1876, when New Hampshire repealed a provision that its governor must be a Protestant, that the last civil disability of Catholics fell away legally in the United States.

As early as 1830, American nativists were becoming alarmed at the influx of the Irish, which did not reach its peak until after the potato famine of 1846. Samuel F. B. Morse, the inventor and painter, was an early and rabid Catholic-baiter. The story goes that on a visit to Rome he did not remove his hat when a papal procession went by, and a member of the Swiss Guard knocked it off.

When Morse got home, he began fulminating against the Pope and the whole infernal system. His hysteria fanned that of other bigots, and soon inflammatory stories were circulating about sinful goings-on in nunneries. A Boston mob burned a local convent to the ground. Morse's rabid essays were published as "Foreign Conspiracy Against the Liberties of the United States."

Maria Monk and the Rise of the Know-Nothings

In 1836 a horror story of convent brutalities and orgies came from a demented Canadian girl named Maria Monk. Her *Awful Disclosures of Maria Monk* purported to be the autobiography of a nun, which she never was. However, abetted and promoted by fervid Yankee divines, Maria, clad in a nun's habit, was a hit on the lecture circuit. All this agitation eventuated in the Native American Party, whose platform offered a solution: raise residency requirements for naturalization of immigrants to twenty-one years.

Rampant anti-Catholicism found expression in schoolbooks, a great many of which were outrageously and specifically anti-Catholic. Catholic children in the public schools of the Protestant Land of the Free were required to recite Protestant prayers, sing Protestant hymns, and read the Protestant Bible. The Catholics introduced parochial schools to preserve their own faith and vainly sought relief from some of the education taxes they continued to pay after their children had left the public schools.

In 1844 nativists formed the American Republican Party, which ran Henry Clay as its presidential candidate. His ensuing defeat was laid to "Abolitionists and foreign Catholics." The party gave way to a secret order whose members were pledged to answer prying questions by saying, "I know nothing about it." Thus the secret society, which formally took the name "Grand Council of the Supreme Star Spangled Banner," entered history as the Know-Nothings. By 1855 the Know-Nothings were riding the crest of a nationwide orgy of Catholic-hating. Their governors sat in seven states, five state legislatures were under their control, and one-third of the Congress were their members or allies.

The madness began to subside when the excesses became ludicrous, as when the Massachusetts legislature created a Nunnery Committee to ferret out of church and convent cellars weapons hidden there to arm the Roman underground for the Pope's coming invasion. The Grand Council could not survive such fatuity, and within a year it was dead—but not the bigotry that had motivated it.

Anti-Catholicism in the Cleveland-Blaine Campaign

The first U.S. presidential campaign in which anti-Catholicism figured importantly was that of 1884. The Democratic candidate was Grover Cleveland, and the Republican was James G. Blaine—who already had plenty of baggage to carry from bribery and corruption scandals described in Chapter 4. Blaine's mother was a devout Roman Catholic, and this fact was used by the Democrats in anti-Catholic areas to make him out to be a Catholic. But in big-city areas with large Catholic and other foreign-born populations, he was just as falsely labeled an anti-Catholic and a persecutor of the foreign-born.

This was the stage on which one of Blaine's Republican partisans launched a fateful sneer at Catholics. The Reverend Samuel D. Burchard, a Presbyterian minister, was an ardent Blaine man, and on the Wednesday before election day he led an elite delegation of New York City's Protestant clergy to call on the Plumed Knight at the Fifth Avenue Hotel in New York City. Before he departed, Burchard issued a ceremonial malediction on Cleveland and his Democratic party, "whose antecedents are rum, Romanism, and rebellion" (Russell 1931, 401).

This slur neatly packaged the Demon Rum and the Civil War with smug, upper-crust anti-Catholicism. Blaine told a friend later that he was stunned and angered at the remark, but he quickly decided that it probably had not been heard by reporters and that repudiation would only spread the story. But a reporter from the *New York World* did hear it, wrote the story, and it spread like wildfire in the six days before the election. Hordes of Democrats of Catholic faith protested—and these were the very strength of Tammany Hall, which was trying to throw the election to the Republican Blaine because of Cleveland's long and potent opposition to that corrupt New York City Democratic organization.

The Catholic defections were enough to give Cleveland a New York State plurality of one-tenth of one percent—a 1,149-vote margin in a total vote of 1,125,000. If even 575 Catholic votes for Blaine were switched by Burchard's sneer at Romanism—a virtual certainty—the remark cost Blaine the presidency of the United States. New York's thirty-six electoral votes gave Cleveland a tally of 219 to Blaine's 182 in the Electoral College. If Cleveland had lost New York, he would have lost the White House, 183–218.

The Ku Klux Klan

Although most Americans probably think of the Ku Klux Klan as a fringe organization predominantly directed against blacks, the latter-day Klans and offshoots have never concentrated wholly on hating or intimidating blacks. They have played an important part in spreading anti-Catholicism and biases against many other religious and cultural groups.

In its original manifestation, the Klan was a secret terrorist organization that sprang up in the South after the Civil War to thwart the heavy-handed Reconstruction of Yankee radicals and carpetbaggers. Its only substantial electoral role lay in its silent menace, underscored from time to time by violence, which persuaded Southern blacks to stay away from the polls, Fifteenth Amendment or not. It went out of business in the 1870s after it had achieved its objective.

The Klan's resurgence in the second and third decades of the twentieth century was, as W. J. Cash put it, an authentic folk movement—at least as fully such as the Nazi movement in Germany, to which it was not without kinship.

Its body was made up of the common whites, industrial and rural. But its blood ... came from the upper orders. And the people who really directed it were very near to being coextensive with the established leadership of the South. People of great prominence in industry and business... usually maintained liaison with it through their underlings and the politicians.... Except in North Carolina and Virginia, the rural clergy belonged to it or had traffic with it almost *en masse*.... [A]nd everywhere the great body of ministers either smiled benignly on it or carefully kept their mouths shut about it. (Cash 1941, 335–37)

The Klan reflected the fears and hates of the time. As Cash notes, it was simultaneously "anti-Negro, anti-Alien, anti-Red, anti-Catholic, anti-Jew, anti-Darwin, anti-Modern, anti-Liberal, Fundamentalist, vastly Moral, militantly Protestant."

The new Klan, overtly political in ways the original was not, swept the South, and, sloughing off its native anti-Yankee aspect, swept on through the Midwest to the mountain and Northwestern states. In Oregon Klan legislators enacted a law requiring all children to go to public schools. It succeeded in softening a denunciation of the Klan in the Democratic platform of 1924 and helped beat back Al Smith's effort at that year's nomination.

Then, at the height of its power, it all began to unravel. On August 8, 1925, after weeks of preparation, transported by fifty or more special trains, 40,000 hooded and sheeted (but not masked) Klansmen, led by the Imperial Wizard of All the Klans, a Dallas dentist named Hiram W. Evans, staged a portentous march on Washington. Late in the day, in the stifling heat, they stood reverently before the Washington Monument and invoked God and General Washington. Thunder

rolled ominously overhead. L. A. Mueller, the Grand Kleagle for Washington, D.C., shouted through loudspeakers. "It will not rain. We shall pray. Never yet has God poured down rain on a Klan assembly." Within minutes the heavens opened, and Klansmen were deluged. Thousands of them broke ranks and scurried for cover, in spite of Kleagle Mueller's shouts for them to remain. Struck by a sense of purpose, Rev. Dr. A. H. Gulledge of Columbus Ohio, got down on his knees on the rostrum. "Oh God," he intoned, "I pray that the remainder of this service will be conducted without rain." Whereupon it rained even harder. (Wade 1987, 250)

The Klan was never the same again, undone by factionalism and occasional embezzlement within and by growing criticism and ridicule from the outside. Its spotty resurgence across Southern states during the civil rights movement of the 1960s and 1970s never approached the membership and influence of 1915–1930.

Catholics and the White House: 1928

In 1928 what was left of the Klan struggled to save the nation again from Al Smith (as it had helped to do in 1924). They swelled the pre-convention chorus of whispers against the Romanist candidate. Their journals, the *Kourier* and the *New Menace*, printed exposés and denunciations of papal plots and Smith's fealty to Rome. They printed anti-Catholic tracts and helped swell the distribution of one sensational forgery, the so-called "Knights of Columbus Oath." This piece had originally been created by an anonymous nineteenth-century author to smear the Jesuits. It purported to be a secret oath that priests of that order had to take, pledging them to persecute Protestants in every way—to flay, lay waste, spoil, burn, and poison.

The Knights of Columbus Oath. At some point the ascription of the oath was shifted from the clerical order of the Jesuits, formally the Society of Jesus, to the lay Catholic order of the Knights of Columbus, and in 1912 a Pennsylvania Catholic who was a candidate for Congress found the spurious oath widely used in the campaign against him. A House election committee exposed the oath as a fraud. The oath and the exposé appeared in the *Congressional Record* for February 15, 1913. In 1928 Klansmen and others reprinted the oath from the *Record*, without the exposé, and cited its appearance as proof of its authenticity.

Newspaper cartoons, speeches, leaflets, and letter-writing and whispering campaigns deluged the country to brand Al Smith the agent of Rome. Some of it was funny. Here and there news photos of construction work on the Holland Tunnel under the Hudson River were identified as the start of a tunnel to the Vatican that the New York governor had ordered.

Mabel Walker Willebrandt, Assistant Attorney General of the United States, went back and forth across the land speaking against Smith before Church and temperance organizations. Her official concern was with the enforcement of the Volstead Act, but her excursions against Smith's Catholicism were entirely compatible. The Anti-Saloon League pulled its strongest support from fundamentalist Protestants, and these were the most apprehensive about the Democrat's religion.

Hoover won, beating Smith by six-and-a-half-million votes.[4] Al Smith's Catholicism contributed to but was far from the only reason for his defeat, which embittered him and helped turn him within a few years to a leading role in the Liberty League, an early precursor of the Radical Right. The greatest damage done by bigotry in 1928 was its rousing the beast in the American polity. As Smith had put it in a speech in 1924, "the Catholics of this country can stand [bigotry], the Jews can stand it, our citizens born under foreign skies can stand it, the Negro can stand it. But the United States of America cannot stand it" (O'Connor 1970, 149).

Catholics and the White House: 1960

The situation in 1960 could not have been more different from that of 1928. John Fitzgerald Kennedy was a wealthy Massachusetts Democrat, a freshman senator with House experience, and the image of style and grace. He was witty, handsome, well educated, widely informed, and an authentic war hero. He was a dream candidate with only one flaw: He was a Roman Catholic.

In 1956 Kennedy was eyeing the vice presidency, and his aides, John Bailey and Ted Sorensen, prepared a private memo to influence Democratic convention delegates. It pointed to Catholic voters the party had lost to Eisenhower in 1952 and suggested that only a promising Catholic—like Kennedy—on the ticket could stem further losses in 1956. Although he did not get the nomination, the Democrats lost again to Eisenhower, and the memo made more sense than ever in 1960. Its logic and Kennedy's wealth and organization prevailed.

Meanwhile, Protestants, Jews, and atheists wanted answers to some questions about Catholic attitudes toward the state. Would a Catholic president place his faith first and his oath of office second? And if not, why had the Pope not said so? For many Protestants pondering these questions, the evidence of recent years argued strongly that a Catholic president would in fact faithfully discharge his oath of office.

The Republicans had already nominated Richard Nixon. He was determined not to exploit anti-Catholicism should Kennedy be named by the Democrats. He remained scrupulous on this point, permitting no deviation from his rigid and unexceptioned policy of leaving the religious issue out of his campaign.

On the Saturday following Kennedy's nomination at Los Angeles, his press chief, Pierre Salinger, asked me to brief him and his staff on prospective pitfalls ahead with regard to the "Catholic issue." Everyone in the room was apprehensive that Nixon would use every opportunity to say something like, "There is no religious issue in this campaign. It is of no importance that my opponent is a MEMBER OF THE ROMAN CATHOLIC CHURCH."

Considering Mabel Walker Willebrandt's part in rousing anti-Catholic bigotry against Al Smith, it was small wonder that the Democrats were apprehensive. But Nixon would not permit his campaigners to stir from his own resolve. He rebuffed every effort to trick him into enlarging on the issue, invariably saying simply and only, "There is no religious issue between me and my opponent."

Early in 1960, with the cooperation of the National Conference of Christians and Jews (NCCJ), the Fair Campaign Practices Committee brought together in Washington a distinguished group of religious leaders and laymen, Protestants, Catholics, and Jews, fundamentalists and liberals, to study and comment on this issue in the campaign.

Charles P. Taft, chairman of the Committee, presided, with the cooperation of the NCCJ head, Lewis Webster Jones. At the close of the two-day meeting, Mr. Taft drew out of the discussions a brief set of principles for considering "the injection of religious issues into the 1960 campaign." The statement condemned "stirring up, fostering or tolerating religious animosity, or injecting elements of a candidate's faith not relevant to the duties of the office he seeks." And it called for "intelligent, honest and temperate public discussion of the relation of religious faith to the public issues" (Felknor 1966, 266–67). It appeared widely in the press, general and secular, and without doubt was a substantial influence for calm.

But millions of Americans were not disposed to be calm. They took seriously the lurid leaflets flooding the country with the history of Catholic perfidy: Catholics murdered Abraham Lincoln after he had warned against the Pope; Catholics slipped Franklin Roosevelt a poisoned drink; Catholics paralyzed Woodrow Wilson with a nerve drug; Catholics injected Harding with a drug that caused his fatal heart attack.

Anti-Catholics distributed the Knights of Columbus oath in fifty or more versions. An anonymous pamphleteer purported to exhort Republican Catholics to kick over the party traces and vote for Kennedy so "we Catholics" can have it all our way and to Hell with the wretched Protestants. A similar fake urged Catholics, "Elect Kennedy so our Blessed Lady Ever-Virgin Mary will be the First Lady of our Land." Naturally, both documents were distributed only to Protestants. These variously sick, vicious, and lying pieces circulated in the untold millions of copies. The Fair Campaign Practices Committee collected some 1,500 different editions of scurrilous and distorted anti-Catholic propaganda during 1960.

Wisconsin was one of a dozen states where these rabid tracts were everywhere. Many of them figured in some cynical mischief by Kennedy forces during the primary campaign, which Kennedy's people saw as their opportunity to lay Hubert Humphrey to rest for good. Wisconsin's population was about 32 percent Catholic, one-third greater than the national average, and their residential patterns made it possible to identify and count them with some precision.

Reverse Bigotry

While anti-Catholics were peddling these rabid fliers in Protestant districts, the same pieces began to show up under windshield wipers and doors in the predominantly Catholic districts. They reached many thousands of Catholics by mail, even, so the columnist Marquis Childs reported, being addressed to "individuals in care of the local chapter of the Knights of Columbus" ("The Essential Quality," 1960).

Sardonic journalists covering the campaign suspected, but could not prove, that the Kennedy forces were covertly distributing these pieces to enrage Catholic Republicans into voting in the Democratic primary, as Wisconsin law allowed. But neither reporters, Republicans, nor repeated phone inquires by the Fair Campaign Practices Committee found any hard evidence.

Several years later Paul Corbin, the advance man who worked the Catholic districts for Kennedy, confessed to friends that he—at the direction of Bobby Kennedy—had arranged the distribution of the leaflets to Catholics. John Kennedy's friend and biographer, Ted Sorensen, recalled the advance man's resourcefulness. Corbin invited "all the Reverend Fathers at a Catholic seminary to attend a rally in their town that weekend, [and] added, 'But fellows, please wear your sport shirts,' " (Sorensen 1965, 136).

The Catholic manipulation worked. Kennedy won all six heavily Catholic districts and lost all four of the Protestant ones. And the national publicity accruing to the bigoted leaflets created a wave of sympathy among unbigoted non-Catholics in the rest of the United States. The cost was minor. One of Kennedy's friends and advisors withdrew from the campaign in protest at the reverse bigotry.

But the problem of John Kennedy's religion was real enough. The wild pamphleteers only steamed up the bigots. There was a large middle ground of apprehensive Protestants who might be persuaded either way. The latter received much attention from, among others, an organization called Protestants and other Americans United for Separation of Church and State (POAU; later shortened to Americans United). POAU cautioned citizens against the "so-called Knights of Columbus 'oath,' " which, being "fraudulent," should not be distributed. Along with the warning, POAU distributed the oath.

It also circulated leaflets of its own. If the Catholics took over, "Protestants would be treated with snide amusement and official contempt," read one.

They would be reduced to second-class citizens and treated as damned souls. Their young would be cajoled and bribed to leave their traditional faith. They would be steadily, systematically whittled away. They would be left at length a devout but inconsequential minority, just as Protestants are in Spain today.

After 50 percent—*that*! (Cited in Felknor 1966, 61)

A group of Protestant ministers associated with Norman Vincent Peale had expressed great concern over how a Catholic president would affect freedom of religion for non-Catholics, and in early September Kennedy told Sorensen he had decided to meet this problem head-on. He accepted an invitation from the Houston Ministerial Association to address it and respond to any and all questions.

On September 12, he appeared before an audience of some 600 and spoke briefly of his vision of "an America where the separation of church and state is absolute—where no Catholic prelate would tell the President how to act, and no Protestant minister would tell his parishioners for whom to vote." And he answered often difficult questions fully and frankly. When he finished he had, Theodore H. White wrote, "won the applause of many and the personal sympathies of more; the meeting had closed in respect and friendship" (White 1965, 262).

He also had compiled a basic campaign document, for the entire proceeding had been filmed. It was a triumph, and printed excerpts and film clips from it became major weapons for the rest of the campaign. Kathleen Hall Jamieson analyzed the use of the basic television film of the confrontation.

"Leonard Reinsch, Kennedy's TV and radio adviser, confirms that more total time was purchased to rebroadcast Kennedy's September 12 performance in Houston than any other single piece of campaign propaganda." It was aired in thirty-nine states, most heavily in those identified in the original 1956 Bailey-Sorensen memo as states where Catholic votes could swing the state for a Catholic Democrat (Jamieson 1984, 136; [JFK at Houston 1960]).

THE POLITICS OF RACE

When James Thomson Callender, the roving smear artist described in Chapter 3, turned against his sometime sponsor, Thomas Jefferson, he turned his formidable research capacity loose on the persistent rumors that Jefferson had enjoyed a long-standing sexual relationship with one of his slaves, an especially comely one named Sally Hemings. As the rumor spread, she became known as "Black Sal" or "Dusky Sally" to many Federalist campaigners and writers—and their readers. What was scarcely controvertible was that one of her light-skinned sons, Tom, bore a notorious resemblance to their master.[5]

Tales of Sex with Slaves

Ironically, Callender first learned of the Jefferson-Hemings liaison while he was imprisoned (under the Alien Act) in Richmond, and shortly after his release he went to Charlottesville to nose around at Monticello, where he accumulated much supporting detail from the president's neighbors.

In September 1802, with the election of the Eighth Congress only weeks away, the turncoat pamphleteer loosed his new bombshell, the sensational Sally Hemings story. It was circulated, reprinted, told orally, talked about, and denied across the country—though Jefferson himself, convinced that a denial would only keep the tale alive, never denied it publicly.

During the presidential campaign of 1804, the Jefferson story was still circulating, but it was old news. The president, the libidinous Jacobin to the Federalists, had his revenge at the polls, where he smothered them. Callender was dead by this time, having drowned in July 1803, while drunk, in three feet of water in the James River, where he had gone ostensibly to bathe.

A generation passed before interracial sex figured again in a presidential campaign. When Andrew Jackson decided against a third term in the White House, he was popular enough to preselect the Democratic ticket for 1836. For president he picked his own vice president, Martin Van Buren, who to Southerners was a smooth and shifty Yankee. Even worse was his choice for vice president, Colonel Richard M. Johnson, a hero of the War of 1812.

What was wrong with this for white Southern consumption was that Johnson lived with a woman named Julia Chinn, a mulatto slave he inherited from his father, and by whom he had two daughters, whom he and Julia raised. When the Democratic convention nominated him, the Virginia delegation walked out (DAB 1928–58; Meyer 1932). But Van Buren and Johnson won the nomination and the election.

From the mid-nineteenth century on, a variety of election cartoons and gimcracks taxed candidates with pro-Negro attitudes unpopular with most voters, especially in the South. Currier and Ives did a cartoon in 1860 titled, " 'THE NIGGER' IN THE WOODPILE," showing a grinning black squatting inside a stack of rails just split by Abe Lincoln and representing the Republican platform (Minnigerode 1928, 384). An early campaign button for the 1904 Democratic candidate, Alton B. Parker, represents a wedding cake with a bridal scene appearing beneath a portrait of each rival candidate. Beneath Parker is a happy bride and groom, both white. Beneath the wild Republican, Teddy Roosevelt, is a black groom with a white bride. The legend: "It's Up to You" (Friz 1988).

Attributions of Negro Blood

Black ancestry has been attributed to a great many U.S. presidential candidates starting with Jefferson himself, but none more than Harding. On August 22, 1920, the *New York Times* ran a Harding genealogy attempting to lay the ghost by delineating the five generations between the senator and the first Harding to land at Haddam, Connecticut ("Haddam Home of Hardings," 1920).

Harding's special nemesis was a monomaniac on miscegenation, one William Estabrook Chancellor, a professor at the College of Wooster (Ohio). Chancellor appeared sane enough apart from his morbid loathing for any prospect of black contamination of white blood. Beyond mere segregation, he wanted all blacks and mulattoes disfranchised. He had assembled a genealogical sketch imputing several strains of Negro blood to Harding. He printed thousands of these tracts, but they sat unread as Harding's prospects for the Republican nomination seemed to dwindle in the GOP preconvention maneuvering of 1920.

Suddenly—out of the famous or fancied smoke-filled room—lightning struck, and Harding was the candidate. Just as suddenly, the tracts about his supposed black blood were everywhere. Rumors and whispers of black ancestry had dogged every political campaign Harding had waged, but while troublesome they were never decisive. As Chancellor's fliers swept the political world, one of them reached President Wilson's private secretary, Joseph Tumulty, who rushed to his crippled boss, waving the tract gleefully.

"Governor, we've got 'em beat!" he cried. "Here is a paper which has been searched out and is absolutely true, showing that Harding has Negro blood in him. This country will never stand for that!"

Wilson responded deliberately. "Even if that is so," he said, "it will never be used with my consent. We cannot go into a man's genealogy; we must base our campaigns on principles, not on backstairs gossip. That is not only right but good politics. So I insist you kill any such proposal" (Wilson 1939, 305–6).[6]

Equal Rights: LBJ and the Invisible Sell

The Texas Lyndon Johnson was an important asset for the Kennedy ticket in the Deep South. He spoke for equal rights there, but he spoke "Southern." Peter Lisagor of the *Chicago Daily News* recalled an incident from that 1960 campaign that reveals a lot about Southern political rhetoric in action. Style is more important than content; for generations the goal of the Southern stump-speaker has been to leave the audience limp and swooning with delight, even if oblivious to the content of the message.

When the perspiring Johnson, who had worked his [South Carolina] audience up to a frenzy with his shouting, slashing attack upon the GOP ticket, spoke of "human rights" and the justice of treating everyone equally, regardless of race, religion or region, the farmers were whooping and applauding. So were the two governors [of South Carolina and Georgia].

Later, when a couple of reporters buttonholed one of the governors and asked why he applauded so vigorously at the point of Johnson's demand for equality "for colored and white babies," the governor seemed flustered, and said, "why . . . why, he didn't say anything like that." His uncertainty suggested that he was so wrought up by Johnson's passionate oratory that he didn't really hear what the senator was saying. And one had to conclude, sadly, that maybe the farmers hadn't heard rightly, either ("1960—When Johnson Told Dixie His Views," 1965).

Exploiting Race

Earl Long was willing to use the bigotry of some of his constituents to advance a political cause, but—like Jimmy Carter a couple of generations later—the Longs were not bigots themselves or Ku Klux Klan supporters. Huey despised the Klan for its bigotry and violence. Once when the Imperial Wizard of the Klan offered to come to Louisiana to campaign for him, Long rejected the offer as follows: "Quote me as saying that that Imperial bastard will never set foot in Louisiana, and that when I call him a son of a bitch I am not using profanity but am referring to the circumstances of his birth" (Williams 1970, 703).

Until the civil rights revolution of the 1960s, the only kind of political mischief directed against blacks in the South was to intimidate them into staying away from the polls. But manipulating white racism was another matter. In 1946 when Georgia's notorious bigot Gene Talmadge was running for governor, he was opposed in the Democratic primary by one James V. Carmichael. Talmadge came across and hired a man who was a dead ringer for Carmichael. The double's job was to drive two black men around Georgia in an open-topped touring car, stopping in every town, while the blacks would loll arrogantly in the back seat, puffing great clouds of smoke from big cigars. In the primary the real Carmichael was snowed under.

Jimmy Carter's successful campaign for the presidency in 1976 received generally admiring media coverage, which gave voters outside his native region little cause to suspect that he was, as I wrote four years later,[7]

as sophisticated as any Deep South politician about "old-fashioned Georgia straight-razor politics," as it is sometimes known on its home soil. Home folks have known all along that Carter learned that game quickly when he virtually was robbed of a primary victory in his first run for the Georgia Senate in 1962. He learned more in his unsuccessful bid for governor in 1966 and in his 1970 primary campaign for the governorship.

Once scurrilous distortions have been repeated until they are familiar to everyone, they are replayed in voters' minds every time a candidate brings them up to disavow them. The tactic is one of the ancient tricks of the smear artist, and the [1980] Carter campaign... used it brilliantly to depict [Ronald] Reagan as bigot and warmonger.

Innuendo suggesting that blacks should fear Reagan appeared early, but was really orchestrated beginning in Chicago on Monday, October 6, when Carter told a Democratic rally: "You'll determine whether or not America will be unified or, if I lose the election, whether Americans might be separated, black from white, Jew from Christian, North from South, rural from urban..."

Tuesday and Wednesday, as the Chicago quote ricocheted around the country, the President acknowledged to various interviewers and audiences in Washington and Nashville that he had gotten "carried away," had made comments about Reagan "that were ill-advised," and wanted to get his campaign "back on the track."

Then on Thursday in Bristol, Tennessee, he put forth a reminder positively phrased: "I want to see the nation united, North and South united, black and white united, rural and urban united."

The next day, Friday, Carter's former U.N. ambassador, Andrew Young, campaigning for the President's reelection [before a heavily black audience] in Columbus,

Ohio, took up the theme. A questioner, presumably spontaneously, asked Young to interpret a speech Reagan had made 10 weeks earlier at the Neshoba County Fair in Mississippi. Young [a black veteran of the 1960s Civil Rights Movement] had a ready answer: In Philadelphia, Mississippi, where [in 1964] three civil rights workers were murdered "by the sheriff and the deputy sheriff and a government posse protecting states' rights, that looks like a codeword to me that it's going to be all right to kill niggers when he (Reagan)'s President."

Five days later . . . the White House disowned the Young comment: "The remark attributed to Mr. Young does not represent the President's view." There was more. "At his last press conference, the President made clear that he does not believe that Governor Reagan is a racist or is running a campaign of racism. He has also stated that he regrets the injection of racism into the campaign and would like to see it eliminated."

By [that time] the idea that Reagan was bad news for blacks was everywhere and Carter could avoid the subject entirely, leaving it to his surrogates to keep it alive with a subtle reminder now and then. ("Election '80: Dirty at the Top; Below That, Cleanest in Decades," 1980)

Black Racism

Abraham Lincoln's Emancipation Proclamation and the Reconstruction efforts of Radical Republicans left newly freed Negroes oriented toward the Republican party when they did vote. Northern cities posed for blacks few of the obstacles to voting that real and implied threats by the Klan did in the South. Then when the social and social welfare legislation of Franklin Roosevelt's New Deal began to make Democrats of voting blacks, and when World War II industrial development in the urban North drew floods of black migrants from the rural South, very large blocs of faithful black Democrats suddenly appeared in Northern industrial cities.

An immediate effect of the 1960s civil rights revolution was the election of black officials in the black constituencies. This was not limited to black mayors and city council majorities in overwhelmingly black Southern cities—though it was most dramatic there—but to all electoral positions in the urban North as well. Increasingly, redistricting after each census created black congressional districts in major cities, and black membership in the House of Representatives went from four in 1963 to sixteen in 1973 to twenty-three in the 101st Congress in 1989.

A powerful and persuasive black politician could put the same sort of lock on his—later his or her—House seat that white political bosses could do. Sometimes one or another found it expedient to campaign against the white establishment, whether it offered an immediate threat or not. Adam Clayton Powell, who represented New York's Harlem in the House for twenty-two years from 1945, was a pioneer both as a black congressman and at subtly or flamboyantly sticking it to Whitey for the delectation of his constituents. A vengeful House establishment set a select committee to investigate his affairs, and the House excluded him from the Ninetieth Congress in 1967—an action his supporters called racist and the Supreme Court called unconstitutional.

Black congressmen in massively black districts are free if they choose to campaign by baiting white media people, white colleagues, the whole white establishment, and whites in general, and when faced with a black primary opponent to label him or her an Uncle Tom and a tool of white interests. A prime example of the success of this approach is a South Side Chicago congressman named Gus Savage, elected to his fourth term in the 101st Congress.

Black candidates who elect to campaign against Whitey really have only two threats to worry about. One is the prospect of black middle-class inroads into their districts—and this kind of demographic change proceeds at a glacial pace. The other is to be gerrymandered out of office after the next census, a prospect slightly but not much more likely.

However, black candidates who have an eye on statewide or national office never play the black racist game in seeking office, concentrating instead on building a record of interracial cooperation and accomplishment. Edward W. Brooke III, a senator from Massachusetts in the 1960s and 1970s, comes to mind, as do longtime Los Angeles Mayor Tom Bradley and the Virginia governor elected in 1989, Douglas Wilder. There are hundreds more, at least, on their way up the political ladder around the United States, but the nature of media coverage of politics requires a string of successes on the lower rungs of that ladder before the political comer of whatever color becomes visible at all to the general public.

7

The Many Uses of Distortion

The art of distortion in political campaigning is painting a false picture with daubs of truth. Each daub is a fact taken out of a setting where it is part of a truth and carefully inserted into a new setting where it becomes part of a deception. The 1964 presidential campaign was one of the most sharply polarized in U.S. history, and like any such campaign it saw the wholesale use of distortion as each side tried to paint the other as the essence of evil. Modern visual media lend themselves well to this task because they are so effective at stimulating and exploiting emotion. And they are especially well suited to distortion because the moving images they present seem fully credible.

DISTORTING CHARACTER AND MOTIVE

Goldwater's puritan zealots of 1964 wanted to rally moral America to strike down the evil Johnson, and they contrived a television motion picture titled "Choice" to do it. Two weeks before the election it was screened for the Washington press corps—but by the Democrats, for whom Dick Tuck had obtained a copy.[1]

Savaging Johnson

The film was a morality play, made for Goldwater's campaign organization, albeit without his specific knowledge. A sponsor, Mothers for a Moral America, had been created to present it to the nation's housewives on afternoon television. In September a Citizens for Goldwater aide named Russell Walton had commissioned a trio of filmmakers to create a "documentary" that would stress, as he put it to them, juvenile delinquency, crime, moral degeneration, narcotics; and the facts that women are afraid to walk on the street at night, the parks are empty after dark—parents are fearful for their children, husbands for their wives... the country's moral standards are in a serious decline.... Remind the people of the moral crisis in America, the rising crime rate, rising juvenile delinquency, narcotics, pornography, filthy magazines. We want to just make them mad; make their stomachs turn. (Felknor 1966, 230)

Walton referred to recent race riots in Harlem, and he cautioned against any shots that might look like police brutality, then spoke of audiences, rural audiences.

They think that the big city is something evil, that it is a sinkhole, it produces narcotics and crime. This film will obviously and frankly just play on their prejudice. ... We are catering to the Midwest. We should carry the Midwest like nothing. They have a very high level of morality in the Midwest supposedly, so we are just going after that too.... The basic emotion is the fear and the anxiety of parents for their children's safety, for the safety of their wives, the safety of their homes. "Tonight maybe the glass will shatter and someone will come into our bedroom." Then we provide them with the solution for it: morality must start at the top, it must start with the White House, and the Administration. (Felknor 1966, 231–32)

After discussing how to blame all these moral failures squarely on Lyndon Johnson, Walton concluded that John Kennedy, like him or not, was "moving America to a period of greatness [while] this guy Johnson is nothing but a political animal."

Producer Raymond R. Morgan spoke: "He said, 'Ask not what your country can do for you, but what you can do for your country.'"

"I think you can twist that," Walton said, "You can twist it subtly because Kennedy is respected by both parties."

The resulting film followed the story line brilliantly. It was narrated by the actor Raymond Massey, with somber power and righteousness. The Kennedy image was deftly invoked and twisted. Over a score of strident and frenetic jazz, a black sedan careened through the night, empty beer cans flying out the window. A riot scene is there, blacks looting and smashing. Strippers, wild teenagers, bizarre dances. Rioting whites, looting blacks. Topless bathing suit, drug paraphernalia, a male reveler in a fig leaf, a rack of dirty books (Felknor 1966, 230–33; [Choice 1964]).

When the Fair Campaign Practices Committee (FCPC) challenged the Republicans to avow the film, Goldwater screened it and repudiated it as "racist." The only actual audiences were at Democratic fund-raisers showing copies of the original film purloined by Dick Tuck.[2]

This anti-Johnson film—notwithstanding the fact that it was not broadcast—was made to distort both the character and motives of the president. The video distortion of the anti-Goldwater campaign—which had Johnson's express approval and was broadcast—distorted the character, though not the motives, of the Republicans' nominee. This was accomplished principally in a series of thirty-second television ads, the most lethal of which, the Little Girl and the Daisy, is described in Chapter 3.

Savaging Goldwater

The second spot, like Daisy, was shown only once, and it had similar emotional impact. Another winsome little girl appeared, this time with her mommy and an ice cream cone. Mommy quickly pointed out that ice cream cones used to be poisoned with strontium–90 but not any more. However, there was "a man who wants to be President and if he's elected they might start testing [atom bombs] all over again." The only way to prevent a new wave of bomb tests, with strontium–90 coming back to poison little girls, was to elect President Johnson [Strontium–90 1964].

There was a flood of protest, and as with Daisy, the spot was not rescheduled. Democratic Chairman John Bailey pointed out to critics that the Democrats merely exploited the image Goldwater had created, and that was true. But when the Democrats of 1960, confronted with the "Catholic issue," insisted that the opposition and the voters accept John Kennedy's word as to whether he would be the Pope's servant first and America's second, the Republicans did so and the issue was abused mainly by bigots. Nixon's GOP could have conjured up some unforgettable television spots with burning martyrs. But it didn't. In 1964 Goldwater simply could not get any Democrats to pay attention when he outlined his views on nuclear responsibility, views that were so fully disguised in the Democrats' notorious spots. If the Republicans had responded in kind they might have actually run their "morality play," or a series of them, over and over, until the (strontium-laden) cows came home.

DISTORTING ATTENDANCE AND VOTES

Attendance

Negative campaigns often make much of missed votes or committee hearings. A consistent pattern of missing important votes on important measures, or of missing key hearings or committee work sessions can indeed be an indication of serious shortcomings in a legislator. But no gross statistic such as "Senator X missed seventy-two record votes" has any significance whatever unless it is analyzed and qualified. Moreover, the modern Congress tends to run as a "Tuesday to Thursday club," allowing long weekends for "back-in-the-state" activity, during which only a national emergency could assemble a quorum in Congress. And everybody but workaholics leaves early or returns late once in a while.

Attention-grabbing television spots belabor the missed votes theme in every campaign. A favorite device is a pack of bloodhounds trailing the missing lawmaker to bring him back to the job. In almost every case, these commercials, which seem to imply serious dereliction of duty, have virtually no significance [Hound Dogs 1982].

Distorting the Meaning of Votes

There are as many ways to distort the meaning of a vote in Congress as there are steps in the legislative process. A "yea" at one stage or another may reflect support or opposition to the substance of the bill. The smear artist uses the intricacies of the process to deceive the public. In self-defense, the citizen needs to know a little about how a bill becomes law.

While an important bill is being considered, numerous attempts will be made to amend it—either to "fine-tune" it, expand it, contract it, or sabotage it. When its final shape is agreed on, the question of adoption remains. But there are still several ways to kill it besides voting a flat no on the last roll call. A motion to table the bill may be made, or to recommit it, that is, send it back to the committee that handled it originally.[3]

This is only the sketchiest summary of ways to alter, kill, or maim a piece of legislation—usually without leaving a trace, for few of the steps will entail roll-call, or record, votes.

Various party and interest-group researchers compile voting records of incumbents they hope to defeat and supply them to challengers of their own persuasion. But they are tricky to use and may distort even with the most scrupulous intentions. Since World War II a number of ideological and special-interest groups have promulgated indexes of this kind that purport to rate members of Congress on a single scale: how "right" they are in terms of the rating group's own biases. The prominence these indexes once received in the news media has declined. Still, hardly a congressional election year goes by without some use of this approach to pry a legislator out of office. A sophisticated example was at the core of a highly visible—and ultimately successful—U.S. Senate campaign in 1964.

Kennedy vs. Keating in 1964: A Textbook Case

A few months after his brother's murder, Robert F. Kennedy resigned as attorney general of the United States and moved to New York to claim the U.S. Senate seat occupied by the Republican Kenneth B. Keating. "Bobby" was disliked by some liberals who had opposed his brother, the president, and he faced predictable anti-Catholicism. He was vulnerable to the "carpetbagger" label, having lived in New York only as a schoolboy.

His own and Keating's pollsters knew that in New York Bobby had a high "antipathy quotient." To nullify his reputation for ruthlessness, he opened his campaign on a conciliatory note. He launched a gentle and serious campaign and treated the Republican incumbent, Senator Keating, with propriety and respect.

Keating's campaign was a generally good-humored projection of his consistent moderate-to-liberal record, generally paralleling that of his Republican senior colleague, Jacob K. Javits, but a little less ardently liberal here and there. Keating played standard New York politics in appeals to the state's long list of ethnic groups—including choosing Italian audiences to charge accurately that Attorney General Kennedy's Cosa Nostra hearings had led to nothing but headlines endlessly repeating Italian underworld names.

The senator, whose own civil rights record was solid, told civil rights workers that the attorney general had walked out on their fight so he could seek the New York Senate seat. Both of these charges angered Bobby, but what hit him hardest was press coverage of Keating's criticism of his negotiations to sell certain German assets seized during World War II.

Keating had helped legislate permission for the attorney general to sell a chemical company owned by the German I. G. Farben cartel without waiting for protracted legal actions to end. Now he said, in effect, that Bobby had moved so quickly and carelessly that the proceeds—some $60 million— were in danger of falling into the hands of surviving Nazis.

Keating did not question Kennedy's motives, but the case was too intricate for political reporters, for whom the key words were *Kennedy*, *$60 million*, and *Nazis*. Kennedy was furious. Innuendo about Nazi affinities had dogged his family for decades, since remarks attributed to his father when he was ambassador to Great Britain in the early war years.

The Kennedy organization cried foul over the Nazi, Italian, and civil rights charges. They did not file a complaint with the Fair Campaign Practices Committee because, as one of the team later said, "We didn't want to look like cry-babies." Bobby Kennedy said later that when Keating began to attack him personally, he was freed to enter into an aggressive campaign. He did.

What ensued was described by a liberal magazine, the *Reporter*, as "the sudden deliberalization of Senator Keating" ("The Reporter's Notes—Kennedy vs. Keating (con[tinued])," 1964). It was accomplished by prestidigitation with Keating's recorded votes over eighteen years in the House and Senate.

The voting-index trick underlay a newspaper ad and a flier that called Keating an ultra-conservative even "by right-wing standards" on the basis of a conservative group's "high award" to Keating three years earlier when it listed him thirty-third on its index. (His conservative rating was exceeded occasionally by the Kennedy-Johnson administration's Senate majority leader.)

A vote against one version of a bill Keating thought unfair to New York was interpreted to mean he had "opposed federal aid to education since

1947." Actually, he supported it. A vote by Keating (and Bobby Kennedy's brother Teddy) to *increase* funding for higher education was represented as a vote "to cut $600 million from the Aid to Higher Education bill." Time after time, votes against weakening amendments were presented as opposing the underlying bill. It takes weeks of research—as Walter Quigley knew well—to weave such a carpet of lies out of threads that are only partly true. It takes similar weeks of research to ferret out the whole truth, and neither reporters nor voters in the midst of a campaign have that time to spare.

The Kennedy distortion that got the greatest mileage related to the landmark Nuclear Test Ban Treaty that John Kennedy signed shortly before his murder. Keating had been cool and sometimes caustically critical about it, but early in 1963 he began to come around and finally supported it firmly.

In a speech at Syracuse University on October 19, Bobby Kennedy attacked him for ridiculing the treaty for years but acknowledged, according to the text he gave the press, that Keating's "final response was adequate." But Kennedy went beyond that. The Associated Press said "Kennedy also charged the [*sic*] Keating 'ridiculed' the Nuclear Test Ban Treaty and did not speak out for it until after passage was assured." And the Syracuse *Herald Journal* said Kennedy in two speeches "accused Keating of voting against Federal Aid to Education, housing, urban renewal, the Nuclear Test Ban Treaty." (Dispatch No. 280, 1964; "Keating Statements In Cuban Crisis Were Inaccurate, Kennedy Says," 1964).

Keating complained to the Fair Campaign Practices Committee of distortions by the attorney general on the subjects of education and the Nuclear Test Ban Treaty. Ironically, a few days earlier FCPC had gone to the Keating organization about a smear directed at Bobby Kennedy, a scurrilous pamphlet by a professional anti-Communist named Frank Capell, "The Strange Death of Marilyn Monroe." The pamphlet suggested that Bobby arranged the murder of the actress after an unsatisfactory liaison.

Committee agents in New York and Los Angeles had been informed that the pamphlet was about to be injected into the New York campaign. The committee notified the Keating forces, which prepared a repudiation of the Capell tract to release if it did appear.

Keating released to the press his complaint about the Kennedy charges for Friday morning, October 23. The Kennedy apparatus had its response in the same editions. The FCPC staff first learned of the exchange in the morning papers, and before long messengers from both camps elbowed each other into the committee's Madison Avenue offices.

Near the end of a campaign, the committee staff worked through the weekend and often around the clock. The Keating charges were necessarily complex and based on numerous citations to the *Congressional Record*. Both the committee's researcher, Frederick F. Andrews, and I spent the weekend studying the complaint, assembling further documentation from Keating and studying that.[4]

The Kennedy answer was short and simple. It jibed at Keating for "running to the Fair Campaign Practices Committee to complain about documented recitation of the facts about his record" while Keating was making "false charges" about a Kennedy " 'deal' with the Nazis, being anti-Italian, running out on the civil rights program," and telling Jews that Kennedy was supported by Egypt's President Nasser. (The Nasser allusion related to a sort of jurisdictional dispute between Nasser and American Arabs over who hated which Senate candidate more.)

Then Kennedy said Keating was only "an interested observer" of the test ban debate "until the day before the voting began." His Syracuse text had confined "ridicule" to 1959. Now he stitched together three isolated passages from a Keating speech in the *Congressional Record* to support his claim that Keating had "ridiculed" the treaty just before its endorsement by the Senate in 1963.

The excerpts Kennedy cited were snipped and pasted in the classic style of the political dynamiter to fashion ridicule out of a plea for support.

Monday morning I dispatched a letter to Kennedy asking documentation on his education charge against Keating, then turned to the Test Ban Treaty. I said I read his statement with dismay, and that

Mr. Keating has provided documentation for his complaint . . . which demonstrates conclusively that your description of his position on the Test Ban Treaty is not only false and distorted, but also appears to be either a deliberate and cynical misrepresentation or the result of incredible carelessness, touched with luck.[5]

I pointed out that whoever put together the quotation attributing ridicule to Keating "had to pore through 240 lines of the senator's *Congressional Record* speech of September 20, 1964, beginning at page S16713, before finding the first of three isolated passages which you lump together to describe his attitude."

After summarizing the Keating speech, my letter concluded: "I trust you will be able to correct the grievous flaw in your research operation that this dishonest and unfair distortion reveals."

The Fair Campaign Practices Committee never issued findings in disputes about campaign tactics and was debarred from doing so by the law under which it was tax-exempt. Therefore, I naturally intended the letter to be personal and confidential, for the eyes only of Kennedy, whoever opened his mail, and whoever else relayed it to him. Within a couple of hours his researcher, Adam Walinsky, a brilliant young lawyer who had left the Department of Justice with him, was on the phone to justify the contention that the excerpts from the Keating speech reflected Keating's own views and that they indeed amounted to ridicule.

By this time the committee had full documentation from Keating and partial documentation—from its own resources, based on Kennedy staff citations of dates and votes—on the Kennedy complaint. A Keating campaign figure phoned to inquire whether the committee would brief the editorial writers of the *New York Times* and the *Herald Tribune* on the situation.

For years the committee had given occasional briefings to reporters on the background of campaign controversies, but never outside its own offices. I was asked to go to the papers for the briefing. I refused and was reminded that the committee had the only complete set of the Keating documentation in New York. (It had been assembled between Friday and Monday.) Unwilling to let the material out of the committee's possession until the tangled education matter could be reviewed further, I relented and agreed to let Fred Andrews go to the papers with the files and answer questions of fact purely for background.

In the confusion and haste of the moment, my copy of the confidential letter to Kennedy found its way into one of the file folders Andrews would take with him. He left for the papers and was met in the *Times* lobby by a Keating staffer.

At the *Times* the basic questions were answered, and when he left, Andrews inadvertently left part of the Keating documentation behind.

Two blocks south, at the *Herald Tribune*, Fred Andrews was embarrassed to realize he had left key material at the *Times*. The Keating man asked about the committee's communication to Kennedy, and Andrews confirmed that such a letter had been sent. The editorial writer asked to see it, and Andrews showed it to him, stipulating that it was off the record, that is, not for publication.

A reporter, Martin Berck, was in the room and asked if he might see the letter. As Andrews put it later in a memo to me, "in the confusion surrounding what part of the conversation was on the record and what part off," he handed the letter over. Berck asked if he might copy it. Andrews, assuming that it was clear that the letter and any committee response to questions was off the record, permitted him to do so. Berck announced that he intended to print the letter; he had seen it, had gotten it honorably, and could not erase it from his memory. Andrews demurred, Berck insisted, and the interview ended.

An hour or two later when I began to find out what had happened, I phoned the *Tribune* to seek withdrawal of the letter. The paper was adamant. I pleaded, blustered, and cajoled, all to no avail. The letter appeared in Tuesday morning's *Tribune*, and the fat was in the fire.

I phoned the committee chairman, Charles P. Taft, in Cincinnati, and we worked out the text of a telegram of apology to Kennedy, making clear that the publication of the letter was unauthorized. I read the text by phone to Kennedy's press man, Debs Myers, who demanded more concessions and a more apologetic tone. I said I wanted to release the statement, but that if Myers wanted to argue for more concessions with Taft he could do so, and gave him the Cincinnati phone number. Myers agreed to call back promptly so a final version could be agreed on.

At this stage, late evening of Tuesday, October 24, the deadlines of the Wednesday morning papers were approaching fast. I had not yet seen Andrews in person to get a blow-by-blow account of how the letter actually got into the hands of the *Herald Tribune*. I assumed the letter had been acquired by some bit of stealth, and the draft of the committee telegram to Kennedy said as much.

A *Times* man, R. W. "Johnny" Apple, phoned from Albany to inquire about the telegram. I read him the draft text, cautioning that the wording might be changed, pending a call-back from Myers at the Kennedy headquarters, and agreeing to call the news desk at the *Times* if the text were changed.

Then Fred Andrews arrived and told me what had happened, including the fact that the letter had not exactly been dishonestly acquired by the *Herald Tribune*. I called Myers to ask about his conversation with Taft. He had not placed the call. I read him the change in wording about the *Tribune*, and he said he would release the telegram at once. The *Times* desk was called to correct the telegram's language.

The *Herald Tribune* phoned, revealing that Myers had already released the telegram in its early version without checking back with the committee. Now in addition to the angry Kennedy forces, the committee confronted a newspaper which found itself accused of dishonesty instead of, perhaps, excessive zeal.

Overnight, so participants told me much later, the Kennedy committee reached the decision that the Fair Campaign Practices Committee had become a liability that should now be shot down. Next morning word reached the committee that one board member, Ralph McGill, had resigned after reading the letter on the grounds that it purported to represent the judgment of the entire committee and that he had not been consulted.[6]

Kennedy campaign staff members and Kennedy partisans on the FCPC board began to arrive, and a hectic conference went on for the rest of the day, interrupted by phone calls and messengers. It was all a misunderstanding. All that was needed was withdrawal of the letter, and perhaps another apology. Perhaps Felknor should be fired or resign. Andrews could be sacked and blamed for the whole thing. The Kennedy staff people said they had new evidence proving that Kennedy had not made the offending statement at Syracuse. Perhaps this could be the basis for a letter of withdrawal. Another Democratic FCPC board member, alerted by Debs Myers, phoned long distance: What the hell was going on?

At length, about 5:00 P.M., an agreement was reached, and the Kennedy people departed. The crux of the statement that I issued jointly with FCPC Chairman Taft was the following:

The letter should not have been written and any accusations in it were necessarily unfair to Mr. Kennedy at that stage. We hereby withdraw it in full.

Additional material has been received from Mr. Kennedy which raises quite different questions of fact.

That turned out to be false, too. The "new material," I finally discovered, was nothing more than a denial that Bobby had ever accused Keating of ridiculing the Test Ban Treaty on the eve of its adoption.

For Kennedy the tactical results of his counterforay were impressive. Shaken by the unfair position in which the publication of my letter had put Kennedy, the committee was for all practical purposes taken out of play so far as the remaining Keating complaints were concerned.

Actually, the committee found itself in a crossfire between Kennedy and the *Herald Tribune*, both playing for keeps. Both were dealing with particles of absolute fact sufficiently isolated from their context to present wholly false impressions. What started out as a misadventure that was unfair to the attorney general wound up as a net plus for him and unfair to Senator Keating because Kennedy naturally claimed the withdrawal of my letter as complete vindication.

After the election, the *Times* and the *Herald Tribune* published interviews in which the new senator-elect said he would have lost if the committee had not withdrawn the letter. This is probably wrong because he won by some 700,000 votes, while Johnson was beating Goldwater in the state by two and one-half million.

The Fair Campaign Practices Committee also was hurt by the affair, both financially because of canceled pledges from Kennedy supporters and by a general (and natural) negative reaction to the mishandling of the affair. By the fall of 1965, the visible negative effects had been overcome, and the committee survived for another fourteen years before effectively succumbing to lack of funds.

DISTORTING ONE'S OWN RECORD

Distortion can be used on one's own record, too, as witness the post-Watergate campaigns a decade after Kennedy's triumph. The "off-year" campaign of 1974

was an exercise in piety and post-Watergate moralizing. The arrogant became meek; veteran pols posed as amateurs. Conservative butterflies crept out of radical cocoons. Once thick-skinned officeholders whined about bland or trivial abuses. It was a year to bring tears to the eyes of an old-fashioned smear artist. ("1974 Campaign: Piety and Post-Watergate Moralizing," 1974)

George McGovern, the arch-liberal target of the Watergate conspirators in 1972, ran a forthright and successful campaign for reelection to his Senate seat from South Dakota. He could not have dissembled his liberalism even if he had wanted to. But many of his ardent supporters masqueraded with great skill. In Colorado his presidential campaign manager, Gary Hart, emerged a moderate after a neat and effective metamorphosis. Next door in Kansas, his neo-moderate sister-in-law, Martha Keys, who had managed the McGovern campaign in Kansas, beat a Republican legislator for a vacant House seat. Colorado also elected another reborn moderate, Eugene McCarthy's 1963 youth coordinator, Sam Brown, as state treasurer.

To be sure, all this is not traducing an opponent by subtracting significant facts from his or her actual record. But it is falsifying one's own record by hiding temporarily unpalatable facts from the voters. And it is still distortion and still deceit.

DISTORTING ABANDONED OR BOGUS POSITIONS

The 1980 presidential campaign in which Republican Ronald Reagan unseated Democrat Jimmy Carter, saw substantial distortion along racist lines, as related in Chapter 6. But there was more. The president's forces probed Reagan on the warmonger theme, not on whether this or that avowed policy of Reagan would risk the possibility of war—a perfectly proper basis for challenge—but, as President Carter put it repeatedly, that the choice between himself and Reagan was the choice between peace and war. Although not the subject of TV spots, the substance was reminiscent of the Johnson campaign on Goldwater.

When Reagan finally cried foul at one of these distortions,

Carter's press secretary called the remark "an overstatement," and staff members openly were delighted that Reagan had risen to their bait. The President then kept the idea alive in less strident language, while his secretary of state took up the hard line, foreseeing as a result of a Carter defeat a United States "endlessly at war all over the globe."

With racist innuendo rallying black voters and the warmonger innuendo winning women to his ticket, Carter then took to distorting even Reagan's gaffes and abandoned positions.[7]

The President carefully misquoted the Republican, in some cases inventing spurious quotations, and attributed to him present intentions and policies the exact opposite of Reagan's own recent declarations. ("Election '80: Dirty at the Top; Below That, Cleanest in Decades," 1980)

He even did so during the only actual debate of the campaign where at last Reagan had a chance to nail Carter's distortions on the spot. Reagan interjected, "There you go again, Mr. President," in a tone of good-humored resignation. The line became famous for the remainder of the campaign.

Given the ripe target presented by some of Reagan's verbal blunders and past positions—quoted precisely and in context—distorting them needlessly appeared not only dishonest but inexplicable and supplied another reason why Carter was so widely criticized for a disreputable campaign, quite unlike the free ride most journalists gave him in 1976. Many presidents have mocked and needled their challengers and assailed their judgment and policies. But the usual practice had been to rely on aides and agents for egregious distortion of their actual words and positions. In 1980 Carter did it himself.

Distorting War and Peace Issues

Distortions in the realm of war and peace, some of them echoing the "big bang" nuclear TV spots of 1964, were rampant in the 1982 congressional campaigns, in which various distortion ploys were used from coast to coast. California's governor, Democrat Jerry Brown, had a following in that state's large anti-nuclear movement, and when he set his sights on a vacant Senate seat, he employed his nuclear arsenal to keep a Republican, Pete Wilson, out of it.

California (and eight other states) had an initiative measure on the ballot that would in effect put the state on record as supporting a bilateral U.S.–Soviet nuclear freeze. The Republican candidate, San Diego's mayor, Pete Wilson opposed the proposition. To dramatize this Brown, who favored it, and to hitchhike on its popularity, used a TV spot featuring a nuclear explosion that recalled Lyndon Johnson's anti-Goldwater bomb spots of 1964. Public response to the ad was immediate and hostile, and though it was withdrawn at once it is thought to have helped defeat Brown. [I Want to Live 1982].

A similar technique was used in a last-minute commercial aimed at ten hawkish Republican senators and representatives by a new PAC, Citizens for Common Sense in National Defense, headed by Philip Stern, a District of Columbia Democrat and one of the Fair Campaign Practices Committee board members involved in the Kennedy sit-in of 1964. Television spots focused on a bus full of schoolchildren about to be blown up in a nuclear confrontation [Bombing the Bus 1982]. But the new PAC's version of hard-ball campaigning was too much so for its intended Democratic beneficiaries who, fearing the spots would backfire, scrambled to prevent their being aired.

A notably vicious Senate campaign in 1984 pitted North Carolina's Democratic Governor James B. Hunt, Jr., against Senator Jesse Helms, the conservative Republican incumbent. Both were powerful, and neither had much personal regard for the other. Commercials for Hunt showed civilian corpses in El Salvador's civil war, while the voice-over blamed their murders on death squads inspired by Helms's "best friend," the Salvadorean right-wing hard-liner Roberto d'Aubuisson. "Helms is a crusader," the narrator declares, "but this is not what he should be crusading for" [Death Squads 1984].

Meanwhile, a rabid Helms supporter who ran a weekly tabloid in Chapel Hill, the *Landmark*, published an article headlined "Jim Hunt is Sissy, Prissy, Girlish and Effeminate." It imputed to the governor both a former homosexual love affair and a current heterosexual (extramarital) liaison with a "former call-girl." Helms disclaimed any connection with the ad, and the editor later apologized tearfully (Snider 1985, 136).

Distortio ad absurdum. In 1982, a New Jersey Democrat named Frank Lautenberg was campaigning against a Republican House member, Millicent Fenwick, for the Senate by charging that she supported the onetime segregationist, South Carolina's Senator Strom Thurmond. Challenged to justify this assertion, Lautenberg said that if elected she would vote for the Republicans to organize the Senate, which would make Thurmond chairman of the Judiciary Committee (as he was in the expiring Congress).

This approach, a staple of campaign distortion, is a sort of perversion of the logical principle of *reductio ad absurdum*. Another 1982 contest offered an outstanding example. Two congressional incumbents had been thrown into the same Massachusetts district by redistricting after the 1980 census. Republican Margaret Heckler ran a television ad that took facts out of context to falsely depict her opponent, Democrat Barney Frank, as favoring prostitution and lenient sentences for rape.

Distorting Sexual Positions

Frank, who had won his original House seat in a campaign that emphasized family values, actually had been advocating legislation he believed would strengthen the hand of municipalities in controlling prostitution by enabling them to establish "Combat Zones" like Boston's, where "adult entertainment" could be confined. And he hoped to make it easier to win convictions for violent rape by reducing maximum sentences from life to twenty years. He made an issue of Ms. Heckler's distortions—and won.

An ironic backlight was cast on this case five years after the fact. In 1987 Mr. Frank, a brilliant legislator and politician and a greatly admired House liberal, answering a question he had planted with a reporter, acknowledged that he was a practicing homosexual. At about the time of this revelation, so his later statements made clear, he had parted company with a male prostitute whom he had patronized once in 1985 and then brought into his home in Washington.

This affair became known in 1989 in a *Washington Times* story. The *Times* quoted the prostitute, Stephen Gobie, as saying he had run a bisexual prostitution ring by telephone from Mr. Frank's town house on Capitol Hill. The congressman acknowledged that this was true but that it had been done without his knowledge. He said he had taken in the prostitute and employed him as a personal assistant for an honorable motive: he wanted to influence Mr. Gobie to "change his life" but had to give up ("Sex Sold From Congressman's Apartment," 1989).

Future opponents might fairly question Mr. Frank's judgment, as Margaret Heckler might well have done in 1982, but not his motives. The effect of the 1982 distortions was to paint the consequences of the legislator's actions in such simplistic terms as to attribute to him either base motives or dangerous irresponsibility.[8]

Many modern critics suggest that casting a pall of opprobrium over the other candidate is furthering the alienation of the voter from the political process. This question is addressed elsewhere in the present volume, notably in Chapters 13 and 15. But whatever the merits of the argument, it is not new. As John Quincy Adams observed of two other candidates at the end of a campaign in 1836,

One can scarcely imagine the degree of detestation in which they are both held. No one knows what is to come. In four years from this time the successor may be equally detested. (Adams 1874–77, 10:366)

8

Political Lies and Liars

Gelett Burgess once observed that half a truth is like half a brick; you can throw it twice as far. That may help explain why full-size falsehoods are seen less frequently than distortion in election campaigns. More importantly, compared to a clever distortion, an out-and-out lie is easy to detect. Nonetheless, candidates often are accused of lying, not infrequently in terms that invoke Adolph Hitler and the big lie—sometimes appropriately.

This chapter deals with several kinds of falsehood, including false statements, disproven charges presented as fact, false claims of authorship, invented history, forgery of various sorts, and fake publications. It addresses falsifying in all media of communication from print to video. The various particular lies of the Watergate affair, however, are treated with the entire scandal in Chapter 12.

Major party organizations are usually responsibly run, but occasionally their fingerprints are found on deliberate frauds. This befell the National Republican Congressional Committee in 1958 when it moved against a West Virginia Democrat, Robert H. Mollohan, who was trying to retire the Republican congressman Arch Moore.

LYING IN PRINT

A four-page special edition of the *United Miners Journal* came out filled with devastating assertions about Mollohan, and people assumed that the mine union had abandoned him to endorse the Republican incumbent. Talk of scandal was rife in the district, which lies in the panhandle country between Pennsylvania and Ohio. The importance of the United Mine Workers (UMW) to elections in West Virginia is great. For the UMW to break with custom and back a Republican could make a vast difference. The truth was that the Mine Workers were supporting the Democrat, Mollohan.

Fake Publications

This special edition was so special that its logotype, *United Miners Journal*, had been cut out and pasted up from a copy of the bona fide UMW publication, the *United Mine Workers Journal*, in the offices of the National Republican Congressional Committee (NRCC) in Washington. The phony publication had been reproduced by photo-offset and distributed throughout the West Virginia district.

On this occasion angry Democrats invoked a federal prohibition of anonymous literature then in effect but rarely enforced. A former staff member of Congressman Moore's named Keith Jacques was indicted and tried. He was acquitted, on the reasonable ground that he had only followed orders and carried material between the district and the NRCC in Washington. The real culprits never came to trial.

Publicizing Disproved Charges

Another approach to lying about a candidate is to publish old charges that have been disproved. This happened to Herschel Loveless, who was running as a Democrat for governor of Iowa in 1956. As his campaign was beginning to take hold, an unidentified handbill appeared around the state identifying him as a thief. The document was a photo-offset reproduction of a clipping from the *Ottumwa Courier* of April 24, 1934. "Ottumwa Man Accused of Cash Theft," the headline read. The article reported that H. C. Loveless had been jailed on a charge of embezzling some $450 from an oil company where he was employed. Its distribution in the campaign jarred his supporters across the state and stirred indignation among Republicans—until all the facts emerged.

The article reproduced was authentic, but what was missing was a correction that had appeared in the following issue twenty-two years earlier. The actual embezzler was found and Loveless completely exonerated within hours of the first story. The same clipping had been used against Loveless years earlier when he was running for a lesser office. That time the GOP's local leader was outraged at the deception and denounced it. In 1956 when the truth was revealed the deception backfired, and Loveless was elected.

Reversing the Truth by Cutting and Pasting

Throughout the time of McCarthyism (c. 1949–57) and for perhaps a decade longer during the heyday of the radical right, a favorite whipping boy of American right-wingers was an organization called Americans for Democratic Action (ADA). Through excessive zeal, careless research, and inattention to true facts, ADA became known in right-wing circles as a pro-Communist organization.

Actually, ADA was established by tough and perceptive liberals in 1947 expressly to prevent further Communist inroads into the U.S. liberal community. American Communists had been using the wartime respectability of the "gallant Soviet ally" to infiltrate many liberal groups and solidify gains they had made clandestinely before the war. Communists were moving to dominate labor, and their effort to infiltrate the Democratic Party and influence its platform and nominations in 1948 precipitated its three-way split that year.

In 1964 a Republican leaflet and a full page newspaper ad zeroed in on this anti-Communist liberal group. "What is ADA?" the headline asked. The answer was alarming: "The political organization, Americans for Democratic Action (ADA), has become a synonym for fellow-traveler, for Communist sympathizer, for advocate of 'soft' policies toward Russia."

The ad attributed the quotation to Robert L. Riggs, chief of the Washington Bureau of the *Louisville Courier-Journal*. The campaign was nearly over when it came to Riggs's attention. At once, he whipped off a steaming letter to Dean Burch, then chairman of the Republican National Committee. "This distortion," Riggs wrote,

is as dishonest a bit of political chicanery as I have encountered in nearly forty years of covering campaigns. It is a cheap trick to make me appear to say the exact opposite of what I actually did say.

Inasmuch as your party scored such a huge success in Tuesday's elections by the use of this distortion, I assume you will file it away for further use in the next campaign.[1] I earnestly request that you file this protest along with the folder containing the ADA ad so that when your people drag it out for the campaigns of 1966 and 1968, they will not be able to pretend they didn't know what a piece of deception it is....

Having covered in 1948 the first convention of Americans for Democratic Action, I was moved on February 2, 1962, to comment upon the hatchet job which had been done on that organization. In my piece, I wrote—

"One of the greatest image-making jobs of *the* current *political* era is the one that has been done on the *organization* named *Americans for Democratic Action*. This job has been done in reverse, performed by its enemies rather than by its friends. So successful has it been that the ADA, which was organized for the specific purpose of forcing Communists to keep their hands off worthy causes, *has become a synonym for fellow-traveler, for Communist sympathizer, for advocate of "soft" policies toward Russia.*" [Italics supplied to indicate which words the Republicans selected for the deception.]

A few months later, when [Republican] Thurston B. Morton was in a Senate race with Wilson W. Wyatt, Morton's people published a pamphlet entitled "The Danger of ADA and Wilson W. Wyatt." Wyatt had been the first president of ADA. To support their contention that ADA was a dangerous outfit, Morton's people quoted me as saying [the doctored quote described above].

Riggs pointed out that on the earlier occasion he had complained both by letter and in the *Courier-Journal* through an editorial but had gotten no response. He concluded, "I just want your records to contain this guidance for someone who might have a relatively weak stomach for distortions."

Republican Chairman Burch did reply to Riggs a couple of weeks later, apologizing for the distortion. He reported that he had taken "what I trust will be effective action to prevent further use of the advertisement," and he deeply regretted "any embarrassment this spurious quote has caused you [Riggs]."[2]

The transient hatchet man thought to have done the surgery on the Riggs quote for the 1962 Kentucky campaign was off the Republican National Committee staff in 1964. But it may be assumed he found work somewhere else.

THE CAMERA LIES

Early in the history of photography it was discovered that changing lighting could alter what the camera saw. Chemical, mechanical, and electronic manipulation enables still or motion photography to be distorted to prescription. Walter Quigley (Chapter 3) was a pioneer in cropping photographs to falsify.

One of the enduring classics of deception by photograph was used to exploit doubts about the loyalty and patriotism of a conservative Southern Democratic member of the Senate in 1950. This was Millard Tydings of Maryland, who was ending his fourth term in the Senate. He had survived a purge attempt in 1938 by President Franklin D. Roosevelt, for whom he was too conservative and too influential.

Tydings, chairman of the Senate Armed Services Committee, also headed a new committee investigating Senator Joseph R. McCarthy's sensational charges of Communist infiltration of the State Department (see Chapter 9). He soon incurred McCarthy's enmity and found himself opposed by one John Marshall Butler, a Baltimore lawyer of modest ability but sufficiently conservative and enthusiastic to win McCarthy's approval and the assistance of the McCarthy apparatus.

There were several substantial falsifications in that campaign, but the best remembered was a composite photograph in a campaign tabloid called *From the Record*, nominally sponsored by Young Democrats for Butler. The picture showed Tydings gazing attentively and respectfully at a rather magisterial Earl Browder, who looked back, soulfully and beneficently, at the senator. Between the figures of the two men was a fine white line, readily detectable by a suspicious person with good vision. Beneath the picture was the following legend:

Communist leader Earl Browder, shown at left, in this composite picture, was a star witness at the Tydings committee hearings, and was cajoled into saying Owen Lattimore and others accused of disloyalty were not Communists. Tydings (right) answered: "Oh, thank you, sir." Browder testified in the best interests of those accused, naturally. (U.S. Senate Hearings [Maryland] 1951, p. 13)

The "Oh, thank you, sir" had ended Tydings's interrogation of Browder and had, of course, appeared in the transcript of the special committee's hearings, which McCarthy's allies had combed, à la Walter Quigley, for ammunition. One of these allies was Frank Smith, chief editorial writer for the *Washington Times-Herald*, who worked hard on the tabloid and the Butler campaign and who later became Butler's administrative assistant. The "thank you" phrase had caught his eye. He showed it to Garvin Tankersley, assistant managing editor and recently picture editor of the *Times-Herald*, which produced half a million copies of the tabloid.

In the production process, "Tank" Tankersley ordered up all available photographs of Tydings and Browder separately and together, and at length came up with two shots that nearly filled the bill. Unhappily, both men were facing the same way. The Browder photograph, made on April 17, 1950, was reversed, so that the Communist, who was facing right when the picture was taken, came up facing left in the print. It was also reduced in size so that Browder and Tydings would appear in the same proportion. The Tydings picture had been made twelve years earlier, under circumstances which explained the senator's attentive expression: he was listening to the election returns in 1938, the year he survived President Roosevelt's effort to sabotage his reelection.

Responsible observers do not contend that the picture or the tabloid made *the* difference in the campaign. In fact, the Butler people believed that only part of the half-million press run was actually distributed. But no one denies that whatever quantity did reach the voters—200,000 or 300,000—the photograph influenced at least some of the 43,000 voters who made the difference and elected John M. Butler, the first Maryland Republican to win a seat in the Senate since 1928.[3]

Frank Smith a few years later wrote a critique on the coverage of the campaign by the press, in which he pointed out that the Butler tabloid was not the only piece of photo fakery in Maryland in 1950. Smith wrote bitterly—and accurately—that the Tydings people themselves had played fast and loose with the facts in a campaign ad that portrayed their senator on the cover of *Time* magazine. *Time*, in a March 3 story, had cited Tydings as one of the ten most effective members of the Senate. Under the tender ministrations of his campaign aides, the gentleman from Maryland appeared in the ad on the *cover* of that issue of *Time*; he was, therefore, presumably the most illustrious of the most effective ten. Actually the March 3 issue of the news magazine carried on its cover not Tydings but King Phumiphon of Siam.

It should be noted that in the Butler-Tydings campaign, the de facto campaign manager, Jon Jonkel of Chicago, was meticulous in not trying to prove that Tydings was a traitor, a Communist, or a pro-Communist; his interest was in exploiting doubt.

TAPING WITH FORKÈD TONGUE

Photography, and along with it photo-offset printing, were merely the first wave of the new technology that brought dramatic new capabilities to the purveyor of political lies. The next wave was electronic, and its effects were sometimes even more dramatic. Audiotape recording made it possible for the technically adept smear artist to use a candidate's own voice to lie about his or her record.

The 1963 campaign for governor of Kentucky was a dirty affair, and nerves were taut over the issue of racial integration. Ned Breathitt, the Democratic candidate, was being depicted as a "stooge" of President John Kennedy and his attorney general brother Bobby. The Kennedy brothers were portrayed as eager to force integration at every level. A fraudulent flier distorted Breathitt's positions on integration and implied that he advocated racial intermarriage.

This was the state of affairs when radio stations all over Kentucky carried a thirty-second radio spot announcement supporting the Republican candidate, Louie B. Nunn. The spot opened with the President of the United States speaking.

[*The President.*] Good afternoon, ladies and gentlemen. I would say that over the long run, we are going to have a mix. This will be true racially, socially, ethnically, geographically, and that is really, finally, the best way.

[*Announcer.*] Breathitt supports this Kennedy policy. Vote against it. Vote Nunn.

Unlike an audio forgery that had come to light a few years earlier, in which opponents of "socialized medicine" had forged an entire radio speech on tape in the name of a United Steelworkers official, the Republican spot in Kentucky used the president's actual voice, from a presidential press conference on September 12, 1963. The official transcript begins thus:

The President: Good afternoon. Ladies and Gentlemen, I want to stress again [the nuclear test ban treaty].

Twenty-two pages later, a reporter engages the president in this colloquy:

Question: Mr. President, a Negro leader who helped organize the March on Washington says that he feels you are greater than Abe Lincoln in the area of civil rights. Apparently a lot of other Negroes support you. The latest poll showed that 95 per cent probably would vote for you next year. Now, in your opinion, Mr. President, does this political self-segregation on the part of the Negroes, combined with continued demonstrations in the North, pose any problems for you as far as the electoral vote in the North is concerned next year?

The President: I understand what you mean, that there is a danger of a division in the party, in the country, upon racial grounds. I would doubt that. I think the American people have been through too much to make that fatal mistake. It is true that a majority of the Negroes have been Democrats, but that has been true since Franklin Roosevelt. Before that a majority of them were Republicans. The Republican Party, I am confident, could get the support of the Negroes, but I think they have to recognize the very difficult problems the Negroes face.

So in answer to your question I don't know what 1964 is going to bring. I think a division upon racial lines would be unfortunate, class lines, sectional lines. In fact, Theodore Roosevelt said all this once very well way back. So *I would say that over the long run, we are going to have a mix. This will be true racially, socially, ethnically, geographically, and that is really, finally, the best way.* [Italics supplied to indicate the sentence the Republicans isolated for their deception.] (Felknor 1966, 238–39)

Such abuses, given the First Amendment to the U.S. Constitution, are difficult and may be impossible to regulate. As with electioneering lies and distortions of every kind, not cynicism but healthy skepticism is the citizen's best defense. A generation earlier Walter Quigley noted that he could find the dynamite to destroy the career of anyone from his utterances over the years. What he would have given for audiotape! With a cheap reel-to-reel tape recorder, a razor blade, and an inch or two of scotch tape, the candidate can be savaged by his own voice.

THE CAMERA LIES: VIDEO

As early as 1934, a deliberate and expert political lie was executed on a very large scale by the motion picture industry. This effort was not made casually. The industry saw itself under siege, for the visionary reformer and novelist Upton Sinclair was running for governor of California. He had been a Socialist for three decades and was that party's unsuccessful candidate in 1930 against Governor James Rolph, who beat him and then died, leaving the office to Lieutenant Governor Frank Merriam.

Although he abandoned none of his Socialist principles or objectives, Sinclair was willing to blur their sharp edges enough to win the necessary converts to get him on the ticket again. He reregistered, this time as a Democrat, and won the gubernatorial nomination with more votes than his eight opponents combined.

His platform was his own utopian program of EPIC, or End Poverty In California, which applied simple Marxist theory to California's poverty. Essentially it called for a vast state social security system providing pensions and payments for the old, the widowed, and the unemployed. Sales taxes would be canceled, and the whole would be funded by taxes mainly affecting the rich: a new, stiff, progressive income tax; increasing the inheritance tax; and making property taxes progressive.

In 1934 this was a wild scheme indeed, and all the more so for an individual state. However, the prospect had enormous appeal to Depression-idled workers and farmers, and Sinclair founded EPIC clubs to promote it throughout the state. By election day there were more than 2,000 of them. These clubs, rather than the tame and anemic state Democratic Party, were the vehicle for his general election campaign. The prospect that enchanted the impoverished scared the very pants off the rich and powerful. All California industry, including the movie moguls, mobilized as if for war. In fact, Woodrow Wilson's World War I "propaganda minister," George Creel, participated in the campaign against Sinclair.

Enormous war chests were raised for the campaign. Propaganda was coordinated by the famous Lord and Thomas advertising agency of Chicago. The new and already formidable political public relations firm of Whitaker and Baxter, a major force in the campaign, mined Sinclair's enormous body of published writings for excerpts that could be used against him. These might be actual, complete statements; partial quotes taken out of context, or ideas for forged quotations that would sound right. The objective was not so much to reelect Governor Merriam, a harmless, superannuated hack, but to defeat Sinclair by making his utopian proposals look even wilder than they were (Harris 1975, 307; Kelley 1956, 33).

Hollywood, led by Louis B. Mayer, made its studios available for the creation of utterly phony newsreels attacking Sinclair and his crazy panaceas, and these were distributed free to every theater in the state. Actors and actresses played the parts of citizens ostensibly selected at random and interviewed "for our cameras." The *New York Times* described the approach in a November 4 story. Neat, wholesome, appealing types saw Merriam as their protector:

[A]n interviewer approaches a demure old lady, sitting on her front porch and rocking away in her rocking chair.

"For whom are you voting, Mother?" asks the interviewer.

"I am voting for Governor Merriam," the old lady answers in a faltering voice.

"Why, Mother?"

"Because I want to save my little home. It is all I have left in this world."

Sinister types with Russian accents praised "Seenclair" and his system, which "worked vell in Russia" ("Films and Politics—Hollywood Masses the Full Power of Her Resources to Fight Sinclair," 1934).

"The most frightening film," writes Sinclair's admiring biographer, Leon Harris, "showed trainloads of hobos on their way to California to partake of the largess Sinclair would provide with the taxpayers' money and to compete for the already too few jobs." California newspapers carried still photos of the hobo scenes—but only sophisticates and constant moviegoers recognized them as Hollywood players, in fact cast members of the Warner Brothers film *Wild Boys of the Road.*

Don Belding, who was Lord and Thomas's West Coast manager, admitted, "We hired the scum of the streets to carry placards through the cities 'Vote for Upton Sinclair,' and speculated that if the campaign had lasted a little longer the whole thing might have backfired and Sinclair been elected" (Harris 1975, 305–6).

But Hollywood's luck held, and its massive tissue of falsehoods, randomly studded with facts, saved the Golden State from the sinister clutches of Sinclairean socialism.

FAKING HISTORY

The presidential election of 1844 became notorious for a sheer fabrication, the invention of the history of a non-event. It also introduced a common noun to the lexicon of election campaigns.

The Tennessee Democrat James K. Polk was opposed for the presidency by Kentucky's Henry Clay, who by now was a Whig. Shortly before election day the *Chronicle*, of Ithaca, New York, published an excerpt from one Baron Roorback's journal of "A Tour Through the Western and Southern States." The baron told of watching the purchase of forty-three slaves by James K. Polk, "the present Speaker of the House of Representatives, the mark of the branding iron and the initials of his name, on their shoulders, distinguishing them."[4]

Other newspapers that shared the *Chronicle*'s Whig leanings just had time to copy its report before the election. In actual fact, the sale never was made, the branding scene never took place, and there was no Baron Roorback.

Polk won the election, but the lie had spread widely enough to besmirch his reputation. The word "roorback" became a common noun, known to succeeding generations of political practitioners and students: roorback, noun, any false or damaging story about a political candidate published too late in a campaign to permit effective refutation.

Faking a War Record—and a Career

In Utah, a little over a century later, a hapless veteran of World War II invented a heroic war record for himself—with considerable help from an admiring public. The tale elected him to the House of Representatives in 1952, and the support it generated might even have reelected him after the story fell apart. The man's name was Douglas R. Stringfellow.

He had been a private in a U.S. Army armored unit who, a day or two after his arrival in Europe and just before being committed to combat, had the bad luck to step on a land mine, which exploded, earned him a Purple

Heart, and crippled him for life. After he returned home to Utah he finished college, got interested in politics, went into broadcasting, and became chairman of the state's Young Republican League. Increasingly, he was seen as a potential candidate for office.

Stringfellow was hesitant to talk about his war wounds and, he later said, found himself almost reluctantly agreeing with sympathetic listeners who would offer hypothetical gallant actions to explain the wounds he was reticent to discuss. The story of his heroism materialized gradually until he became the sole survivor of a thirty-eight-man OSS unit that was parachuted into Germany, where he personally captured a Nazi scientist. His heroic stature grew, and in 1952 when Congressman Walter K. Granger tried (vainly) for the U.S. Senate, Stringfellow ran for his House seat and won.

In the public eye more than ever after the election, he was understandably reluctant to talk about his bravery—which made him all the more attractive and gallant, and he was lionized for his Walter Mitty record. He received a Man of the Year award and was celebrated on a popular network television program, "This is Your Life" in 1954. All this attention stirred skepticism in some veterans' circles, and on October 14, 1954, the once-accidental hoax came apart. On that date an article casting doubt on his story appeared in the *Army Times*. The unlucky Stringfellow confessed at once in a hurriedly arranged, tearful, and dramatic special television broadcast. His plight was received with a lot of sympathy at home in Utah, but he decided to withdraw the nomination for reelection that had already been handed him. He served out the few months remaining in his term and returned to private life in the broadcasting business (Jonas 1966).

FAKING AUTHORSHIP

A bit of plagiarism in 1988—or as it turned out, a few bits—temporarily derailed several American political careers, among them that of U.S. Senator Joseph Biden of Delaware. Biden was one of what U.S. news media called the "seven dwarves" of 1988, lesser pretenders to the Democratic nomination for president. He was widely admired for his oratory, which often left audiences rapt and dazzled. He was chairman of the Senate Judiciary Committee, and one day while he was presiding over the liberal vivisection of a conservative Supreme Court nominee before his committee, he was called from the chamber to learn that his rhetorical borrowings had been discovered.

The loot in this case was an effulgent rhetorical question he had copped and toned down from a Welsh politician, the quasi-moderate leader of the British Labour Party, Neil Kinnock:

Why am I the first Kinnock in a thousand generations to be able to get to university? Why is [my wife] Glenys the first woman in her family in a thousand generations to be able to get to university?

Without identifying his source, the American lawgiver had translated this as

Why is it that Joe Biden is the first in his family ever to go to a university? Why is it that my wife who is sitting out there in the audience is the first in her family to ever go to college? ("Biden's Debate Finale: An Echo From Abroad," 1987)

This trifling rifling was leaked to the press by John Sasso, the campaign manager of the Democratic front-runner, Michael Dukakis, who had come by videotapes of both the Kinnock original and the Biden variation. Then the fact of the leak was leaked and so handled in the news media as to impute scheming most foul to the Dukakis manager, Sasso—who, after a few days of public angst, was temporarily fired by Dukakis. Better poor Sasso had been inducted into the Opposition Research Hall of Fame.

And Biden: had he not been so overcome with guilt, he might have claimed a niche in the Rhetorical Analysis Hall of Fame for cleaning up the mad Welshman's arithmetic. If one accepts thirty-five years as a generation, a thousand generations ago Mr. Kinnock's family was crouching in caves, or perhaps swinging in trees. For in those days—some 32,600 years before Socrates, whatever passed for university was teaching Late Stone Age man to fashion primitive tools from stone and shells. One wonders, indeed, if Kinnock might not have lifted the line from some secret joke book of Stephen Potter (*Gamesmanship*) or perhaps Lewis Carroll (*Alice's Adventures in Wonderland*).

That distinguished authority on political rhetoric, Kathleen Hall Jamieson, takes the Biden case more seriously, in light of the fact that soon after the cloned Kinnockism came to light other Biden borrowings were discovered. The Judiciary Committee chairman had plagiarized from Robert Kennedy and Hubert Humphrey as well as Neil Kinnock.

Of the public personae of three liberals, Biden was fashioning a fourth. No one would fault his choice of ancestors were he not proclaiming that he was self-created. This act of rhetorical parthenogenesis invites us to ask, Is there a person who is Joseph Biden or is he simply a persona constructed of the feelings and history of others? And were he elected, how would we know who it was who was leading? Or whether the person who today is Kinnock and yesterday was RFK might not tomorrow submit to the allure of a new master text? (Jamieson 1988, 222–23)

As for the inherent wisdom of the stolen Stone Age U. quote, a phrase comes to mind from a nineteenth-century American politician who was no less a master of rhetoric than Mr. Kinnock and Senator Biden—and more celebrated for candor than either. It is a capsule book review attributed to Abraham Lincoln: "People who like this sort of thing will find this is the sort of thing they like."

9

Politics and Patriotism

Concerns over loyalty and patriotism have bubbled through the American polity at irregular intervals and levels of intensity since colonial days. The American Revolution itself and the Declaration of Independence were direct products of these internal conflicts. But stewing about what loyalty and patriotism may demand of a free people has never entirely subsided.

At the end of World War I, and following a couple of decades of increasing tension in America between militant Socialists and laissez-faire capitalists, Vladimir Ilyich Lenin announced the Third International and claimed leadership of all the world's Socialist parties. At almost the same instant, Woodrow Wilson made A. Mitchell Palmer attorney general of the United States.

Lenin and Palmer were made for each other. Palmer saw the Red Menace as a clear and present danger and worse. He took direct action without regard to law, Constitution, compassion, or common sense. Using his Bureau of Investigation to swoop down on bands of suspected Communists, he conducted an incredible, lawless campaign of arrest and attempted deportations through the winter of 1919–20. A twenty-two-year-old lawyer, two years in the Justice Department, was made a special assistant to Palmer and cut his eyeteeth in the Bureau of Investigation that winter. His name was John Edgar Hoover.

THE GREAT RED SCARE OF 1920

For Palmer it must be said that he had the wholehearted support of a majority of the American people. Their apprehension was justified by rhetoric from the Communists and fueled further by violent and bloody strikes and riots that were erupting across the country. Eugene V. Debs, the Socialist leader, was in jail for wartime sedition and Wilson refused to pardon him. But other radicals were leading strikes against mines, railroads, and factories. Racial tensions flared everywhere, and as 1919 waned there were devastating riots and clashes between blacks and whites in Chicago, Gary, Mobile, Omaha, and Washington. Bloodshed was part of daily existence, and most Americans were afraid of the Reds.

Palmer's raids netted suspected Reds by the hundreds. On a single January night in 1920, his forces struck in thirty-three cities and made a combined haul of more than 4,000 alleged Communists. In Detroit 300 were jailed for a week—including twenty-four hours without food. All were released when it was proven that they had been arrested on false charges and that all of them were innocent of involvement in any revolutionary movement. In New England and elsewhere, hundreds were arrested who had never had any connection with radical movements.

The hysteria reached state legislatures, which appointed anti-subversive committees that in some cases continued the witch hunt almost uninterruptedly into the 1950s. In New York five Socialist members of the General Assembly were expelled although their party was entirely legal and they had done no wrong. This, notes Samuel Eliot Morison, "went too far, even for conservatives. The *Chicago Tribune*, Senator Harding [to be the next President], and Charles Evans Hughes [the Republican whom Wilson had defeated for the Presidency] denounced their action" (Morison 1965).

Most of those arrested were immigrants and still aliens, and Palmer now set about deporting them. President Wilson was ill and hardly more than comatose; there had not been a cabinet meeting for months. What got done in the name of the chief magistrate got done informally by aides or illegally by the First Lady. Finally, with spring, the president rallied somewhat and by mid-April was able to call a cabinet meeting. There Palmer proclaimed to Labor Secretary William B. Wilson (no relation to the president) that had he only deported more foreign agitators he could have ended a particular troublesome and bloody miners' strike. Secretary Wilson rejoined bitterly that such action would simply have made matters worse. With great effort the president, propped up in a chair, managed to admonish Palmer. "Do not let the country see Red," he said (Smith 1964, 155).

It was too little and too late, but it stiffened the spine of the labor secretary. He and his assistant, Louis Post, began intervening in Palmer's deportation hearings, supplying counsel, and manipulating the cancellation of government actions in the more flagrantly rigged cases, all of which enraged Attorney General Palmer. He demanded the dismissal of Post, and a congressional committee investigated him. Post persuaded them that his actions had been not only just but proper, and he stayed on the job. Eventually, some 600 aliens were actually deported—out of 5,000 arrest warrants that had been sworn out.

Palmer (implausibly, a sort of fallen-away Quaker, right down to using the plain speech) was nothing daunted. He knew full well that his actions, crudely unlawful as they were, had made him a national hero to a frightened citizenry. The 1920 Democratic National Convention was approaching, and he was a real prospect for the nomination. He helped his pre-convention campaign along with a warning. He said he had information that on May Day of 1920 a cabal of radicals was going to launch a coup to overthrow the government of the United States. National Guard units were called up, police forces stood extra duty—New York's entire force was on twenty-four-hour duty—and trigger fingers itched everywhere. The Red Letter day ended without the explosion of a single bomb. Palmer was left like a millennialist preacher on the day after he had promised his flock the world would end. This embarrassing denouement helped prevent his nomination as a presidential candidate, but only narrowly.

GROWING COMMUNIST INFLUENCE AND INFILTRATION

A. Mitchell Palmer's Red Scare left a baneful heritage. Its excesses so offended thoughtful conservatives and liberals alike that it had the effect of blinding many Americans to both the failings of Soviet Communism and the reality of Communist efforts to infiltrate the institutions of the United States and other Western countries. The Great Depression intensified discontent, and various Socialist and Communist parties polled more than a million votes in the presidential election of 1932.

Leftist intellectual ferment in the nation's campuses had permeated to some degree most of the people whose education, training, and convictions made them plausible administrators of the great social and economic experiments of Franklin Roosevelt's New Deal. The administration was careless in a number of ways about Communist infiltration and influence, and it was inevitable that some Communists and more fellow-travelers would slip, fall, or bring one another into positions of some importance in government, the academy, and organized labor during the 1930s. Others entered government during the wartime alliance with Stalin.

Very soon after the end of World War II, U.S. intelligence entities, with growing public support from conservative political and religious circles, were busily trying to measure the extent of this infiltration and identify the infiltrators. By the summer of 1948, former Communist agents had been testifying about espionage, and coincident with the election campaign the House Committee on Un-American Activities, usually called the House Un-American Activities Committee or HUAC, had been pursuing a sensational investigation. A *Time* editor and confessed Communist spy, Whittaker Chambers, charged that Alger Hiss, long a highly placed government functionary, had been his associate in a Communist spy ring.

HUAC had been reluctant to dig far into the matter because of Hiss's persuasive manner and impeccable references. Finally it did so, but only because of the persistence of a freshman congressman from California named Richard Nixon. A month after the 1948 election, Hiss was indicted on perjury counts arising from the investigation. A year later, after a first trial ended in a hung jury, he was convicted of perjury in denying that he had passed government documents to Chambers, then a Communist spy. Another former U.S. employee, Judith Coplon, and a Soviet diplomatic aide, Valentin Gubichev, were brought to trial on attempted espionage charges.

THE RISE OF McCARTHY AND THE ISM

Then, early in 1950, a lackluster, first-term Republican senator from Wisconsin, Joseph R. McCarthy, stumbled across the issue of Communists in the U.S. government. Although he knew nothing whatever about that real but difficult issue, he found it to his liking and, to rescue his short and drab Senate record from general derision, seized on it as a campaign theme for reelection in 1952.

After some slapdash staff research, he tried his wings in February 1950, telling an audience of Republican women at Wheeling, West Virginia, that he had a list of 205 Communists who had infiltrated the State Department. Overnight the speech sparked an uproar of right-wing support and left-wing outrage, and McCarthy thereafter commanded media attention wherever he went.

Over the next three years McCarthy dominated the American political landscape like a killer tornado. The numbers of "card-carrying Communists" he claimed to have on his "list" shifted almost daily; McCarthematics was an imprecise science. Never presenting evidence, he named innocents, ruined reputations, and accomplished what amounted to a reign of terror among liberals and moderates across the land.

The Wisconsin senator and his supporters saw Communists behind every tree. Although in retrospect it is wildly naive to doubt that some of McCarthy's targets—and a great many never on one of his lists—were covert Communists, he never delivered one. Those Communist agents who did come to trial were identified by more responsible agencies, operating with all the frustrating constraints posed by the U.S. Constitution and system of jurisprudence to protect the entire citizenry.

McCarthy's Supporters

Hordes of Americans rallied to McCarthy's spy hunt. Among them were white Anglo-Saxon Protestants whose old American names were waning in power and influence. There were immigrants' children whose war service and rising economic power did nothing for their thirst for status. Irish-Americans, so long contributors to the society yet still denied full equality, united behind the Wisconsin senator, one of their own.

German Americans whose parents and grandparents had been humiliated and harassed by their neighbors in two world wars rallied to McCarthy now as they had to Robert La Follette in opposition to U.S. entry into World War I. Fundamentalist Catholics and Protestants, as Richard Hofstadter observed, "subordinated their old feuds (and for the first time in our history) to unite in opposition to what they usually described as 'godless' elements" (Hofstadter 1963, 80, n.8). So the audience was ready for McCarthy, and the Wisconsin senator, on whom the Communists-in-government issue had dropped out of the blue, was ready for it—in an improvisatory, seat-of-the-pants way.

He was a demagogue of the second water, able to summon passion and outrage in his hearers and grateful, dedicated loyalty in his adherents. He lacked the long-range view and focus that might have made him dangerous for a longer period. He rode the opportunities of the moment. In the light of his initial unconcern with the problem, no one is likely to have been more surprised than he at the genuineness and depth of the cause for concern or at the political payoff waiting for him in what really was a superficial exploration of the subject.

It was said that McCarthy awakened America to the problem of Communists in government, and in a sense he did. He rallied to a political banner a rag, tag, and bobtail of fundamentally apolitical citizens. He also provided a prophetic voice, of sorts, for a sprinkling of disenchanted conservative intellectuals and a heroes' forum for a tattered assortment of gumshoes and recanted former Communists. But his essential lack of scrupulousness—in investigative method, in uncritical reliance on circumstantial evidence, in accepting guilt by association and simple accusation, and in disrespect for due process of law—perverted the awakening into a nightmare.

Damaging His Own Cause

In fact, McCarthy's exploitation of the issue greatly damaged the cause he professed by making it disreputable and making the idea of Communist efforts at subversion and espionage seem ludicrous to many U.S. liberals.

The Republican convention of 1952 rejected the choice of most of McCarthy's followers, Robert A. Taft. The party needed a popular hero to lead its crusade against "the Mess in Washington" and nominated General Dwight D. Eisenhower. People liked "Ike," including Democrats and anti-McCarthy Republicans. Reactionaries who despised all of the above went along; anything to oust the Democrats after five successive administrations.

Much of the campaign was surprisingly bland. As is so often the case, the dirtiest campaigning came from levels below the major candidates. The Communist issue was the most irritating to the Democrats, and the hardest to handle, both because of the way it was presented and because of the underlying facts that enabled it to be an issue. The campaign of the Republicans was keyed to the "where there's smoke, there's fire" approach.

Twenty Years of Treason

There was abundant smoke, in the form of accusations, implications, and some facts. The McCarthy mania was at its crest. The Wisconsin senator referred to "twenty years of treason," and the Republican vice presidential candidate, Richard M. Nixon, spoke of Truman, Stevenson, and Secretary of State Dean Acheson as "traitors to the high principles" of the Democratic Party. To fancy that the phrase would be remembered intact—"high principles," Democratic Party, and all—would have been naive, and to use it knowing it would be forgotten, with only "traitors" ringing in the memory, was simply dishonest.

In his first Senate term, McCarthy had been assigned to the Standing Committee on Expenditures in the Executive Departments. Upon his reelection in 1952, he had enough seniority to chair both it, renamed Government Operations, and its Permanent Subcommittee on Investigations. This became a perfect vehicle for his wildly irresponsible and unproductive Red hunt.

Censured at Last

At last, McCarthy pushed his luck too far by trying to tar the U.S. Department of the Army and the army itself with "coddling Communists." A special Senate committee conducted televised hearings investigating him, for a change, and that did him in. The Senate censured him. He died three years later, broken by alcohol and, finally, contempt.

Joe McCarthy left his name on the era, but he sabotaged his pretended cause by discrediting it. His contemporary, Richard Nixon, was another matter. The disgrace Nixon later brought on himself (see Chapter 12) was after his painstaking and diligent investigative work had taken him to the peak of what U.S. politics has to offer. That work was done on the House Committee on Un-American Activities (HUAC), to which Nixon was appointed when he went to Congress in 1946. He got there by demolishing the political career of a California congressman named Jerry Voorhis, a five-term liberal Democrat. Nixon was a Republican.

THE EARLY CAMPAIGNS OF RICHARD NIXON

As was the practice in California, both candidates filed in both primaries, and Voorhis won the Democratic nomination and amassed a big minority in the Republican contest, which Nixon won. The ensuing campaign was bitter. In the first of a series of "debates," actually a series of joint appearances with questions from the audience, Voorhis protested a Nixon newspaper ad that read, "A vote for Nixon is a vote against the Communist-dominated PAC with its gigantic slush fund."

There were two "Communist-dominated PACs." At this time "PAC" was universally recognized in the United States as the Political Action Committee of the CIO, the Congress of Industrial Organizations (which had not yet merged with the American Federation of Labor to form the AFL-CIO). The CIO had also formed a similar and parallel, but non-union, organization— essentially a front—to broaden its influence; this was called the National Citizens PAC. As to Communist domination, several unions in the CIO in fact had Communist leadership, and considerable influence was exerted in both PACs by both individual Communists and fellow-travelers. This was a subject of considerable public concern and controversy. (The kind of PAC that emerged in the 1970s had not yet been invented.)

Congressman Voorhis pointed out that he had not been endorsed by the CIO's Political Action Committee and had not sought its endorsement. The CIO-PAC had endorsed Voorhis in his previous (1944) campaign, but it did not do so in 1946. However, the Los Angeles County chapter of the closely related National Citizens PAC had ardently and defiantly endorsed Voorhis in 1946.

In the debate, when Voorhis denied the endorsement, Nixon read off the text of the local chapter's endorsement from its bulletin, handed the document to his opponent with a flourish, and went on to cite from its masthead a number of far-left names represented on both boards, suggesting that Voorhis's disavowal of support was meaningless.

Voorhis insisted later that he neither had nor desired the support of the California CIO-PAC, acknowledging that there was "a grave question" of Communist influence over California CIO bodies. But for the remainder of the campaign he was kept busy explaining the facts and denying that he was the PAC's man. Nixon kept the spotlight on the twin questions of Red domination and red-blooded Americanism, with thrusts about the Roosevelt administration and other public officials fronting for "un-American elements" by seeking "increasing Federal controls over the lives of the people" (Felknor 1966, 77).

No one could prove that Nixon ever called Voorhis a "lip-service American," but many voters in the district remembered it that way. In fact, Nixon did toss off several general warnings about "lip-service Americans" without naming Voorhis. Then, with classic last-minute timing, the Nixon forces released a blast at "the insolence of Moscow in telling the American voter to elect PAC candidates, such as Mr. Voorhis," whose record it called one of "consistently voting the Moscow-PAC-Henry Wallace line in Congress."

Nixon's deft and assured footwork in this campaign cannot be ascribed entirely to native shrewdness. The Republicans had assigned a political pro to counsel him, a lawyer and public relations consultant named Murray Chotiner. Nixon's instincts were already sharp; he had identified from the start the need to "blast" Voorhis's "conservative reputation." Chotiner was able to hone these instincts, and Nixon kept Voorhis busy for the rest of the campaign, fighting on Nixon's ground, denying inferences voters drew from what Nixon never quite said.

Voorhis lost. He later observed that he probably would have lost anyway. The district had been gerrymandered into a very conservative one. The winds of change blew Voorhis and a lot of his fellow-Democrats out, and the Republican Eightieth Congress, including Richard M. Nixon, in. He was reelected easily in 1948.

In Congress, Nixon did his homework and paid attention. In HUAC hearings, he was impressed by the character and testimony of Whittaker Chambers, and when Alger Hiss, whom Chambers had accused, was called to testify, Nixon paid the closest scrutiny to gaps and inconsistencies in what he said. Nixon's pursuit led to Hiss's perjury indictment, trials, and conviction early in 1950. (He served three years of a seven-year sentence in federal prison.)

Nixon had thought about trying for a U.S. Senate seat. It was occupied, however, by a popular and conservative Democrat, two-term Senator Sheridan Downey, who had taken it from William Gibbs McAdoo in the 1938 primary. Meanwhile, a three-term Democratic House colleague of Nixon's, Helen Gahagan Douglas, announced her intention to take on Downey in the 1950 primary. Nixon learned that if he were the Republican nominee he would pick up some important support that included the powerful *Los Angeles Times*. One year before election day, he announced for the nomination.

Mrs. Douglas took out after Downey, belaboring him for his support of big business and electric power interests. The vigor of her campaign, and perhaps the awkwardness of opposing an aroused and articulate woman— a celebrated actress—who knew her way around Capitol Hill, took their toll on Downey. He pulled out of the contest, citing the heavy demands of the "personal and militant campaign against the vicious and unethical propaganda" he saw as emanating from Mrs. Douglas and her "extremist" friends.

The Downfall of Helen Gahagan Douglas

Senator Downey was quickly succeeded in the race by Manchester Boddy, editor and publisher of the *Los Angeles Daily News*. He had plenty of financing, the research capabilities of his paper, and the determination of a successful encyclopedia salesman, which he had been. He was spoiling for this fight. Submerging chivalry beneath "Americanism," he swung obliquely at Mrs. Douglas, a vigorous anti-Communist but not his kind of anti-Communist. He assailed "a state-wide conspiracy" by a "subversive clique of red-hots to capture, through stealth and cunning, the nerve centers of our Democratic party" (Felknor 1966, 78). He talked of "the red-hots' blueprint of subversive dictatorship."

Nixon had declared in November with a statement nearly as intense. For him the enemy was not Downey but "planned economy, the Fair Deal, or social welfare—but it is still the same old Socialist baloney, any way you slice it." Now he also cross-filed in the Democratic primary.[1]

Meanwhile, Senator Downey, who later ignored a request from the Truman White House to endorse Mrs. Douglas in the sweet name of party harmony, took to the radio with what became the stop-Douglas theme. He declared she not only had given aid and "comfort to the Soviet tyranny by voting against aid to Greece and Turkey," but she also "joined representative Vito Marcantonio, an admitted friend of the Communist Party," in opposing an appropriation for the House Committee on Un-American Activities "to uncover treasonable Communistic activities" (Felknor 1966, 78).

The foil, Marcantonio, was a onetime Republican who became a New York City congressman in the extreme-left-wing American Labor Party. He had nothing but contempt for liberals, and he particularly despised Helen Douglas. When he read of the efforts of Downey and Boddy to kill her off in the primary by linking her votes with his, Marcantonio, no stranger to demagoguery, chuckled to a friend of Nixon's in the House, "Tell Nicky to get on this thing, because it is a good idea" (Mazo 1959, 81, n.3).

Nicky did. In the primary campaign, Democrats and Republicans rang the changes on the Marcantonio ploy. Almost every anti-Douglas statement tied her to "the notorious radical, Vito Marcantonio;" or "Representative Vito Marcantonio, an admitted friend of the Communist Party;" or "notorious Communist Party-liner, Vito Marcantonio of New York;" or some other variation. In July Mrs. Douglas tried the game herself, and taxed Nixon with voting like the much-aligned congressman (Mazo's phrase) against U.S. aid to Korea and to halve European aid. This also was a classic distortion tactic (see Chapter 7): Nixon had voted for a one-year aid package instead of two.

From the start the direction of Nixon's campaign had been clear. His campaign chairman said Mrs. Douglas's record revealed "the truth about her soft attitude toward Communism." His supporters began to taunt the congresswoman as "the Pink Lady." Then the famous pink sheets appeared. They remain the most remembered aspect of the campaign.

The content of the pink sheet actually was a gift from Manchester Boddy. After the publisher lost the Democratic primary, the opposition research for his negative campaign was secretly turned over to Nixon. A beguiling bit of California political lore relates the circumstances. While attending a political gathering in a supporter's apartment, Nixon learned by a phone call that the promised material was ready. He left the party quietly, made his way stealthily through alleys and backyards to the rendezvous, received the documents, and returned to the party.

The Nixon team's only original contribution to the document was the color of the paper, which Nixon later referred to as "the mordant comment of the color of the paper" (Nixon 1978, 74). The resulting fliers on pink paper, 550,000 of them, were headed "Douglas-Marcantonio Voting Record." They revealed that "Helen Douglas and the notorious party-liner" had cast identical votes in the House 354 times.

The votes were identified with dates and convoluted references whose very awesome detail persuaded lay readers that they were both accurate and significant. Not mentioned was the fact that most of the measures were routine and trivial matters, and that on a great many of them Nixon and most other certified anti-Communists had also voted with Marcantonio and the Pink Lady. Another classic distortion.

Helen Gahagan Douglas was beaten by 680,000 votes and sent to political retirement scarred for life. Nixon, now "Tricky Dick" to Mrs. Douglas's bitter defenders, was scarred, too. The ridiculous oversimplification, the constant implication that beneath ill-advised votes and actions lay treason instead of error or naiveté, the linking technique by which it is argued that identical votes are cast from identical motives—all these originated not with Nixon but with anti-Communist Democrats for whom Mrs. Douglas was too far to the left.

But Nixon used these arguments unstintingly. He stated the issue as socialism from the very first; although Downey and then the Boddy crowd raised the Red flag over her, the Nixon campaign made it her shroud. Marcantonio, not Nixon, was the one who hated Mrs. Douglas.[2] Nixon had no personal animus toward her; he simply wanted the Senate seat she was seeking. To Nixon, as to Marcantonio and her Democratic primary opponents, this kind of campaign appeared necessary to win it. It was a wholly unemotional blend of patriotism and cynicism, all executed, as Mazo and others noted, with surgical precision. The Douglas responses were flailing and inept, possibly because she and her liberal friends were not at ease with the studied application of hyperbole and innuendo.

1950: A DIRTY YEAR

The California Senate contest of 1950 was a dirty campaign in a dirty year. Conservatives as well as liberals were under fire, and as illustrated in California, both primaries and general elections were fought vigorously and often viciously. Joe McCarthy used his growing strength to try to get even with his small but slowly growing band of enemies in the Senate. In addition to the all-out attack of his troops on Millard Tydings in Maryland (discussed in Chapter 8), he campaigned against the Senate's Democratic majority leader, Scott Lucas of Illinois, and Brien McMahon of Connecticut. Everywhere that year the theme was Republican anti-Communism.

"Mr. Republican" as "Fellow-Traveler"

Ohio's Senator Robert A. Taft, commonly styled "Mr. Republican," was opposed by a popular Democrat, state auditor "Jumping Joe" Ferguson. Taft, seeking a third term, was tough, shrewd, untiring, and publicly humorless. His Taft-Hartley Labor Relations Act of 1947, restricting the right to strike, made him anathema to unions and a perfect lightning rod to the whole left. The labor movement had confidently, even arrogantly, put Taft down for extinction and marshalled tremendous resources of money and talent to beat him.

Taft responded with vigor, assailing labor on its most vulnerable flank: Communist influence. At every turn he and his supporters tagged the "get Taft" effort as Communist-inspired. Taft said the campaign against him had been "blueprinted" by U.S. Communist leader Gus Hall in the Red magazine, *Political Affairs*.

Earlier that year the CIO had expelled thirteen unions it found to be Communist-dominated. This brought indignant cries of "purge" and "red-baiting" from the radical left, which in turn angered the union leaders who had managed the expulsions. Taft jumped into the fray and charged that the CIO's Political Action Committee (PAC) was "conceived in Communism, had Communist midwives assisting in its birth, and was carefully nurtured in its formative period by Communist teachers."

Taft had the ammunition. His campaign manager later noted bitterly to a Senate elections subcommittee investigating the campaign that a desperate attempt

has been made [by Democrats and labor] to disassociate the notorious convicted Communist Gus Hall from the campaign. Yet it is impossible to deny his public statement which appears as exhibit 12 of Senator Taft's testimony, and a reprint of Hall's article in *Political Affairs*, Exhibit 14, from the *Daily Worker* dated January 1950, entitled "The Target is Taft—The Year is 1950." Senator Taft referred to this as a blueprint for the campaign. It should be noted with interest that while these statements of Mr. Hall were made early in 1950, there is no disavowal of it [by Democrats and labor] until this late date. (U.S. Senate Hearings [Ohio] 1951, 330)

But in the same *Political Affairs* article Hall had denounced the CIO and PAC leaders as representing "double dealing and disaster."[3]

The Democrats gave Taft as good as they got. Borrowing from Boddy and Nixon, they linked Taft's voting record with that of the "much-aligned" Vito Marcantonio. Like Nixon's pink sheets against "the Pink Lady," it perfectly illustrated the irrelevance of voting record comparisons, demonstrating that "Mr. Republican," too, had voted with the notorious fellow-traveler on issue after issue.

The Democratic candidate carried a magazine photograph of Taft and onetime Communist leader Earl Browder around the state challenging Taft, as a Portsmouth newspaper quoted him, to "tell the people of his meeting with Earl Browder, the Red leader. Maybe Taft's Communist connections are stronger than others."

Taft supporters got up a small cartoon leaflet to show the sinister forces arrayed against him: Communist conspirators, a greedy union racketeer, labor dictators, a whip lashing the poor workers. Labor retaliated with a full-size comic book, which egregiously distorted Taft's position on such key issues as housing, minimum wages, and wartime benefits for armed forces personnel. A million copies of the piece were distributed in the state by unions affiliated with both the CIO and the AFL, then bitter rivals. The piece and the outrage of the Taft people were extensively covered in the press, and the net effect of the cartoon book probably was a severe backfire.

Taft had been traduced by his enemies in the labor movement before. A pair of photographs printed side by side in the *CIO News* of October 14, 1946, showed Taft and, one-eighth inch away, two Nazi leaders, Hjalmer Schacht and Hans Fritzche. The pair of pictures was captioned, "ROBERT A. TAFT AND 'FRIENDS.' " Taft described it to the Senate Elections Subcommittee as "the grand-daddy of all composite photographs." Labor spokesmen denied any intent to imply that there was *really* a link between Taft and the Nazis (U.S. Senate Hearings [Ohio] 1951, 41).

"Red" Pepper

A liberal Florida Democrat who had been in the Senate since 1936 lost his seat in the Democratic primary in 1950. Claude Pepper, an ardent New Deal liberal and one of the most eloquent orators in the Senate, was taxed for his leftist leanings, substantially exaggerated, by George A. Smathers, a young, handsome, U.S. Marine Corps veteran and two-term congressman from Miami. Pepper was attacked as a pro-Communist in a widely circulated leaflet titled "Red Pepper."

One element of that campaign that has found its way into election lore probably belongs in mythology instead of history. According to tradition, one of the things that beat Pepper was a slick and funny back-country gossip campaign that suggestively spelled out Pepper's secret vices. He practiced nepotism (pron. nee-po-tizzum). He had a sister who was a thespian (thez-bian), and a brother who was a practicing homo sapiens. He went to college, where, (get this) he matriculated.

But alas! There is rather persuasive evidence that this tale was worked up for their after-hours entertainment by Northern reporters covering what had become a significant campaign for national media.

THE COLD WAR IN AMERICAN CAMPAIGNS

As the Cold War intensified in the 1960s, it had the effect of freezing the American right wing in its apprehensions about not only Communist aggression but Communist propaganda successes in America. Whether a left-liberal was "soft on Communism" as a mere dupe or was an active traitor grew unimportant.

Many members of the paranoid right ran for office in 1974. The John Birch Society announced its intention to tag the California Democrat, Senator Alan Cranston, as a pro-Communist. Cranston was a founder of the arch-liberal California Democratic Council, an early Nixon target. However, the threat dissipated when the state's conservative GOP governor, Ronald Reagan, publicly declared that the senator was no such thing.

An opponent of a Tennessee Democrat, Senator Jim Sasser, campaigned against him in 1982 with a TV commercial in which a crateful of $100 bills was being parceled out to, so the voice-over related, "committed enemies of our country. Vietnam, Laos, Cambodia, Marxist Angola, and even Communist Cuba." Here greedy hands empty the crate with shouts of delight, and a grinning Castro is lighting a cigar with a $100 bill, saying, "Muchissimas gracias, Senator Sasser" [Beard—"Castro" 1982].

As campaign issues and electioneering slogans retreat into history, it becomes impossible for new generations to comprehend the rage and fury that political slurs of olden days stirred in their objects and their hearers. An 1870 Democrat called a Copperhead might well reach for a gun—yet be unable to savor the flash of hatred that the sneer "Jacobin" would ignite in an 1810 Republican, who might challenge his detractor to a duel. Yet hard-hitting campaigns, colorful invective, fireworks, and circus-like atmosphere have been part of the American political tradition, a virtual racial memory, for more than a century and a half.

A *Chicago Tribune* cartoonist, Carey Orr, saw this perfectly in a 1958 editorial cartoon mocking the young Fair Campaign Practices Committee for what he feared might result if it prevailed: the emasculation of hurly-burly electioneering. A GOP elephant and the Democratic donkey were in a boxing ring, flailing at each other with pillows. "Take that, varlet!" cried one. "Have a care, saucy fellow!" the other cried back ("The Pillow Fight, With a Keg of Horseshoes in Reserve," 1958).

A POST–COLD WAR POLITICS EMERGES

By the time the Cold War of 1945–85 began to recede, what were fighting words in the McCarthy era had less and less meaning for people born in that era—who now were middle-aged politicians, scholars, and journalists. An interesting illustration of this was a flap that erupted in the 1988 presidential campaign over an adjectival phrase much flaunted by Joe McCarthy.

The Wisconsin demagog would assail this or that government agency as hiding 35 or 207 "card-carrying members" of the Communist Party. He and his sycophants repeated the accusation so often that it entered the language like a common obscenity and raised the blood pressure of dedicated liberals whenever they heard it.

Early in 1988, the Democratic nominee, Michael Dukakis, who was seventeen years old when Joe McCarthy launched his "crusade," used the term in a gently ironic sense to proclaim himself a "card-carrying member" of the American Civil Liberties Union (ACLU). Because the ACLU's increasing activism over the preceding two decades had made it a lightning rod for conservatives, the GOP campaign of George Bush bounced the phrase back and forth for the rest of the year to depict the Democrats as soft on criminals, pornographers, and drug dealers and hard on the God-fearing and law-abiding citizen.[4]

Aging liberal pundits, in whom "card-carrying" woke the most sinister and visceral echoes, were appalled. Seeing the Bush campaigners' deft and sardonic pickup of Dukakis's only attempt at humor as a malevolent descent into a new McCarthyism, they nursed their angst for months. One person's meat is another's poison.

When news of the bloody massacres of the French Revolution reaches North America by sailing ship, thoughts of the Jacobin awaken terror in the Federalist breast. When Allied propagandists portray the merciless Hun bayoneting Belgian infants, German names are a handicap to Midwest politicians. When a Jane Fonda poses with North Vietnamese soldiers manning an anti-aircraft gun, the instant transmission of the resulting propaganda photo stirs rancor toward young American radicals in surviving American veterans.

As wars and great national stresses wax and wane, so do both the currency and the potency of loyalty and patriotism as political issues. Traitor: in peacetime the definition remains, but its ability to summon passion, rage, and electoral action lies dormant, awaiting the next great crisis.

Part III

Political Chicanery: Disrupting the Machinery

The following two chapters turn from denunciation and deception to actual intrusion and interference in the electoral process. Chapter 10 deals with political intelligence, in the sense of espionage, and chicanery, in the sense of sabotage of an opponent's campaign.

Chapter 11 considers sabotage in another dimension: disruption of or interference with the actual casting and counting of votes. While this is fraudulent by definition, in some circumstances it has been viewed as droll or colorful, too, variously creating difficulties and entertainment.

Espionage and Sabotage

Every sophisticated politician recognizes that effective intelligence—usually meaning espionage—is essential to a successful campaign. It is of great value to know what the opposition is about to do. Sometimes, given early and accurate warning, a damaging blow can be forestalled completely or perhaps twisted to the rival's disadvantage. The converse is obvious: one's own operation needs to be protected from discovery and infiltration by the camp of the opposition. This means counterintelligence. But it is easier said than done.

Like military intelligence, the political variety revolves around much that is mundane and utterly boring. Endless review of print, video, and radio records of speeches, interviews, voting records, and news releases is an important element and usually is handled by researchers with the party committee, consultant, or other campaign organization. But this opposition-research staff must have a sharp eye for that occasional faint glimmer among all the dull detail that may prove to be a useful lead.

In the United States, the two national party committees have exchanged news releases for years, as a sort of professional courtesy. Each knows the other would be able to acquire each new handout shortly, and each benefits by saving the time and effort necessary to secure copies from other sources.

POLITICAL ESPIONAGE

Only rarely do flesh-and-blood spies augment this unwritten exchange agreement. Even more rarely do such espionage capers by undercover agents come to light. One that did in 1964 unraveled almost before it got off the ground. A Reuters teletype operator, Louis Flax, was moonlighting at the Democratic National Committee, relaying plans and schedules to the Democrats' network around the country every night.

A GOP agent reached Flax and sounded him out about covertly sharing each day's important developments. When Flax demurred, the agent referred to "certain things" in his background that might jeopardize his regular job if he did not cooperate. The teletypist had been imprisoned on a bad check charge. Flax was taken aback. "Wouldn't you consider this something on the order of blackmail?" he asked.

The caller was offended at this interpretation, but he persisted and persuaded Flax to call the head of security at what turned out to be the Republican National Committee and to identify himself as "Mr. Lewis."

Flax informed the Democrats' communications chief, Wayne Phillips, that he had been approached. Phillips suggested that he pretend to play along. Flax's affidavit tells of his reception at GOP headquarters by John Grenier, the executive director; "Mr. Lewis" agreed to cooperate, and the plan was cemented.

Two days later double agent Flax-Lewis delivered the first shipment of The Papers: a sheaf of carbons of secret messages already screened by Wayne Phillips. When Flax-Lewis left the office, a man he had seen inside slipped him $1,000 in bills.

After two weeks of this, Phillips invited news people to witness the next payoff. But Republicans had learned about the scheme and none of them showed up. Grenier, questioned by journalists later, responded insouciantly that he knew no one named Flax.

Political intelligence operations seem to emulate the politico-military model in scrutinizing the sexual proclivities of their subjects. Plenty of promising careers have been derailed as a result of the inopportune discovery of sexual profligacy, whether hetero- or homosexual.

Ferreting Out Sexual Deviations

In the politics of the American right wing, there has long been an almost obsessive concern with sexual aberrations. One longtime staff member of the Republican National Committee who somehow escaped the postconvention purge by Goldwater's people in 1964 complained to a friend that there was no time for developing legitimate political issues because the research operation was so absorbed with probing for sexual anomalies in the Johnson administration. One recalls the equation in the McCarthy era of homosexuality with treason: "89 communists and perverts. . . . "

Washington is naturally a security-conscious town, and it has two police departments: the Metropolitan or District Police and another force that is part of the National Park Service. Both protect the populace against being overrun by sex deviates. Sometimes they have nearly overrun each other, with decoy cops from the two corps trying to compromise and arrest each other.

Not all the arrests have comic overtones. On October 7, 1964, police officers stationed at peepholes—which they manned regularly—in a public men's room near the White House collared two men they had been observing. One of them was Walter Jenkins, right-hand man, confidant, and trusted friend of the president of the United States. Nothing appeared in the press for a few days, and Republican "anonymous tipsters" then telephoned local newspapers and suggested they check out the police morals squad blotter for October 7.

As the story was just beginning to leak around town, the first press query reached the White House—where it was relayed to Jenkins himself. At once, he called Abe Fortas and Clark Clifford, eminent Washington lawyers who were both friends and Democrats. They asked the newspapers to hold the story temporarily, which they agreed to do—but only temporarily.

When nothing showed up in the evening papers, Dean Burch, the GOP chairman, released a statement citing a "report sweeping Washington that the White House is desperately trying to suppress a major news story affecting the national security." Burch's statement pried the story loose, and United Press International (UPI) put it on the wire at 8:09 p.m.

The unfortunate Jenkins was put into a hospital by his physician for nervous exhaustion. President Johnson, who had been out of town campaigning, accepted his resignation with regret. Goldwater greeted the news with restraint and decorum, but his wild California supporters fashioned a bumper sticker, "Johnson is King and Jenkins is Queen." In Louisiana at a Goldwater dinner, the notorious segregationist Leander Perez passed out three-dollar bills good for "three bucks at Jenkins House" and bearing a photo of the President and a drawing of the White House under the legend "BAKER & JENKINS HOUSE" (Felknor 1966). A new campaign button appeared:

> All The Way With L.B.J.
> But Don't Go Near the Y.M.C.A. (Friz 1988)

The thoroughness of Republican research in this case was not revealed for some time. The recordbook containing the blotter entry disappeared from the police station later in 1964, but not before Republican agents had photographed the page. Walter Jenkins had been arrested on the same charge in the same YMCA men's room in January 1959 but had forfeited bail to avoid trial. Nearly a decade after the fact, on November 7, 1973, this was dredged up and placed in the public domain, via the *Congressional Record*, by the Honorable Carl T. Curtis, a right-wing Republican stalwart and senator from Nebraska (p. S20080).

SABOTAGE: DIRTY TRICKS AGAINST AN OPPONENT

Dick Tuck, the legendary Democratic prankster discussed below, did not originate the kind of trickery that made him famous. In 1928, some forgotten

Republican master in Louisville pulled off an epic ploy that generated a lot of heat, no light, and a hearty laugh for all but the Democrats.

Al Smith was coming to town to address a late summer rally in the municipal auditorium. When the Democratic candidate arrived, the hall was packed—and uncomfortably hot. The heat seemed to increase, and when Smith was introduced, it was hotter than ever. H. L. Mencken was on Smith's campaign train and covered the meeting for the *Baltimore Sun*. He wrote later that before Al was

half way through his speech he was sweating so copiously that he seemed half drowned. The dignitaries on the platform sweated, too, and so did the vulgar on the floor and in the galleries. Minute by minute the temperature seemed to increase until finally it became almost unbearable. When Al shut down at last, with his collar a rag and his shirt sticking to his hide, the thermometer must have stood at 100 degrees at least, and there were plenty who guessed it stood at 110. (Mencken 1943, 288–89)

Only when the candidate and his entourage had returned to the train did they learn what had gone wrong. The Republican city administration had, as Mencken put it, "had its goons fire up the boilers under the hall, deliberately and with malice prepense" (289).

Dick Tuck: Vintage Harassment

Dick Tuck first made news in California in the 1950s. For years he made a major avocation of harassing Republican candidates, Richard Nixon more frequently than most. Once he managed to switch signs on a pair of waiting buses during a Nixon campaign tour. One, labeled "NIXON," was ready to rush the candidate to a live television appearance. The other, labeled "VIP's," was standing by to take celebrities to a hotel.

In 1962, Nixon was challenging the incumbent Democratic governor, Edmund G. ("Pat") Brown. One Tuck scheme led to a news photo of an ebullient Nixon beneath a sign in the Chinatown of Los Angeles. "Welcome Nixon," it read in English. But the sign also bore Chinese characters reading, "What about the HUGHES LOAN?" in reference to Democrats' allegation about improper financial aid for Nixon's brother.

A campaign train, the Nixon Special, was making a whistlestop at San Luis Obispo. Nixon, standing on the observation platform of the last car, began his speech to an attentive crowd. Tuck was there and merged into the crowd wearing a railroad trainman's cap. He worked his way through the crowd, emerged on the engineer's side of the train, adjusted his railroad cap, and signaled the engineer to pull out and head for the next stop. He did.

Two years later, Barry Goldwater was emphasizing old-fashioned values and virtues, and his campaign planned what must have been the last significant use of the railroad for presidential whistlestopping, through several vitally important Midwest states. Dick Tuck was working as an advance man for the Democrats, and he proposed another train stunt. After some debate, Democratic National Committee planners concluded that it was unlikely to backfire when exposed—as it surely would be.

A pretty, twenty-three-year-old woman named Moira O'Connor, a fashion advertising writer from Chicago, was a volunteer at Democratic headquarters and offered to take on the train job. She covertly obtained GOP press credentials as a free-lance magazine writer so she could ride the Goldwater Special.

Not long after the Goldwater train left Washington, bemused reporters found under their compartment doors copies of an en-route publication, *The Whistle Stop*, dedicated to keeping them "advised, informed, protected, and, with considerable help from the senator himself, amused." A bulletin happily reassured the reporters that fluoride, a dental-health water additive then a bête noire of the right wing, had not been added to the train's water supply. A second edition was promised for delivery "at breakfast tomorrow." Assistant press secretary Vic Gold began to prowl the corridors before dawn in search of the culprit.

Instead he found copies of a second edition, with a scoop on how the Republican nominee had arranged to avoid confusion as the train rolled westward into the Central time zone: "The senator has decided to use Washington time. George Washington, that is."

Gold and his colleague, press secretary Paul Wagner, had been doing their homework, ticking off familiar faces on the train in a process of elimination, and now they checked certain vacant compartments, including one that held luggage filled with future "Whistle Stop" editions.

The two located Miss O'Connor at breakfast. "This is your last delivery, dear," said Gold. He gave her five minutes to pack and put her off the train at Parkersburg, West Virginia (Felknor 1966, 46).[1]

Nixon Strikes Back

Nixon and various of his key supporters have repeatedly acknowledged the tactical brilliance of Tuck's harassment, and their own efforts to emulate it have proven disastrous—as became painfully evident in the Watergate affair (Chapter 12). Nixon himself is not without experience in a kind of harassment, though with a harder edge, as is typical for the GOP.

During his unsuccessful California gubernatorial race in 1962, conservative Democrats began receiving in the mail a postcard questionnaire, including a reply card addressed to the sponsor, a Committee to Preserve the Democratic Party in California. Among other things, the questionnaire asked Democrats whether they approved of admitting Red China to the

United Nations and "allowing subversives the freedom of college campuses."
A yes answer, it was made plain, was "the CDC leadership viewpoint."
Part of the mailing was devoted to soliciting funds to cover its cost.

CDC was the California Democratic Council, which after World War II
became the largest volunteer political movement in the United States. It was
ardently liberal and strongly influenced, but never quite dominated, Democratic politics in the state. Republicans were always looking for ways to
divide the party by pitting conservative Democrats against the CDC wing.

The postcard poll was singing this song. A multiple-choice question asked:
Can California afford to have a governor indebted to the CDC? Possible
answers were (1) to demand that Democrats repudiate the CDC; (2) to
refuse support to Democratic candidates who fail to denounce CDC; or (3)
to support "a Republican candidate rather than sell out the party and the
state government to CDC objectives."

When the poll appeared the Democratic State Central Committee got a
temporary court order restraining its continued circulation and freezing the
bank account of the Committee to Preserve the Democratic Party. This was
enabled by the postcard's pitch for money; California law forbade seeking
funds in the name of a party organization without the party's authorization.

A California court later found that the poll had been "instigated, financed,
prepared, implemented, supervised and executed by" Nixon committees and
that "this postcard poll was reviewed, amended and finally approved by
Mr. Nixon personally." The judge found that while the polling company
billed the Nixon campaign for a "statewide mailing to 900,000 *conservative*
Democrats," the returns were publicized by the Nixon people as the "voice
of the *rank and file* Democrat" (italics added). The judge awarded the
Democrats all contributions raised by the poll—$368.50, which disap-
pointed Roger Kent, the party vice chairman who initiated the suit; he had
hoped for much more (Felknor 1966, 113–14).[2]

Espionage, Sabotage, and Race

Until the 1960s, "black votes" was an oxymoron in the white South. But
the modern reality is that black votes are essential to Democratic victories
in Southern elections. Before this became fully apparent, die-hard segregationists among white Southern Democrats continued to play fast and loose
with the race issue, as their forebears had done ever since the Reconstruction
Amendments made voting a theoretical possibility.

This political sea change was not far advanced in 1964 when Lyndon
Johnson of Texas ran for president on a civil rights platform. Democrats
in segregationist areas found themselves sorely tempted by the Goldwater
campaign, which in Southern states went out of its way to avoid offending
white supremacists.

Neither candidate was a racist by any reasonable stretch of the imagination, but both campaigns had Southern operatives perfectly willing to stretch things a bit more than that to take the luster off the other candidate. What the Johnson people needed in still-segregationist areas was a way to tie Goldwater to civil rights and black aspirations. Inadvertently, a Republican gave it to them.

Carl Shipley was chairman of the Republican Central Committee for the District of Columbia, whose population was predominantly black. He ordered up a leaflet emphasizing Goldwater's long and consistent efforts to advance black rights and opportunities, desegregating the Arizona National Guard among them, and distributed it in black sections.

Washington news media played up the contrast between the Southern campaign, where the Goldwaterites acted as though their senator had voted against the Emancipation Proclamation, and Washington, where they were draping him in Lincoln's mantle.

Many GOP politicos immediately recognized the explosive potential if the Democrats should obtain this D.C. Goldwater-for-the-Negro pitch and distribute it to Southern whites. So, of course, did the Democrats. They set out to find and reprint the leaflet for wide circulation among their own segregationists, who were defecting in droves. The Republicans halted the D.C. distribution and tried desperately to retrieve every copy they had already passed out.

After a frantic scramble for copies the Democrats managed to acquire a single leaflet. It was printed mainly in light blue ink, which was difficult to copy by photo-offset, so they reset the type word for word. They printed untold thousands of their version, with only one change from the original text. Beneath the Republican identification on the back fold was a new credit line: Reprinted by the Democrats as a public service.

OUTSIDE INTERFERENCE: FOREIGN MEDDLING

Sabotage of an American election is by no means the sole province of candidates or their agents—or even U.S. citizens. Foreign governments have intervened in American elections since the very first contest for the presidency. Barely a week before election day in 1796, the minister of France's revolutionary government to America, Pierre-Auguste Adet, engaged in an egregious bit of meddling clearly planned to swing the presidential election to Jefferson. Adet intended to do so by influencing voters in key states to vote against Adams, who was Washington's vice president. The French minister's prime target was Pennsylvania, which was thought to be safe for the Federalist Adams. Fifteen electoral votes were at stake.

In the form of letters to the American Secretary of State, Timothy Pickering, Adet issued a series of proclamations to the American people attributing a recent decline in Franco-American relations to the hostility of President Washington and the Federalists. Those relations, he suggested, would be signally improved if Jefferson were President. If Washington's policies were not abandoned, he warned, the Directorate ruling France would retaliate in a variety of harsh and unpleasant ways.

Adams was confident that this brash tactic would backfire on the meddling French, and he scoffed that Adet's threats amounted to no more than casting "some electioneering nuts among the apes." Federalists circulated copies of the letters in the hope that the impudent French diplomat's intervention would backfire, but Pennsylvania did go for Jefferson, electing thirteen Republicans among the state's fifteen electors. Adams won, but by only three electoral votes, 71–68 (Minnigerode 1928, 42–62; Smith 1962, 2: 899).

The president-elect's confidence in a backfire proved right, but barely, and the episode left him alert to future French meddling. In his inaugural address at Philadelphia, March 4, 1797, he cautioned that if Americans' votes

can be obtained by foreign nations by flattery or menaces, by fraud or violence, by terror, intrigue, or venality, the Government may not be the choice of the American People, but of foreign nations. It may be foreign nations who govern us, and not we, the people, who govern ourselves. (U.S. Congress [House] 1961, 9)

If confirmation were needed that Adet's manipulations were no accident, it came a century later when his correspondence with the Directory was published. Adet had written that he expected France's threats of hostility to "have a great influence on the choice of the President who is about to be elected.... that the electoral votes will be given to Jefferson."

After the election, in which his strategy failed so narrowly, he explained his Pennsylvania letter to his government.

I had it printed in order to arouse public attention at the moment when electors were to be chosen who are to select the President, and at the same time to judge by the effect it would produce on the Government what results I might expect from the second session of Congress. (Minnigerode 1928, 62; AHA 1904)[3]

In 1808 James Madison was the subject of whispers about his putative support for the Jacobins; he was even denounced as a "Frenchman." The *Albany Register* declared—and recanted only much later—that the Jacobins had made naturalized French citizens of him, along with Thomas Jefferson, in 1793 while they were, respectively, vice president and secretary of state. The truth was that the French had made *honorary* citizens of Adams and Jefferson, as well as President Washington (Brant 1941–61, 5:434).

The Meddlesome Citizen Genet

Still more French mischief was in store for Madison, who was seeking the presidency as a Democratic Republican against his Federalist colleague among the Founding Fathers, Charles Pinckney. The miscreant this time was the meddlesome Citizen Genet. By now Edmond-Charles Genet had become a naturalized U.S. citizen and a resident of New York. He had been a hereditary bureaucrat before the French Revolution, and he was sent by the revolutionary government as chargé d'affaires to America, where admirers of the French radicals dubbed him Citizen Genet, the French Revolutionary title analogous to "comrade" in the Russian Revolution.

As a diplomat, Genet had intruded wherever he could to derail President Washington's neutrality in the French war with Britain, to arm privateers in U.S. ports against British ships, to maneuver America into war against Britain, and more. When his mischief grew completely intolerable, Washington asked the French to recall him, and Genet, realizing that—at best—he would face jail at home, elected to become an American citizen.

He never did stop meddling, and in 1808 he undertook to do Madison out of the presidency. Genet's former diplomatic contacts and his social position (he married a daughter of Governor Clinton of New York) gave him access everywhere, and he came by a copy of notes kept early in the Constitutional Convention of 1787 by New York's late Chief Justice Robert Yates, who had been a delegate.

Genet fabricated a clever forgery out of Yates's notes concerning Madison's actions in the early days of the convention. In effect cutting and pasting snatches of Madison's actual words together in a different order, he "cleverly pieced [them] together in such a way as to represent Madison as the leader of the national party in the Federal Convention and working for the annihilation of the state governments." This fraudulent pastiche was published by Genet in 1808 as "A Letter to the Electors of President and Vice-President of the United States." Note that Genet, whose eye was always for the biggest deal, did not bother with the citizenry or the press but addressed delegates to the Electoral College (Farrand 1966, 1:xiv; 3:410).

American Manipulation of Foreign Influence

Near the end of the nineteenth century, an American citizen manipulated the British government into an indiscreet revelation that helped the Republican Benjamin Harrison interrupt Grover Cleveland's eight years in the White House. The year was 1888, and the GOP was still smarting over the Democrat Cleveland's defeat of James G. Blaine in 1884 with the help of a last-minute shift of Irish-American votes.

A California saboteur named George A. Osgoodby set out to decimate Cleveland's strength among the Irish. Osgoodby was sure that the British government would much prefer that Cleveland stay in office. But how to smoke out some statement to that effect, which would drive every Irish American out of Cleveland's camp?

Using the pseudonym Charles F. Murchison, Osgoodby wrote a letter to the British ambassador, Sir Lionel Sackville-West, posing as a naturalized American of British birth, and asked the ambassador's advice on how an affectionate son of England ought to vote as between Harrison and the Democratic incumbent, Cleveland.

Sackville-West was completely taken in. The anglophobic adventures, in America as well as the British Isles, of Ireland's Fenian Society, predecessor movement to the Sinn Fein, had long irked the ambassador, and he seized this opportunity firmly. On September 13, Sir Lionel answered "Murchison" that Cleveland's return to the White House would serve British interests well.

The Republicans kept the letter secret until October 24, two weeks before election day, and then trumpeted it far and wide. President Cleveland, shocked at the ambassador's intrusion in U.S. politics, handed Sackville-West his passport the same day the story broke. But the damage was irreparable. New York's big Irish vote swung heavily against Cleveland, and Harrison nosed him out.

Osgoodby's motive in tricking the British ambassador into endorsing (and defeating) Cleveland was partisan. Other Americans have tried to manipulate U.S. elections for the benefit of foreign countries they favored. Examples include pro-British Federalists, pro-French Jeffersonian Republicans, pro-Soviet U.S. Communists, German-American Bundists of the 1930s, partisans of the Spanish Republicans during the Spanish Civil War, and supporters of Hanoi in the Vietnam War. Because the U.S. citizen is free to advocate *any* foreign or domestic policy, judgments and even discussion about such electoral actions are extremely difficult. Before the U.S. entry into World War II, some Americans saw Lend-Lease and Bundles for Britain as unconstitutional. Others read the isolationism of America First as active support for fascism.

The Influence of AIPAC

Probably no advocacy organization of the 1980s had greater impact on U.S. foreign policy than the American Israel Public Affairs Committee (AIPAC). It is not a political action committee in the sense of existing to raise and contribute funds but a lobby that unfailingly supports the Israeli government and promotes U.S. funding and other support for it. AIPAC does not contribute directly to candidates, but its activist members and supporters control many individual PACs and can induce the contribution of campaign funds that dwarf those of most ordinary PACs. Its director after 1980, Thomas A. Dine, had considerable Senate staff experience in foreign policy, and he quickly made it one of the most influential voices in the entire U.S. foreign policy community.

The organization's interests do not coincide with all American Jewish interests because there are some anti-Zionist Jews; a good many others ardently support Israel but differ sharply with various Israeli governments about policies affecting the West Bank, Lebanon, "land for peace," and negotiating with the PLO.

AIPAC itself, suffering no agonies of indecision about such questions, is quick to identify and extirpate—or, in the case of "dissident" Jews, virtually excommunicate—what it sees as Israel's enemies. These have included some of its most thoughtful supporters—those with the fatal blemish of not being uncritical advocates.

Paul Findley was an eleven-term congressman whose home district sprawls across thirteen south-central Illinois counties from east of Springfield to the Mississippi River. He was the third-ranking Republican on the House Foreign Affairs Committee, and he made the mistakes of proposing Israel-PLO talks and advocating pressures on Israel to withdraw from Lebanon. In 1980 he faced a Democratic challenger who, as he wrote, advertised for campaign contributions

in Jewish newspapers from coast to coast, stirring up interest by calling me "a practicing anti-Semite, who is one of the worst enemies Jews and Israel have ever faced in the history of the U.S. Congress." He drew funds from each of the fifty states. In all the campaign cost $1.2 million—the most expensive in Illinois history. We each spent about $600,000. (Findley 1985, 17)

Findley was reelected, but his share of the vote, 70 percent in 1978, dwindled to 56, and in 1982 he

lost by 1,407 votes, less than one percent of the total cast. In a vote that close, almost any negative development could account for the difference. The attack by pro-Israel activists was only one of several factors. Nevertheless, [AIPAC] claimed credit for my defeat. In a report to a Jewish gathering in Austin, Texas, a few days after election day, Thomas A. Dine ... concluded, "This is a case where the Jewish lobby made a difference. We beat the odds and defeated Findley." (Findley 1985, 21–22)

In 1984, AIPAC took on another Illinois Republican, Senator Charles H. Percy. Percy won by a landslide in 1972 but by a scant 53 percent in 1978—when he received 61 percent of the state's Jewish vote. He lost in 1984. That was after he had supported President Reagan's approval of selling AWACS aircraft to Saudi Arabia, and "AIPAC decided that Percy was too dangerous in his role as chairman of the Senate Foreign Relations Committee."

Percy survived a bitter primary, in which fifty-five pro-Israel PACs put up $285,000 for his rival, Congressman Thomas J. Corcoran.

Letters went out all around the nation, their envelopes emblazoned with the question, "CAN YOU NAME *ISRAEL'S WORST ADVERSARY* IN CONGRESS?" An enclosure seeking support for Corcoran declared that "more than any other officeholder in Washington, Percy has worked to destroy the special relationship between the United States and Israel." (Tivnan 1987, 190)

In the general election campaign, a friend of AIPAC who had been one of its largest contributors, a young California contractor named Michael R. Goland, spent at least $1.1 million of his own on an independent campaign against Percy, without giving any of it directly to the senator's Democratic challenger, a former teacher and editor named Paul Simon. Goland's campaign blanketed the state with television and other ads taking former Percy statements out of context to suggest he was an admirer of the PLO leader, Yassir Arafat.

Percy, long one of Israel's most thoughtful and influential friends in Congress, lost. Afterward, in a speech to a Jewish group in Toronto, AIPAC's executive director, Thomas Dine, boasted, "All the Jews in America, from coast to coast, gathered to oust Percy. And the American politicians—those who hold public positions now, and those who aspire—got the message" (Tivnan 1987, 191).

Two years after the Percy defeat, Michael Goland was in action in his own state, California, to put down a strong challenge to AIPAC's staunch friend Senator Alan Cranston. Goland was later convicted in Federal District Court in Los Angeles of the misdemeanor of giving in excess of the allowed $1,000 to the campaign of a third-party candidate, an ultra-rightist and anti-Zionist named Edward B. Vallen.

Cranston's serious challenge came from Republican Congressman Ed Zschau, and Goland gave $120,000 to the Vallen campaign in order to draw off anti-Cranston votes from Zschau. Vallen, the *Los Angeles Times* reported, "got 109,516 votes, about 5,000 more than the margin by which Cranston defeated Zschau," in a total vote of 7 million.[4]

Testimony at Goland's trial revealed that after his role in Senator Percy's 1984 defeat, Goland had warned several senators that if they voted for a proposed 1985 Saudi Arabia arms deal, "I will do to you what I did to Charles Percy in 1984" ("Goland Gets Jail Term For Illegal Campaign Gift," 1990).

OUT OF LEFT FIELD: OUTSIDE INTERFERENCE
BY INDIVIDUALS

Individual domestic intruders into electoral politics show up at irregular intervals and often inject substantial confusion into the process. Sometimes they are motivated by hate, a sense of irony, or some combination of economic and social interests. When labor was patching over its differences trying to beat Robert Taft out of his Senate seat in 1950, one of the era's most flamboyant union chiefs, John L. Lewis, the powerful head of the

United Mine Workers, learned that Taft was scheduled to address a group of miners at their work site. He quickly squelched that notion with a thinly veiled threat in typically florid prose, to the president of the Ohio Coal Operators Association:

Taft's secret political handlers propose to have him enter coal mines to cozen the men underground. This will be bad from the standpoint of coal production.

Taft was born encased in velvet pants, and has lived to rivet an iron collar around the necks of millions of Americans. He is the relentless, albeit witless, tool of the oppressors of labor.

You should refuse him entry into mines where Americans toil. The underground workings are necessarily confined, and the air therein is easily contaminated. The effluvia of the oppressor is ever disagreeable and could enrage the men to a point of evacuation of the mine. This we would both deplore. (U.S. Senate Hearings [Ohio] 1951, 40)

Stalin in Arizona, 1958

One of the most incredible boners of modern politics grew out of another set of labor-management tensions in Arizona in 1958. Barry Goldwater, seeking his second Senate term, was opposed by the man he had defeated in 1952, the veteran Ernest McFarland. The Phoenix newspaper, the *Arizona Republic*, had given outrageously one-sided coverage to Goldwater. One day that newspaper ran a banner headline across page one: "GOLDWATER HONEST, SINCERE, MINERS SAY." The small print revealed that a mine union chief didn't like Goldwater but believed that he was honest and sincere enough so you always knew where he stood.

The "Miners" reference was to the Mine, Mill and Smelter Workers Union (hereafter Mine, Mill), important in the state because mining is a major economic factor there. This was one of the unions that had been thrown out of the CIO for its control by Communists, and it had not been readmitted. The *Arizona Republic* was hostile to unions of any stripe and especially to those with Communist leadership. It also had lately been attacking anti-Communist labor leaders on its front page, among them some who were enemies of the Mine, Mill leaders.

One Arizona trade unionist, an aircraft worker named Frank Goldberg, who belonged to the International Association of Machinists (IAM), was infuriated by the *Republic's* use of a Mine, Mill leader's words—and a distortion at that—to push Goldwater, who was anathema to virtually all unions, and especially when the paper had been traducing union leaders who were as anti-Communist as Goldwater himself.

Goldberg recalled a recent IAM journal containing a cartoon of Joseph Stalin, grinning, winking, and suggesting that good union members should support "right to work" laws, which hampered union power in a number of American states and made it a joke in all Communist countries. The

aircraft worker arranged with a friend employed by the machinists' union
to have the cartoon reproduced on a sheet with the "Honest, Sincere"
headline from the *Republic* across the top. In the new version, Stalin would
be saying, "Why not vote for Goldwater?" And at the bottom of the page
would be a line citing the newspaper's use of the miners' union "endorsement" to support Goldwater, noting that "Politics makes strange bedfel-
lows."

Shortly before election day, the job was ready, and the sheet was distributed in Phoenix and a few other areas. It was immediately interpreted as
suggesting that Barry Goldwater had Communist support. Goldberg had
no idea that federal law required him to put his name on the document and
that he had broken the law (later repealed).[5]

Goldwater was furious, and he assumed that McFarland had sponsored
the flier. McFarland assumed that Goldwater had created the piece as a
reverse smear to discredit the McFarland campaign. Goldwater summoned
the FBI and McFarland the Senate elections subcommittee. A committee
investigator arrived and could only find copies of the sheet in the hands of
newspapermen to whom Goldwater had sent them as evidence of Mc-
Farland's rotten smear. By doing so, even on this small scale, Goldwater
also had broken the law by distributing anonymous campaign literature.

The FBI quickly found Frank Goldberg and his ally, Earl Anderson, the
IAM employee. They were indicted, tried, and convicted of violating the
federal statute. A final irony remained. Anderson had the printing done by
a Los Angeles firm he dealt with on union business, and through error the
IAM had been billed—and paid for—the smear sheet. The ultimate moral
was clear: If you don't know your way around the legal pitfalls when you
are tempted to get involved in a campaign, don't make a move without
your lawyer.

The trouble Frank Goldberg got himself and his friend into by remaining
anonymous was avoided by a vengeful Minnesotan in the same year. A
Democrat named Joseph Robbie was running against the veteran Republican
Congressman Walter Judd.[6] A Twin Cities man named Earl Joseph Seymour
French was persuaded, for whatever personal reasons, that Robbie's election
would be a major misfortune. He trotted off to a neighborhood print shop
and ordered a quantity of handbills, which he then set out to distribute:

> Jos. Robbie
> Not a State Man—from S. Dak.
> Ran for all sorts of offices in So. Dak.
> Claims he is a Lawyer.

Earl Joseph Seymour French, in compliance with Minnesota and federal
law, signed his name and address to the sheet and peddled his papers wherever he thought they might embarrass Robbie. Robbie assumed, naturally

enough, that this was the work of a Judd henchman and challenged Judd to repudiate the tactic. The Republican congressman, who, like Robbie, had agreed to abide by the Code of Fair Campaign Practices, reviewed the code's plank on repudiating unfair tactics. It committed a candidate to repudiate unfair tactics used *on his behalf.* Judd reflected on the fact that he had never even heard of French, and the fact that the handbill did not so much as mention Judd, and refused to repudiate it.

It turned out that French didn't think much of Judd either; he simply didn't like Robbie and found this a good time to say so. Judd won. As an aftermath, Judd's decision not to repudiate the handbill led the Fair Campaign Practices Committee to amend the code for the only time in its existence (1954–78) to commit candidates to repudiate unfair tactics used either for them or against their opponents.

11 _____

Buying and Stealing Votes

Public concern over money in politics began to rise in the first decade of the twentieth century, and it has not subsided. Concern has focused on who gives, who gets, and what the money buys. Votes? Influence? Access? Civic pride? Costs have escalated relentlessly, and the money to defray them has never been lacking. Nor have public and media fascination with the subject.

What precipitated this attention were press reports soon after 1900 that corporations and other moneyed interests—then often seen as the last of the robber barons—were making enormous contributions to politicians for campaign expenses. Reformers in and out of Congress sought legislative remedies, and counter-reformers sought to derail them. Before long scholars began to examine the phenomenon of political money.

THE STUDY OF FINANCING ELECTIONS

Four political scientists stand out in that company. James K. Pollock of the University of Michigan got the ball rolling, publishing *Party Campaign Funds* in 1927. Two important works came from Louise Overacker of Wellesley College, *Money in Elections* (1932) and *Presidential Campaign Funds* (1946). Alexander Heard of the University of North Carolina and later chancellor of Vanderbilt University, wrote the definitive *The Costs of Democracy* (1960). Heard was a prime mover in establishing a unique institution, the Citizens' Research Foundation (CRF).

CRF is devoted explicitly to study and publishing in the once arcane field of electoral finance. That the field is no longer arcane may be attributed largely to the foundation's work. Originally situated at Princeton, N.J., since 1978 it has been part of the University of Southern California, where its director, Herbert E. Alexander, is a professor of political science. Alexander was Heard's protégé in a research project on money in politics at the University of North Carolina. Out of that project the CRF emerged, and Alexander has been at its center ever since.

The CRF's major publications are Alexander's books *Money in Politics* (1972) and *Financing Politics* (1984); the latter has been updated frequently. The foundation issues monographs and other studies from time to time. Since the 1960s it has been a fount of information for all serious students of its subject—including the Federal Election Commission, both major parties, the news media, and the U.S. Congress itself. Its studies can be found in every adequate academic and public library.

The reader interested in how political money is raised and the particulars of its application is referred to these works. The present book does not address this field but is concerned instead with the dirtywork that all that money can buy.

BUYING ELECTIONS

Henry B. Payne bulks large in the annals of buying votes, but in his case it was the votes of a state legislature. In the 1850s he was a state senator from Ohio who failed to persuade his colleagues to elect him to the U.S. Senate. He tried and failed to be elected governor. He did win a single term in the U.S. House of Representatives. When the voters refused him a second term in 1876 the House named him (a lame-duck representative) to the Electoral Commission appointed to resolve the fraudulent presidential election of 1876, which is described below. With this educational background, a decade later he tried again for the U.S. Senate, and this time he made it. Reliable tradition has it that Harry Payne walked into the Ohio State Capitol with two suitcases full of money and walked out with a Senate seat.

The half-century following the Civil War was an era of fraud and manipulation in American politics that would leave a modern electoral swindler gasping with envy. An occasional hiccup intruded on this grand bacchanale, like the election of 1884, which put a Democrat and notorious reformer, Grover Cleveland, in the White House. Republicans were sure his election had been fraudulent, and they were determined not to be had again.

By 1888 things were moving their way: Cleveland was in trouble. He had been elected by the narrowest of margins. The New York–Irish vote, which had swung to him on a fluke, was now swinging back against him; anti-Blaine Republicans who supported him then did not now. His reforms had alienated machine politicians, his naming New York's Boss Manning secretary of the treasury had alienated reformers, and his gathering attacks on the trusts had driven off moneyed Democrats.

The Republican strong man of the hour was Pennsylvania's state treasurer, Matthew S. Quay, who "controlled men by his refined understanding of their private vices," which he catalogued in a huge card file in his Harrisburg office (Josephson 1938, 407). He regularly bribed legislators. He was newly elected (by them) to the U.S. Senate. Simultaneously he became chairman of the Republican National Committee.

Matt Quay was running a hard and lavishly financed campaign to elect Benjamin Harrison, a benign, naive, and harmless Hoosier grandson of William Henry Harrison. Quay knew that a crucial key to regaining the presidency for the Republicans was the "independent vote" and that it could be purchased if the campaign fund had enough money. He knew the levers to pull to get the money together, and he pulled them all.

The non-partisan ballot, supplied by the government and listing the candidates of both sides on the same sheet, had not yet been imported from Australia. That would happen in another five or six years throughout most of the United States. In 1888 the political parties still printed their own ballots, and party workers thrust the party ticket into the hands of voters approaching the polling places. If a voter accepted the Harrison ticket and rejected the Cleveland ballot proffered by Democratic workers, the Republicans could be sure he had voted right.

Voting the Floaters

Matt Quay had long since perfected the application of this system to harvesting the "floating vote." In those days very large numbers of citizens, identifying themselves as independents, allowed themselves to be persuaded by party bag men. Their votes were quite literally for sale, and the going price in the inflation-plagued year of 1888 was either three of the new $5 gold pieces or a crisp new $20 bill.[1]

Beating the opposition to sign up the floaters in a given area, and keeping them under control until their ballots were in the box, was critical. Boss Quay's treasurer at the Republican National Committee, Colonel William W. Dudley, was up to this challenge. "In the effective use of money for the purchase of purchasable votes there is no man in the country superior to Colonel Dudley," said an admiring contemporary (Josephson 1938, 423). His style can be seen in a letter he wrote—on National Committee stationery—to an operative in Indiana, the candidate's home state, which looked to be very nearly even, but had to be carried.

New York, October 24, 1888

Dear Sir:

I hope you have kept copies of the lists [of floaters] sent me. Such information is very valuable and can be used to great advantage. It has enabled me to demonstrate to friends here that with proper financial assistance Indiana is surely Republican for Governor and President, and has resulted, as I hoped it would, in securing for Indiana the aid necessary. Your committee will certainly receive from [Indiana Republican State] Chairman [James N.] Huston the financial assistance necessary to hold our floaters and doubtful voters, and gain enough of the other kind to give Harrison and Morton 10,000 plurality. . . . [D]ivide the floaters into blocks of five and put a trusted man with the necessary funds in charge of these five and make him responsible that none get away and that all vote our ticket. . . .

/s/ W. W. Dudley, Treasurer ("The Political Campaign—Damaging Exposure of Republican Plots," 1888)[2]

Unfortunately for the diligent colonel, his instructions became famous as the "Blocks of Five Letter." It fell into the hands of a Democratic spy, a clerk on a railway mail car who regularly examined interesting-looking envelopes for useful secrets. Democratic (and even several Republican) newspapers made much of it for the five days remaining before election day. The shock waves from this scandalous revelation were not enough to offset Colonel Dudley's labors, but they did shock the president-elect, who persuaded state party leaders to disavow the colonel and bring him to trial in an Indiana court.

Dudley was incredulous. He vowed he would be no scapegoat and that if this foolishness were pursued he would "explode a lot of dynamite" that would blow the lid off and reveal "the entire inside workings of the Republican National Committee" (Gresham 1919, 2:605). He was tried in federal court, where he escaped punishment through a smart lawyer and a legal technicality.

Dudley's jeopardy lent point to a comment of Quay's. When he congratulated Harrison, the president-elect breathed, "Providence has given us the victory!" Quay later snorted, "Think of the man! He ought to know that Providence hadn't a damned thing to do with it!" The president-elect, he said, was a "political tenderfoot" who would "never know how close a number of men were compelled to approach the gates of the penitentiary to make him President" (Josephson 1938, 433).

A certain elegant simplicity shines through campaign finance in the Quay era: one man, one vote, twenty dollars. However, as the march of technology opened new possibilities to the electioneers, it also steadily increased costs. High-speed printing, radio, air travel, television, polling techniques—the price of winning elections increased at every turn. When regulation intruded to level the playing field, exceptions continued the advantages of the really rich, whether rich from family wealth or friendly support. The candidate of modest means confronts a simple choice: find the money or get out of the race.

MUCH ADO ABOUT NOTHING: THE NIXON FUND FLAP

One ingenious effort to solve part of this problem for a young senator, Richard Nixon, blew up on him when he became a vice-presidential candidate in 1952. Several of Nixon's California admirers had put together a fund of some $18,000 to cover political expenses he could not charge to his Senate budget and could not afford himself. The fund was created to cover postage, extra travel to and within the state, and other such mundane and essential expenditures that added up quickly.

Reporters friendly to the Democrats discovered the "Nixon Fund" in mid-September. After all the perks and payoffs of twenty years in the White House, that party was smarting badly from the holier-than-thou strictures the Republicans were ladling out about mink coats and morality in government. The Nixon fund story was manna from Heaven, and the Democrats laid on heavily about slush funds and the like.

The war hero, General Dwight Eisenhower, was the Republican presidential nominee, and he was urged by some key advisors to dump this young opportunist Nixon with his slush fund. While the general pondered publicly, Nixon arranged for television time and defended his own probity and the propriety of his fund before the nation. At the end of the show, he urged watchers to tell the Republican National Committee whether he should stay on the ticket or not. They immediately deluged GOP headquarters with expressions of support, and the political issue was resolved.

As the audience response makes clear, the Nixon speech reflected a masterful reading of the popular psyche. It placed Nixon firmly among the large majority of Americans as a family man of meager resources. It evoked image after image of the common people, including his wife's non-mink "respectable Republican cloth coat" and a quote from Lincoln. It acknowledged receiving one gift, a little cocker spaniel dog named Checkers, which his kids loved and which he was going to keep, come what may. Years later in his memoirs, Nixon acknowledged a big gift from Franklin D. Roosevelt, that is, using the dog—man's best friend—to deflect partisan attacks (Nixon 1978). (Roosevelt's ringing defense of his little dog, Fala, is recalled in Chapter 4.)

The emotional content of the Nixon defense distracted attention from the real merits of his case: the plight of a poor candidate in politics. The speech was immediately disdained by the Democratic elite, but, as noted, the popular response to it ensured his place on the ticket.[3] It is often forgotten that just before the speech a similar fund came to light that had been created by friends of the Democratic presidential candidate, Adlai Stevenson, when he was governor of Illinois—and Stevenson was a man of some wealth.

The Stevenson fund was dug up by the staunchly Republican *Chicago Tribune*, and Nixon alluded to it discreetly in his speech, inviting the governor to emulate the senator and bare his own finances. But the Democrat's fund received only modest and intermittent news coverage. Gradually, over the next few years it became apparent that almost every politician operating at a national level had some such source of money for essential political expenditures between campaigns.

An alternative, of course, is personal wealth, which, as Herbert Alexander observes in *Money in Politics*,

confers still another advantage, illustrated by John F. Kennedy from 1956 to 1960 and Nelson Rockefeller from 1960 to 1964. Money permits a potential candidate to maintain a large staff between campaigns, which generates publicity to make his name and actions known. He can put task forces and experts to work on policy development and fact finding. A less affluent potential candidate cannot as easily buy a build-up between campaigns; for example, Estes Kefauver was unable to remain in the public eye between the primaries of 1952 and 1956. (Alexander 1972, 41)

ON STEALING ELECTIONS

Voter turnout, ever a goal of reformers, since time immemorial has been a particular pride of the vote thief. The dead have voted. Dogs and cats have voted. Criminals have voted under their rightful names and under aliases. Fictional characters have voted. New York City, a sometime bastion of electoral respectability, also has shone in terms of voter turnout. In the rarely equaled get-out-the-vote drive of 1844, there were nearly 41,000 qualified voters. Making necessary allowances for the suddenly ill, the lazy, and the disaffected, the turnout was amazing: 55,000. The dead filled in for the sick.

Often in the twentieth century, Republican indignation at Democratic vote-stealing in Chicago has focused unwelcome attention on that city's voting peculiarities. In many wards virtually every voter is a Democrat. It has been literally impossible for many years to find Republican poll-workers and watchers for these precincts, and in this situation the only limits to skulduggery are the imaginations of the skulduggers. After almost every Chicago election the GOP launches a cry that it was stolen, as it often was.

There is a strong likelihood that but for the Chicago anomaly Illinois would have gone for Nixon in 1960. The city delivered a Democratic plurality of 319,000 for Kennedy—enough to offset the Nixon vote in the rest of the state and put Illinois's twenty-seven electors in the JFK column with 9,000 votes to spare. Had Chicago fallen short of this sterling clutch performance—say someone had miscalculated and underestimated the vote needed to counter downstate—and come through with a Kennedy plurality of only 309,000. Nixon would have carried the state, and the close electoral count of 1960 would have been even closer: 276 to 246 in Kennedy's favor.

Although many, perhaps most, of Nixon's advisors disagreed violently, he refused to pursue an investigation of the Chicago chicanery. As he put it in his memoirs:

We had made a serious mistake in not having taken precautions against such a situation and it was too late now. A presidential recount would require up to half a year, during which time the legitimacy of Kennedy's election would be in question. The effect could be devastating to America's foreign relations. I could not subject the country to such a situation. And what if I demanded a recount and it turned out that Kennedy had won? Charges of "sore loser" would follow me through history and remove any possibility of a further political career. After consulting these and many other factors, I made my decision and sent Kennedy a telegram conceding the election. (Nixon 1978, 222)

Chicago and other big cities enjoy no monopoly on vote stealing; they are more widely known in these terms because the word leaks out faster from a city than from the wide open spaces where men are men and not given to loose talk. There are six states each of which turns out a smaller presidential vote than, say, Marion County, Indiana (Indianapolis). They elect twelve U.S. senators, six House members, and eighteen presidential electors. Elections in these and other smaller states often are decided by a few thousand—and occasionally a few hundred—votes. At this level counting is simple. So is cheating.

1876: Stealing the Big One

The election of 1876 probably will stand as the all-time high-water mark in terms of plain and fancy thievery of votes, popular and electoral, in American presidential elections. There were four candidates, of whom only two, fielded by the Prohibition Party and the Greenbackers, knew they had lost honestly. The major party candidates were Samuel J. Tilden, Democrat, of New York, and Rutherford B. Hayes, an Ohio Republican.

Northern support for the Reconstruction was dwindling, and liberal Republicans were reacting against tales of excesses by carpetbaggers. In the South, the Amnesty Act of 1872 had enfranchised white Confederate veterans. It was obvious that the Reconstruction was unraveling, but white Southern manhood would wait no longer. The Democrats

openly threatened that they would "carry the election or kill the last damned Republican in the South." The Klan brought its intensive campaign of terrorism to a whirlwind climax. Shipments of arms hurriedly dispatched to military units were confiscated by Klansmen who had been tipped off by railroad officials. On Election Day the locations of many polling places were suddenly changed without notice in an effort to lose the Negroes. The whites appeared with rifles in hand and turned away prospective Negro voters. Many Negroes who sought to vote under escort of United States Marshals were shot, and the Marshals with them. (Kennedy 1946)

Tilden won the election but was about to lose the count. In an electorate of a little over eight million, he polled a popular plurality of a quarter-million over the Republican Hayes.

Each major candidate clearly carried seventeen of the thirty-eight states. Tilden had 184 sure electoral votes—one less than a majority. Hayes got

163 firm electoral votes. The dispute arose over four states. Florida, Louisiana, and South Carolina had 19 electoral votes among them. Tilden had carried the states, and Democratic election boards certified that his electors had been chosen. Republican election boards managed to disqualify enough Tilden votes to certify Hayes's electors. So Florida, Louisiana, and South Carolina sent two delegations apiece to the Electoral College, one Republican and one Democratic.

The fourth contested state was Oregon, which the Republicans had carried beyond question. The Democratic governor, acting wholly illegally, arbitrarily disqualified one of the three Republican electors—possibly feeling that if Southern Republicans were going to play the numbers game, a Western Democrat could do likewise. He certified a Democrat in place of the ousted Republican. Had this gambit been sustained by Congress, Tilden would have been the nineteenth president of the United States. His 184 undisputed votes, plus that of the one unlawful elector from Oregon, would have given him the majority required by the Constitution: 185.

The election was thrown into Congress. The Constitution set forth the procedure: "the President of the Senate shall, in the presence of the Senate and the House of Representatives, open all certificates and the votes shall be counted."

The Constitution, however, did not specify who should do the counting. The Senate was heavily Republican, and would be sure to count Hayes in. The House, as heavily Democratic since the election of 1874, would certainly elect Tilden.

The unprecedented deadlock alarmed Congress, as partisans and as national legislators, so it set up an Electoral Commission, designed to be as scrupulously bipartisan as possible. Five of fifteen members came from each body of Congress, and five came from the Supreme Court. The Democratic House chose three Democrats and two Republicans. Reciprocating, in the interest of fair play, public necessity, and political realities, the Republican Senate picked three Republicans and two Democrats. The Supreme Court members were to be two Democrats and two Republicans, with these four to pick the fifth—tacitly but firmly understood to be Justice David Davis, an independent from Illinois.

However, the Illinois legislature, with an eye on the state's twenty-one Republican electoral votes, opportunely elected Justice Davis to the U.S. Senate, class of 1876. The four remaining justices then picked a Republican colleague, Justice Joseph P. Bradley of New Jersey.

Early in the actual life of the Electoral Commission, Justice Bradley wrote an opinion supporting Tilden's election. Shocked at this blindness to all but the facts and figures, Republican political leaders remonstrated with Justice Bradley, who ultimately found for Hayes, thus tidying up the commission tally to a party-line 8–7, eight Republicans versus seven Democrats.

So it was demonstrated that who votes is not so important as who counts, a lesson learned with diligence and application by many a political trickster since 1876. However, the increasing use of computer voting and counting, coupled with the vigilance of the news media, have made the Hayes-Tilden manipulation a thing of the past. Never since has a president been elected with fewer popular votes than his rival, even though the Electoral College system leaves room for that eventuality.

Cleaning Up (In) New Orleans

In his heyday, Huey Long owned Louisiana as completely as though he had bought it. He ran the state by remote control from the U.S. Senate. Members of the state legislature were known as Huey's "trained seals." The governor, O. K. Allen, was probably the most manipulable public servant since the horse that Caligula made a Consul of Rome. Even the Longs laughed about his pliability. As Huey's brother Earl put it, "A leaf blew in the window of Allen's office one day and fell on his desk. He signed it."

About the only dissent to Huey's rule came from the "Old Regulars" political organization that dominated New Orleans. The Kingfish decided to cripple the organization and demanded an immediate crackdown on the gambling and prostitution that kept city taxes low by keeping public officials' take-home pay high.

Mayor T. Semmes Walmsley defied Long's edict. Huey, via the obedient Governor Allen, dispatched the Louisiana National Guard to take over. Infantry, artillery, and cavalry units surged into the old city and took over all municipal functions. By a happy chance, the date of the primary election was at hand, and one of the seized offices was that of the registrar of voters. This enabled Long to prevent election "frauds" that might have returned the popular Mayor Walmsley to office. Instead, of course, Long's man won. Louisiana's "dictator" had saved the Crescent City's ballots from any thieves but his own.

Lyndon Johnson's Stolen Election

One of the lurid features of the 1964 presidential campaign was a rash of paperback books traducing Lyndon Johnson and liberals. These books swept the country from improvised facilities—desktop publishing twenty years before its time.

The last of the big three of these paperbacks, and the only one focused completely on Johnson, sold more than six million copies. It was *A Texan Looks at Lyndon*, by a sometime Texas historian, J. Evetts Haley, who saw Johnson as wholly immoral and wholly cynical. He even saw sinister implications in the fact that Lee Harvey Oswald had made an overnight stay in Jim Wells County, Texas, where, Haley said, Johnson stole his first election to the Senate in 1948. Here Haley, a conservative Texas Democrat who was a delegate to the 1948 state convention that eventually and barely certified Johnson's miraculous victory, was onto something substantial.

This stolen election story, while old news in Texas, scandalized millions of other Americans who read the book or read about it in the general press. It became a substantial underground issue in the 1964 campaign. The Fair Campaign Practices Committee took note of it in response to numerous complaints and inquiries. At that time the FCPC published a bulletin called *Fair Comment*, for which the author Robert Sherrill, a Texan and at the time a Miami newsman, reviewed the book. "An impressive amount of research has been ruined by Haley's hatred for his subject," he wrote. "The result is a book of grotesque perspective . . . a book in which normal actions, seen through a steaming mirage of hate, take on strange and dreadful shapes."

The story was part of right wing exploitation of cloudy passages in Johnson's electoral history. In various versions, including books and campaign tabloids, the tale must have reached a circulation of 20 million or more. Basically, the Johnson miracle at the polls revolved around poll box number 13 at Alice, Texas, and enabled the young congressman to win his Senate seat by an eighty-seven-vote margin.

Sherrill's review in *Fair Comment* put it in perspective.

Johnson defeated former Governor Coke Stevenson with the help of George Parr, South Texas' political czar, who "discovered" 203 more votes—all but one for Johnson—several days after the balloting was over. These 202 Johnson voters had, amazingly enough, voted in alphabetical order. For good reason Stevenson challenged the vote, and he might have won in a court showdown if Justice Hugo Black . . . had not ruled that federal courts have no jurisdiction in a strictly party primary.

Unquestionably the election was cloudy, but if it cannot be forgiven at least it can be better understood if restored to its historical context.

First of all, when Johnson lost to Pappy O'Daniel in the Senate race of 1941, the tables were reversed. The morning after the election, Johnson was ahead by 5,000 votes. Four days later he had lost by 1,311 votes. Satisfied with this lesson in practical Texas politics, Johnson did not ask for a recount. But next time he was ready. When he went out for the Senate again, it was against Stevenson, an old hand at dealing with the peculiarities of South Texas voting, who had, when being re-elected governor in 1940, carried Parr's home county, Duval, by the friendly ratio of 3,643 to 53 over his primary opponent. ("Teetering Piles of 'Proof,' " 1964)

Peculiarities of South Texas Voting

Non-Texas journalists, and through them the U.S. public at large, were scandalized again a quarter-century later when the second volume of Robert A. Caro's biography of Johnson appeared, devoting much of its bulk to the notorious Senate election—and casting the wily and dexterous Stevenson as something of a noble martyr (Caro 1990).

Curiously enough, Caro did not so much as take note of the Haley paperback of 1964, which covered much of the same ground and a number of the same sources and in the process scandalized 1964 America from sea to shining sea—except in Texas, where it was old hat. The "peculiarities of South Texas voting," in Robert Sherrill's perfectly tuned phrase, have long been celebrated there. In fact, an old Texas joke was resurrected in 1964 to explain them.

Little Pedro is crying. "Why are you crying, Pedro?" asks a local resident. "I am crying for my poor dead father," says Pedro. "But Pedro," comes the response, "your father has been dead for ten years." "That's just it," Pedro sobs. "Last night he came back to vote for Lyndon Johnson (Coke Stevenson, Rutherford B. Hayes...) and he didn't come to see me."

Tampering with returns, like any other bit of dishonest electioneering, is always subject to improvement by the innovative mind. In a 1982 New York City primary election for a state senate seat, Vander L. Beatty, a tame candidate of the Democratic machine in the Bedford-Stuyvesant section of Brooklyn, was defeated at the polls but sought vindication in a post-election canvass. Beatty's agents reviewed the voter-registration records at the Board of Elections—but only after the winner's people had checked the same records and found no error.

Working over the weekend, the Beatty crew found—mirabile dictu—1,591 extremely conspicuous forgeries, 141 more than needed to overturn their defeat. This was enough to require a special election, which—according to the peculiarities of South *Brooklyn* voting—organization candidates always win ("Stealing an Election," 1982).

The American tendency is to believe that any problem can be corrected by legislation. But when the Australian ballot was adopted in order to end stolen elections, crooked election clerks found they could invalidate ballots by defacing them with a bit of pencil lead wedged under a thumbnail. When the voting machine arrived, it was quickly found that a hairpin or a paper match could jam it beyond immediate repair.

Delaying the Vote Made Easy

Another old favorite, still in use even though machines are harder to beat than ever, and requiring no mechanical dexterity whatever, is to delay the line of voters awaiting their turn by running in a batch of organization workers to ask any stupid question to slow up the line. The pace becomes so slow that people who must get to work or have other things to do—the kind of voters presumed to be against the organization candidate—will give up in disgust as the minutes stretch into hours.

This was brilliantly executed in New York after Bobby Kennedy won his Senate race in 1964. Before he could take over the New York State Democratic Party (also on his agenda, and necessary because it was leaderless) he had to make peace with the reform Democratic clubs that had opposed his importation, so he struck an alliance with them

> over a surrogate court judgeship, and Kennedy (although out of the country during most of the campaign) brought all of his considerable resources to the race: the campaign staff was made up of the same people who had managed the Senate race. On the day of the primary, a busload of sixty-five workers from the farm club in Boston came down to "help out at the polls." The "help" included suggesting to those standing in line that they should be prepared to be fingerprinted, or having a photographer wander up and down the line snapping pictures. It was politics of the old school—before Watergate gave 'dirty tricks' a bad name—but in retrospect, the campaign marked the passage of power from one generation and style of politics to the next. (Kayden and Mahe 1985, 47)

Registration abuses were long a standard device for locking out prospective voters that might oppose the local organization. In general, such abuses have been on the wane in the United States since around the end of World War II, finally even including the South. There, the early increases in black registration were fought hard in a delaying action by segregationists, but were finally overcome by sheer weight of numbers. From that moment dates the election of black officials in Southern communities with black majorities.

Registration irregularities sometimes occur in rural sections of both North and South, where small numbers of voters and limited outside scrutiny still offer opportunities to the ballot thief. The general pressure for ease of voter registration invites fraud, but computerized lists and professional scrutiny discourage it. In the nineteenth century there were voter identification requirements but generally no voter registration requirements. This is how Colonel Dudley and his people were able to vote floaters with such ease.

Permanent voter registration through a national identity card has been used in Europe, and some variation, such as a driver's license for identification, may yet be adopted in the United States. But most of the proposals along these lines involve problems or objections of one sort or another.

FOREIGN ELECTIONS AND THE U.S. MODEL: THE WORLD CHANGES

Foreign interest in American electoral practices increased sharply beginning in 1989 with the rapid decay of one-party Communist governments around Europe, the coincidental glimmerings of unrigged elections in Mexico, and here and there in Central and South America.

Mexico had been governed rigidly since 1929 by the Institutional Republican Party (Partido Revolucionario y Institucional, or PRI). Its automatic electoral landslides were not even plausibly challenged at the polls for six decades. But by the 1980s the monolithic one-party control of the

PRI was being examined at last, both by losing independent parties no longer content to lose endlessly and by an entity of the Organization of American States (OAS).

In 1990, the Inter-American Human Rights Commission responded for the first time to the complaints of Mexico's perennial-loser parties. It sharply criticized varieties of electoral fraud that even such former meccas of hanky-panky as Chicago, Boston, and New York sadly relinquished long ago— apart from an occasional nostalgic revisitation in extreme circumstances.

In Mexico most of the favored tricks were routine: ballot-box stuffing, keeping non-PRI election officials out of the polling places, forging signatures of bona fide judges on altered vote counts, removing potentially hostile voters from registration lists, and using the police to intimidate non-PRI voters. The only element in the list of Mexican frauds not an old standby north of the border was the occasional use of army units to intimidate voters.[4] What Quay and Hanna could have done with this!

Similar arrangements have been widespread in Latin America, as they have been everywhere in the present and former Communist countries of East and West, most African countries, and the rest of the Third World.

The hesitant, gathering, stirrings of democratic and republican demands that began at the close of the 1980s inevitably looked to U.S. elections as a model, down to the point of the engagement of American political consultants. Some of these ordinarily jaded latter-day pols returned from voluntary or paid consulting chores in Central Europe wide-eyed at the preciousness that peoples of the Old and Third Worlds perceive in a process that many of the Yankee or Gringo pros have long considered common as that old Yankee political staple: dirt.

But the Old World's newly free dreamers hope they have seen the future, and they dream that it really works.

Part IV

Mischief and Reform; Reform as Mischief

As bacteria develop immunities to drugs designed to kill them, so political systems adapt to survive prescriptions for reform. But the effort goes on, spurred from time to time by some new epidemic of abuses grown too troublesome to tolerate. One such was the Watergate scandal of 1972. Although widely misunderstood and misinterpreted, then and since, it provoked a great wave of electoral reform.

The four concluding chapters of this book examine the scandal, the resulting reforms and their effects, our sources of information and understanding about both, and prospects for further reform. Chapter 12 deals with Watergate: what went wrong and why and how; and Watergate as the new mandate for reform. One of the mischiefs of that reform is a Congress whose members are nearly immune to defeat (Chapter 13). The evolution of modern news media and the often skewed political perceptions they transmit are treated in Chapter 14. Finally, Chapter 15 offers perspectives on further reform.

12

Watergate: Mandate for Reform

If their own explanations are pieced together, the perpetrators of the Watergate scandal were not there because they were busy correcting the wrongs of two centuries of political vandals, whose great heritage was being destroyed by its beneficiaries, ungrateful wretches. The whole thing was a high public service, and this is the thanks we get!

If their popular prosecutors, the avengers of truth and virtue, are taken at their word—an equally risky proposition—it was a conspiracy driven by evil never before seen on Earth and carried out by men whose greed, guile, and wickedness we had been taught was a figment of fundamentalist orthodoxy and therefore did not exist. If only we had thrown Nixon off Ike's ticket!

The ingredients of the scandal were the essence of paradox. A political campaign managed for a master campaigner by a circus troup of naifs and thugs. Lawyers, marketers, and closets stuffed with money. A desperate, half-billion-dollar effort to win a fight already publicly thrown by the opposition.

What became the Watergate affair began in secret shortly after Nixon's first inauguration in 1969. Its first public notice was the needless and meaningless burglary of the Democratic National Committee at the end of May three years later. This was largely left unexplained and unexamined by the news media and the electorate until the winter's nagging by the *Washington Post's* Carl Bernstein and Bob Woodward. Nixon got his landslide.

A few days before the election, I wrote about the unanswered, even unasked questions of Watergate in my biennial roundup of campaign mischief for the North American Newspaper Alliance.

Yes, it is properly styled the Watergate mess and not caper, and it is something ugly and frightening, more substantial than mere vilification and the theft and purchase of votes. It is a problem that demands the attention of the President, who alone can reduce it to the proportions of a set of nasty excesses that have been sharply disciplined.

The American people will forgive the President the opportune delay of his attention until after he had won his coveted mandate. But they will not forgive his dismissing it with the know-nothing gambit. And the forum in which they will call him to account is the only one in which they can force his attendance: history. ("McGovern Paid the Price for Rhetorical Excesses," 1972)

He chose the know-nothing gambit, the people did force his attendance in that forum, and in less than two years he had resigned in disgrace.

THE CLIMATE AND THE OVERREACTION

The civil dissent and disturbances that had driven Johnson out of the running for a second term continued throughout the election year of 1968 and into and past 1969. Nixon's inauguration also inaugurated fifteen months of sporadic rebellion, including more than 4,300 successful bombings, nearly 1,500 bungled ones, and 35,000 bomb threats. In the summer and fall of 1970 a federal office building and some dozen university research centers were blasted, some demolished, by bombs. Even the U.S. Capitol sustained bomb damage in March 1971.

It is essential to remember that President Nixon perceived this astonishing level of public vandalism by American anti-war militants—what some called at the time the "kill for peace crowd"—as not only the gross disruption of public order but sabotage and subversion on behalf of hostile foreign governments. There was much credible evidence to support this view in some of the cases that kept erupting.

Desperate to restore order, the Nixon administration overreacted. Other presidents had confronted grievous challenges to national security and public order. John Adams, faced with extensive foreign meddling and subversion by agents and domestic admirers of France, got the Alien and Sedition Acts adopted and extended naturalization requirements from five to fourteen years. Lincoln (in the midst of an undeclared and unpopular war) called out U.S. troops to suppress draft riots in 1863. The oppressions of the Great Red Scare of Wilson's last year are discussed in Chapter 9. The problem facing Nixon was neither imaginary nor inconsequential.

Still, he overreacted. The president embraced, then under pressure backed away from, Draconian new security measures proposed by a young zealot on his staff, Tom Charles Huston. It would have footnoted the Bill of Rights with exceptions. It was too much even for J. Edgar Hoover. Nixon's stalwarts, preparing to reelect him by an unprecedented landslide, were determined to outdo even the self-brutalizing Democrats at destroying the Democratic ticket.

With a pre-campaign treasury so rich they were embarrassed to ask for money, All the President's Men, in Bernstein and Woodward's phrase, spared no expense to silence enemies, sabotage hypothetical rivals, and ferret out secrets to remove the minutest mathematical chance of anything but a thundering mandate for their leader.

Bernstein and Woodward listed thirty-five president's men in their Watergate cast of characters. Most remarkable about almost all of them is their utter invisibility in American electoral politics before 1972.

IMPEACHMENT: THE PROCESS IN ACTION

The following analysis originally appeared over my signature in the *Britannica Book of the Year 1975* and is reprinted here by permission.

On August 9, 1974, Richard M. Nixon resigned as President of the United States of America. He alone, among the thirty-six men who have held the presidency, was driven from office by Article II, Section 4 of the U.S. Constitution.

The fact that Nixon resigned before the full House of Representatives could act on the three articles of impeachment recommended by its Judiciary Committee in no way alters the fact that it was the process that forced him out. The House would have impeached him by an overwhelming margin and he realized this even before new evidence revealed that he had deceived his own defense counsel and chief defenders about his involvement in Watergate. After those revelations, conviction by the necessary two-thirds majority of the Senate shifted from likelihood to virtual certainty. But before those last steps—formal impeachment by the whole House, the public spectacle of a trial before Senate and nation, and the degradation of conviction—the President chose what in effect was a plea of nolo contendere, no contest, and resigned. In this step, too, he was the first.

Origins and Meaning. Impeachment found its way into law in England in the fourteenth century, where it was used intermittently until 1806. In 1787 it was built into the U.S. Constitution. Its purpose was to make possible the punishment of a guilty President (or other federal official), whose lesser accomplices would be brought to justice in ordinary courts of law. At the same time, the process would allow for acquittal if the accused were adjudged guilty by less than the overwhelming margin of 2–1. Benjamin Franklin reminded the Constitutional Convention that prior to the adoption of impeachment, whenever a first magistrate was brought to justice, "recourse was had to assassination in which he was not only deprived of his life but of the opportunity of vindicating his character." James Madison saw the need to defend the community "against the incapacity, negligence or perfidy of the chief magistrate."[1] The convention agreed by a vote of 8–2 [states] that the executive be removable on impeachment, with only Massachusetts and South Carolina dissenting.

The idea of impeachment for incapacity was omitted from the final drafts of the Constitution, and incapacity itself is really only dealt with there in the Twenty-Fifth Amendment, ratified in 1967. It was under this amendment that Nixon named Gerald Ford to succeed the disgraced Spiro Agnew when he was forced to resign as Vice President in 1973, but it also provides for orderly succession if a President is gravely ill or otherwise incapable of discharging his responsibilities.

The roots of the word impeachment are in the Latin *impedicare*, "to fetter," and not in the Latin *peccare*, "to sin." It comes to English through a Middle French word meaning "hinder." Thus its connotation is close to "impede" and far from "peccable" or "peccadillo." To the founders of the Constitution, it meant both punishment and suspension or displacement, "degradation from office," in Gouverneur Morris's term.

Article II, Section 4: The President, Vice President and all civil Officers of the United States, shall be removed from Office on Impeachment for, and Conviction of, Treason, Bribery, or other high Crimes and Misdemeanors.

The meanings of treason and bribery are clear enough; what then are "high crimes and misdemeanors?" One constitutional lawyer has said that a collection of unanswered traffic tickets would amount to "high misdemeanors" if the U.S. Senate said it did. When Gerald Ford was serving in the House of Representatives, he led a pious and vain effort to impeach Supreme Court Justice William O. Douglas for allowing some of his writings to be published in a magazine Ford considered pornographic. At that time he declared that "An impeachable offense is whatever a majority of the House of Representatives considers it to be at a given moment in history."

The Johnson–Nixon Comparison. "Strict constructionists"—notably the defenders of Presidents fighting impeachment—argue that high crimes and misdemeanors must be indictable offenses—explicit violations of law. This was the case with Nixon's defenders as it had been with those of President Andrew Johnson 106 years before. The eleven articles of impeachment against Johnson attempted to identify specific acts as high crimes (two) and misdemeanors (nine), each article ending with some such stipulation as "did then and there commit and was guilty of a high misdemeanor in office." Although the argument about what constituted high crimes and misdemeanors raged across the country as well as in Congress, no consensus ever developed.

Some of Nixon's last-ditch defenders have argued that the Ninety-third Congress with its top-heavy Democratic majority was nothing but a lynch mob, determined to drive him from office at all costs. A review of the history of the Fortieth Congress, which impeached Johnson and barely acquitted him, is instructive in this respect.

... The seventeenth President was a Tennessee Democrat who was elected Vice President under the Republican Lincoln in 1864, and served all but the first six weeks of Lincoln's second term. All seats in both houses of Congress apportioned to the eleven Confederate states were vacant during the Civil War, and when the Johnson impeachment came to issue before the Fortieth Congress in 1867 and 1868, only Tennessee had been readmitted to the Union. Thus in the House, fifty-one normally Democratic votes were vacant seats, as were twenty in the Senate. The Republicans had a "veto-proof Congress," with 74 percent of the votes in the House and 78 percent in the Senate. By contrast, in the Ninety-third Congress, which forced Richard Nixon to resign, Democrats controlled the House with only 57 percent and the Senate with 58 percent, margins that are trifling by comparison.

There are a few parallels between the two cases, separated by slightly more than a century in time. Although Lincoln and Johnson had won the 1864 election with 55 percent of the popular vote, the Tennessee Democrat did not inherit even the modest popularity that the murdered Lincoln had gained. From the start his relations with Congress had been difficult and his foot-dragging and outright interference in the Reconstruction course set by Congress made him enemies by the dozen.

Nixon, who had gained reelection with a historic landslide, was nevertheless personally unpopular, the beneficiary in 1972 of a massive resistance to his opponent rather than a personal or political endorsement for himself. The arrogance of his principal aides reduced his congressional defenders.

In the case of Johnson, his sympathetic support for Southern leaders so recently rebels became increasingly apparent. This, and his manifest distaste for the Radical Republicans' program of enfranchising and otherwise aiding Southern blacks, moved the Northern press to step up editorial demands that he be impeached. The roster of newspapers thus assailing Johnson included many that had previously supported him, such as the *Chicago Tribune*.

In the Nixon impeachment, as the President's innocence of ordering or leading the coverup of Watergate and related excesses became more and more problematical, public support dwindled fast. First, there was damaging testimony before the Senate Watergate committee, then incriminating tape transcripts, and finally the evidence presented to the House Judiciary Committee. The totality of all available information painted a dismaying picture of complicity and deceit. As this happened, the moderate and conservative press that had held out hope for his exoneration deserted him and began demanding his impeachment—again including, as 106 years earlier, the *Chicago Tribune*.

Although the party alignment against Nixon was less heavily weighted than the hostile imbalance that faced Johnson, the GOP ranks of the Fortieth Congress were split much more deeply than the division between Southern and Northern Democrats in the Ninety-third on which some of Nixon's supporters hoped to rely. The Radical Republicans in Congress in 1867–68 were counterbalanced almost evenly on key Reconstruction issues by conservative Republican fellows. Then, as in 1974, economic and other problems impinged on the impeachment question: a severe post–Civil War recession and sharp controversy over monetary policy.

However, the actions for which Johnson was impeached had been not only public but flamboyant. The Congress had legislated its program for reconstructing Southern society, giving the blacks meaningful freedom, and uniting a country shattered by civil war; the President had impeded, delayed, and countermanded. Congress enfranchised blacks and sent Union troops to oversee their voting; the President named Southern politicians as governors and changed military orders; he fired Republican postmasters and named Democrats in their stead, and threatened more of the same in order to garner local support for his programs. The Congress legislated the Tenure of Office Act, requiring Senate approval for the dismissal of any presidential appointee who had to be confirmed by the Senate. It later became apparent that the act was unconstitutional, but Johnson both observed it and scorned it, striking no consistent pattern. Finally he fired his secretary of war, an act of defiance provoking the ultimate collision.[2]

In the Nixon case all the transgressions had been secret. The President's men had engaged in a host of unlawful actions to ensure what was already certain: that he be elected not narrowly but by a landslide. They had, in effect, set aside the operation of the Constitution and laws as they related to adversaries of the President—whether political campaign opponents, or just detractors, or even suspected traitors against whom the law seemed to find no effective sanctions. The original actions on behalf of the President had been covert; then they had been disguised and covered up; finally it became apparent that the coverup, clearly involving obstruction of justice and a variety of illegal actions, and had been participated in, and even led, by the President of the United States.

Here was the difference: secret abuse of law by Nixon and his men, flagrant rejection of law [questionable or not] by Johnson. Libertarians among the Republican conservatives of 1868 hesitated to join the vengeful Radical throng, and although most senators voted "guilty" against Johnson, he was spared because one [Republican], Edmund Ross of Kansas, voted with the Democrats.

The same kind of legislators—libertarians among 1974 Republicans—were first stunned, then outraged, by the abuse of civil liberties on behalf of a Republican President, who then urged on a conspiracy to cover its own tracks. Republicans gamely insisted on his innocence, and then, as they realized they had been deceived, [sadly or angrily] decided to vote to impeach.

Defenders of Nixon who continued to see him as innocent, as conspired against and traduced by the press, argued that the House Judiciary Committee had been weighted against the President, and that the whole excursion had really been a hanging party. But by comparison with the only other presidential impeachment, the 1974 "Affaire Nixon" was a very model of comportment, of discreet conduct and determination to be fair. A scant handful of Democrats on the Judiciary panel—notably Jerome Waldie of California, Robert Drinan of Massachusetts, and Elizabeth Holtzman of New York, and occasionally Charles Rangel of New York and John Conyers of Michigan—revealed constant animus and fiery rhetorical flights against the iniquity of the President. Most Democrats, however, seemed subdued and uncheered by the prospects.

In the Johnson impeachment, bias was evident everywhere. In the House the Radical Republicans who had successfully pressed for impeachment were exultant in their declarations. One saw the Johnson administration as "an illustration of the depth to which political and official perfidy can descend." Such florid proclamations embarrassed the conservative Republicans, one of whom wrote to his wife, "They are determined to ruin the Republican party." Like others, he was much dismayed by Andrew Johnson who, he wrote, "*does* continue to do the most provoking things. If he isn't impeached it won't be his fault."

When Johnson's trial actually took place in the Senate it was presided over, by constitutional mandate, by the Chief Justice of the United States, Salmon P. Chase—who had let it be known to one leading Democrat that if Andrew Johnson were denied the Democratic presidential nomination later in 1868, he would be willing to accept it.

Under the succession laws then in force, an impeached Johnson would be succeeded, there being no Vice President, by the president pro tempore of the Senate, Benjamin F. Wade—who sat in the Senate during the trial and voted for impeachment. He came within one vote of becoming President himself. The prospect was not lost on conservative Republicans who mistrusted him; more than one observed that but for Wade's obnoxious character Johnson would have been convicted. Senator David T. Patterson of Tennessee, Johnson's son-in-law, also took part in the trial—and voted for acquittal. Senator Ross—who has been immortalized as the courageous Kansan who cast the crucial vote against conviction—was a conservative Republican who shortly thereafter switched his alignment to Democratic.

Portent for the Future. If the Johnson impeachment left no precedents to be emulated in future exercises of that awesome responsibility, it did leave some horrible examples of conduct the future might shun. And these were indeed shunned during the Nixon impeachment proceedings. In 1974 lamentations were heard among the more partisan Democrats and other antagonists of the former President, that he had been allowed to resign and had thus escaped the actual mill of impeachment.

This line of reasoning argues that Nixon was not suitably punished. The hue and cry escalated again when Gerald Ford subsequently granted him a full and complete pardon for any crimes he may have committed during his tenure in office. "Suitable punishment," of course, is a subjective judgment. It is not difficult to imagine that the disgrace of being forced from the presidency of the United States was, of itself, harsh and sufficient punishment on a man who long looked wistfully toward the history books. Consideration must also be given the U.S. Constitution's concern for protecting the republic from the miscreant and his coadjutors, which the founders put coequal with punishment. Again, that concern is met equally well by forced resignation.

As for justice, "Shall any man be above justice?" George Mason of Virginia asked his fellows in the Constitutional Convention in 1787. "Shall the man who has practised corruption & by that means procured his appointment in the first instance he suffered to escape punishment, by repeating his guilt?" The impeachment process answers "No" quite convincingly, and it should serve to warn future holders of the presidency that impeachment is not some relic of the past or historical curiosity but, rather, a part of the U.S. Constitution—one that still works. (Felknor 1975)

THE MISCHIEF-MAKERS: NON-POLITICIANS

The first lesson of Watergate is an argument against depoliticizing politics.

The virtual absence from Nixon's entire entourage of people steeped in political tradition, with long experience in government, is of the greatest significance. Robert H. Finch was a conspicuous exception. He was a seasoned and responsible politician, former Los Angeles County Republican chairman, and had been Nixon's administrative assistant as vice president, his campaign director in the squeaker election of 1960, and lieutenant governor of California. He was Nixon's secretary of health, education, and welfare, but he left the administration early in 1972. On election day, he tried to see Nixon to counsel coming clean about Watergate, but Haldeman, his old friend, on learning his intention would not let him see the president (White 1975, 208).

Haldeman, though he had been advance man and manager of Nixon campaigns, was an advertising and marketing executive, a manager and not a "creative person." So were most of his hirelings. His total experience in government was the Nixon White House, where he held the keys to the inner sanctum and was the president's get-it-done man. His arrogance was reflected in those he hired and ran, and their collective arrogance variously irritated and alienated a generation of Republican and other politicians and such journalists as he encountered.

Nixon saluted John Mitchell as a wise man who understood politics. But Mitchell's political wisdom came as the slick savvy of a municipal bond lawyer. His specialization was in creating and using public authorities to evade the constitutions of states and cities and their strict limits on public debt. Governments often must borrow sums far beyond their usually ancient constitutional limits, and lawyers like Mitchell make that possible by the creation of public authorities that *seem* to be backed by the "full faith and credit of" the state or city whose constitution forbids such backing. In other words, Mitchell's vaunted political background was in legal inventions to subvert and evade the constitutions of U.S. states and cities.

Nixon himself acknowledges the facts of the Watergate scandal and accepts overall responsibility for it, particularly in *In the Arena*, but elsewhere, too (Nixon 1978). In *Arena* he states early, "I failed to take matters firmly into my own hands and discover the facts and to fire any and all people involved or implicated in the break-in" (Nixon 1990, 33).

But his fundamental error was opening the Pandora's Box out of which swarmed and flew the incredible cloud of mischief-makers that ended his presidency, the non-politicians he entrusted with his political life.

Nixon and the "Myths" of Watergate

In *Arena*, Nixon is at pains to deny what he calls the myths of Watergate, which he says his adversaries use to depict his administration as "the most corrupt in American history." Such a charge is preposterous, for corruption in any ordinary sense is not really part of Watergate. Some of the "myths" relate to "corruption" and can be dismissed: that he sold ambassadorships, profited monetarily from his public career, and tried to cheat on his income tax.

His denial of some of the "myths" that do relate to Watergate can be accepted without affecting his central responsibility (which he has acknowledged). These include that he *personally* ordered the break-in and that he erased that famous eighteen-plus minutes of tape (which I consider neither credible nor plausibly motivated, and which at worst would only have been extra poison frosting on an already lethal cake).

Others require more analysis. He says it is myth that he illegally used the Internal Revenue Service on his enemies. His suggesting targets for IRS curiosity was surely not illegal and has abundant bipartisan precedent going back almost to the Sixteenth (income tax) Amendment, ratified in 1913.

The "myth" that he was the first president to record White House conversations is manifestly myth. Although it is widely known that Franklin D. Roosevelt recorded from the Oval Office, his well-deserved reputation for checking up on everybody has been widely forgotten. It is clear that FDR had intelligence reports—probably including wiretapping reports—

assembled on a number of his political foes, some of whom suspected it at the time.

Indeed, his press secretary, Charley Michelson, and other members of the president's political apparatus believed that he routinely spied on them. In *The Ghost Talks*, Michelson related that in 1932 the Democratic National Committee's executive committee chairman, Jouett Shouse, told him "that the Governor [FDR] had a spy in our office reporting to him on all we did. That sounds quite probable, for he never was a man to take chances" (Michelson 1947). Hamilton Fish, FDR's Republican congressman and one of his first purge victims, was outspoken in accusing the president of having his phone tapped. We know that John Kennedy taped White House conversations occasionally and that, through the agency of his zealous brother, the attorney general, he engaged in widespread bugging and wiretapping. We know that Lyndon Johnson taped Oval Office conversations selectively.

Nixon assails as myths three accusations that are both germane and widely believed: that he ordered massive illegal wiretapping and surveillance of enemies, including the covert break-in at the office of Daniel Ellsberg's psychiatrist; that he ordered hush money paid to Hunt and others; and that he ordered the CIA to obstruct the FBI's Watergate investigation.

The first of these he denies flatly. While he denies ordering either of the other actions, he does acknowledge considering them and discussing them with staff, which he admits was wrong. Of the last, he says he erred in following staff recommendations but that the CIA did not accede to such requests from the White House.

Underlying Guilt: Creating the Organization

Nixon's underlying guilt was in creating the organization, that bizarre congeries of non-politicians that scrupled at nothing to serve him. He had no want of knights to silently answer Henry II's question, "Who will free me from this turbulent priest?" As Theodore H. White observed, "In 1946 when Nixon began in politics, 'how things work' was simple; the lessons came from the school of Whitaker and Baxter" (White 1975, 63). And that was guidance enough for his men.

The remaining myth Nixon denies is that he deliberately lied throughout the Watergate period, although he admits an "error of recollection" about a seminal phone conversation of June 23 (Nixon 1990, 33–40). There is no reason this cannot be believed. Ultimately he did "let it all hang out," as a phrase of the day had it. Whether he lied is essentially immaterial, for the essential truth is that he had surrounded himself with a staff perfectly willing to lie or do almost anything else for him.

Nixon comes close to acknowledging even this, but then, almost in the same breath excuses it, in a single passage in *Arena*. It constitutes the bulk of a single paragraph, but I shall parse it here to consider it point by point:

"What happened in Watergate—the facts, not the myths—was wrong." The basic fact, on which we all can agree.

"In retrospect, while I was not involved in the decision to conduct the break-in ... " We can accept this as true but not material.

" ... I should have set a higher standard for the conduct of the people who participated in my campaign and administration." Ah, yes; the key.

"I should have established a moral tone that would have made such implications unthinkable. I did not." Right, and right.

"I played by the rules of politics as I found them." The critical phrase here is not "rules of politics" or "found them," but "as *I* found them." Just as Teddy White pointed out, Nixon found them as Clem Whitaker and Leone Baxter taught them (by example, and occasional pronouncement) and practiced them.

"Not taking a higher road than my predecessors and my adversaries was my central mistake." Nixon and his people assuredly were not following the standards of Washington, Adams, Lincoln, or Cleveland. Indeed it is by following the lowest standards of many of his predecessors combined that the Nixon crew destroyed the Nixon presidency. But note: he was not the captive but the captain of that crew.

"For that reason, ... " Again, the cop-out, amassing all guilt and all responsibility under the single failure to follow a higher standard than his predecessors.

" ... I long ago accepted overall responsibility for the Watergate affair. What's more, I have paid, and am still paying, the price for it" (Nixon 1990, 41). True, and fair enough. Case closed.

Taken item by item, hardly anything that happened in the Watergate scandal was without precedent. The break-ins may well have been; but we do not know. The taping and bugging is addressed above.

Even the notorious Huston Plan had something of a precedent in the last months of Woodrow Wilson in the White House. Although the president certainly did not approve it, and indeed was hardly competent to prevent or stop it, Wilson, all unwitting, did have something like the Huston Plan in the depredations of A. Mitchell Palmer and his Great Red Scare of 1920. In Palmer's case it was easier. So many of his putative anarchists and Bolsheviks were aliens that it was a simple matter to deport them summarily.

Watergate as Tuck Envy

As to the Watergate "dirty tricks," we know that Dick Tuck, at first indulging his own whimsical bent and later as a Democratic Party advance man, originated exploits of political mischief that were variously embarrassing and harassing for their mostly Republican targets—mostly Nixon, in fact.

The degree to which the news media found Tuck's tricks vastly amusing inspired the Nixon campaign's heavy-handed sophomoric efforts by Donald Segretti to emulate them. Tuck's work of sabotage—a "minor dark art" in Teddy White's phrase—was sophomoric, too, but always with sparkle and wit. Without doubt some of the Tuck gambits—merry pranks to Democrats—were deeply offensive to Nixon. Yet the media merriment they sparked made emulating Tuck important on the Nixon team's agenda, as is reflected again and again in their Senate Committee testimony and other writings. Witness Haldeman before the Senate Committee:

The repertoire of the political prankster includes such activities as printing up embarrassing signs for the opponent, posing in trainman's clothes and waving the campaign train out of the station, placing an agent on the opponent's campaign train to produce witty newsletters mocking the candidate, distributing opposition signs at rallies for use by members of the crowd, encouraging band leaders to play rival songs at rallies and so forth.

The activities we had in mind, and for which we drew careful boundaries, specifically excluded anything remotely connected with the Watergate type of activity. (U.S. Senate Hearings 1973, 2876)

But here again, as so often, they missed the essence. Here, the *delicatesse* that characterized Tuck's work was

degraded to buffoonery by ... Donald Segretti (hired by his USC classmate Dwight Chapin), who had no experience in politics, a thirty-year-old man of outstanding naiveté and stupidity. Segretti was the kind of man who, coming into a strange city (like Tampa, Florida), would simply telephone local Republican headquarters and ask the anonymous answering voice on the phone (as he did) to recommend a trustworthy individual to do "part-time work" in his secret enterprise. (White 1975, 155)

DRAWING MORALS FROM WATERGATE

What are the morals to be deduced from the Watergate scandal? Several are apparent, and one is as important inside as outside the world of active politicians: Trust the system to work—in the fullness of time, perhaps, but eventually.

For the president and future presidents: A staff too large, too autonomous, and too self-directed is an extremely dangerous booby-trap.

For the media: It is true that—eventually—as Broder wrote, in Watergate "investigative reporting had scored its most important victory and become an indelible part of Washington reporting" (Broder 1987, 141). Upton Sinclair, himself a quondam journalist, believed that reporters needed to be protected from their capitalist bosses. But for Walter Lippmann, out of his far more sophisticated concern for professionalism in journalism, "the problem ... was much more severe. For Lippmann, journalism did not have to be rescued from capitalists but from itself" (Schudson 1978, 153).

For the Democratic Party: Remember, or learn again like a brain-damaged patient in therapy, that when Democrats elected presidents their constituency was near the center and not an elite of liberal theorists and a surly mix of alienated and dropout clients. Democrats elected presidents six of nine times from 1932 to 1964 by claiming the center.

For conservative Republicans and others on the right-hand edge of the American polity, those for whom an Eisenhower is a liberal sap and even a Reagan is suspect: Remember Goldwater and Landon. When Republicans won five of six presidencies from 1968 through 1988 voters thought Republicans represented the center.

And finally, for reformers: Heed Samuel Johnson's caveat: Hell is paved with good intentions. (It was Karl Marx who watered it down to "the road to hell." Stick with Johnson.) The reform heroes Hiram Johnson and Bob La Follette, fighting off the robber barons, worked out a way to take the politicians out of politics and paved the way for Goldwater in 1964 and McGovern in 1972.

They also—as unwitting as Woodrow Wilson while his attorney general was scourging Reds and making them martyrs—opened a new political freeway that led from Whitaker and Baxter all the way to Watergate.

13

A Result of Reform: Invincible Incumbents

The framers of the U.S. Constitution envisaged Congress as a citizen legislature of amateur politicians, with distinctly different qualifications for the two chambers. At the Convention of 1787 there was considerable discussion of long terms for senators—life, or during good behavior, or fourteen years. Several delegates thought senators should not be compensated, that they would serve out of a sense of responsibility.

There was general agreement that terms should be short in the House of Representatives; the first proposal was for one year. Three years was much discussed because terms in the Continental Congress during the last half of its fourteen-year existence had been limited to three years in any six. For the new Congress Elbridge Gerry said New England would never consent to a three-year term. He considered, so Madison recorded, "annual Elections as the only defense of the people agst. tyranny. He was as much agst. a triennial House as agst. a hereditary Executive" (Farrand 1966, 1:214). Two years was a compromise. The Founders wanted turnover in the House.

This, like many a dream, eventually got interpreted to death. The modern U.S. House of Representatives has a turnover rate approaching that of the United Kingdom's House of Lords, where death is the only way to lose a seat. In practical terms, the only way other than death that American House seats are vacated is the retirement or elevation of the incumbent. In 1986, of the 435 House members, 408 ran for reelection; 402, or 98 percent, won.

The number of defeated incumbents in 1988—six—equalled the count for 1986 and was the lowest ever recorded (Ornstein, Mann, and Malbin 1989). In 1990 the percentage of winners slipped to 96 percent.

The Founders knew that, absent the three-years-in-six limit introduced by the Articles of Confederation in 1881, some outstanding congressmen would be reelected time after time. As Hamilton (or Madison) put it in *Federalist*, No. 53, "A few of the members, as happens in all such as-

Table 13.1
House Service in the 1st–10th Congresses

Terms Served	9	8	7	6	5	4
Congressmen	1	4	6	5	9	30

Source: *Biographical Directory, U. S. Congress*, 1989.

Table 13.2
Service in the 80th and 101st Congresses

	House Service in 2-Year Terms					
No. of terms	21+	16–20	11–15	6–10	3–5	1–2
80th Cong.	1	8	28	85	166	147
101st Cong.	2	12	40	141	155	85
	Senate Service in 6-Year Terms					
No. of terms		5+	4	3	1–2	
80th Cong.		2	9	15	74	
101st Cong.		6	14	18	62	

Source: *Congressional Directory*, 1947, 1989.

semblies, will possess superior talents; will, by frequent reëlections, become members of long standing; will be thoroughly masters of the public business."

But 96 percent?

TURNOVER IN THE EARLY CONGRESSES

There were 106 House seats among sixteen states after the first census (1790).[1] After the second census (1800) 142 seats were divided among seventeen states. In the course of the first ten Congresses (1789–1809), only fifty-five men were elected to as many as four terms. Only one served as many as nine (see Table 13.1).[2]

In contrast, in the 101st Congress sixty-three members had served more than ten terms (see Table 13.2). One, Jamie L. Whitten of Mississippi, had served twenty-five terms (fifty years) and thirteen others more than fifteen terms.

Only thirty-three (7.5 percent) were serving their first term in the 101st Congress. Fifty-two more were in their second term. The situation is different in the Senate, where only thirty-seven of one-hundred members of the 101st Congress had served more than two terms, and the import and reasons for this will be discussed below.

But for the House of Representatives, the truth is that Congress is in the age of the invincible incumbent. This is a recent development, which Richard Nixon calls the "incumbency lock," believing it

another highly negative characteristic of today's politics. Congress has become an incumbent's protective association.... Forty-two years ago, one hundred five new congressmen were elected to the much-maligned eightieth Congress.[3] Fifty-two of them defeated incumbents. Two of them went on to become President. Ten became senators. Five became governors. Most of those who defeated incumbents would have no chance to be elected today. (Nixon 1990, 200)

This situation evolved in two stages, the first before the middle of the nineteenth century. Instead of what the Founders expected would be the new Citizen Legislator, much on their own model, there evolved what we may irreverently call a "New Class." Milovan Djilas's phrase is a little pungent for the American experience, but this class was indeed a new political bureaucracy (cf. Djilas 1957, 38). It was the profession of political leadership and management.

Michael Schudson has commented on this development as it arose along with and as a result of changing political party organization, once real parties came to exist. This set in with the retirement of John Quincy Adams and the other surviving Federalists. It coincided with electoral law changes— popular voting for presidential electors, and the adoption of universal white manhood suffrage—which we think of as grotesquely primitive; but then it was a remarkable democratic innovation.

The New Professionals circa 1840

This development, Schudson reminds us, moved Richard Hofstadter to propose "Martin Van Buren, rather than Andrew Jackson, as the representative figure of Jacksonian Democracy. Van Buren was one of the 'new breed' of political leaders. He and other members of New York's 'Albany Regency' were prototypes of the new class of professional politicians" (Schudson 1978, 47). They came from no social elite, had no elegant education, and some were rough country boys; but they took to the new politics like ducks to water.

They were, in short, modern political professionals who love the bonhomie of political gatherings, a coterie of more-or-less equals who relied for success not on the authority of a brilliant charismatic leader but on their solidarity, patience, and discipline. Their party gave them a creed, a vocation and a congenial social world all in one. It is hardly surprising that they should have developed a firm and self-conscious awareness of the imperatives of party organization, and have laid down a comprehensive set of canons for its management. (Hofstadter 1972, 242)

Here Schudson points out that "these new professionals did not reestablish old parties run by personal cliques but invented new organizations, popularly based and democratically run" (Schudson 1978, 48). It is interesting, and not irrelevant, to note that as this was happening to politics in the 1830s, important changes were afoot in the press. Newspaper reporters were beginning to be paid for their work. Journalism was inventing itself and becoming a profession (see Chapter 14).

THE MISCHIEF OF MODERN REFORMS

The second stage in the evolution of the invincible congressman is quite recent, stemming from a significant change in party alignment in the House of Representatives and from other coincident and closely related developments in the American polity. These include the great enlargement and proliferation of professional congressional staffs and propaganda resources, which have completely changed the nature of the game. Their effect has been to make incumbents virtually invulnerable. Thereby they have created a new necessity for "negative campaigning" if a challenger is to have any chance. This places a premium on the skills of professional campaign managers and media artists and has given them a large role in controlling the electoral process.

Post-Watergate reforms created Political Action Committees (PACs), thus handing lobbying interests, ever willing to finance the increasing cost of campaigning, a large role in setting national priorities. Simultaneously, this development took a large part of campaign finance out of the hands of the parties.

Reform efforts such as the primary election already had done much to eliminate the seasoned judgment of professional politicians from selecting candidates. The consequent decline of party discipline over errant Congressmen or candidates exacerbated the negative effects of all the other elements. Although the parties—whose emergence in the 1830s and 1840s started the ball rolling—are not dead, they are vastly different from what parties were through the approximately one-hundred years ending around 1968.

What has been shunted away from everyone's attention by all this change is the original role and the raison d'être of the House of Representatives. The consequential change in its alignment mentioned above occurred in 1974. It was only one of many shifts in the twentieth-century makeup (that is, partisan balance) of the House, and far from the largest. Actually, the House was designed to reflect sharp changes in popular sentiment. In 1904 Teddy Roosevelt brought in forty-three new House Republicans with him. Together, the successive House elections of 1910 and 1912 swept in 118 new Democrats.

The next election—1914—swept more than half of them right back out. The Harding election of 1920 added 63 Republicans in the House, and 75 new Democrats displaced them two years later. The elections of 1930 and 1932 swept in an additional 146 Democrats—one-third of the whole House.

In the Ninety-third Congress (after the election of 1972), the Democrats controlled the House by the comfortable margin of 242 to 192 (there was one independent). The post-Watergate election of 1974 added forty-nine

Democrats and gave that party more than 2–1 control of the House in the Ninety-fourth Congress, 291 to 144. But the numbers were not as important as the mood of the Watergate babies and the massive changes already under way in augmenting technical support, staff size, and budget.

The mood was anti-politics and anti-politicians. We have noted elsewhere the pretense of 1974's challengers that they were outsiders—anything to avoid looking or sounding like a politician, for the politicians brought us Watergate. Once on the inside, the disguise disappeared, and it became clear that the newcomers were hardball politicians of the first water. What they were not was politicians of the old school—deferring to senior colleagues, go along to get along, take a back seat for the first term, and don't make waves. Indeed, many of them had never held public office but had cut their political eye teeth as agitators for consumer rights, for peace and against the Vietnam War, and for environmental and assorted other "good causes." Veteran officeholders, no; politicians, yes. They proceeded to take over.

THE WATERGATE BABIES TAKE OVER

The Watergate freshmen got together a month after their election to organize, and by January 20 they were ready. Although net Democratic gains only totalled forty-three seats, the Watergate class of new freshmen numbered seventy-five, the largest infusion of newcomers in many years. They had identified their prospective allies carefully, and they were helped by a significant shift to the left in the Republican House delegation. Many of the new Democrats had been elected from formerly safe Republican districts, and they had more in common with some of the new Republicans than with the old guard Democrats they had ousted.

In the Democratic Caucus they used all their muscle and elected the slick and canny Philip Burton to its chair. Then, in meetings of the Democratic Strategy and Policy Committee and the Democratic Caucus just before and after Congress convened, they went on to sack three of the most powerful Democrats in the House, all old autocrats whom they stripped of their chairmanships. These were Felix Edward Hébert (Louisiana), chairman of Armed Services; Welsh R. Poage (Texas), of Agriculture, and Wright Patman (Texas), of Banking. They nearly, but not quite, also got Wayne Hays of Ohio, chairman of House Administration.

House Speaker Thomas P. "Tip" O'Neill, Jr., candidly acknowledged his surprise at their success. "In all my years in the House, this was one of the few times when I was genuinely caught by surprise" (O'Neill 1987, 284).

In an interview with David Broder four or five years later, O'Neill also was candid about dealing with them as Speaker.

They don't think about party loyalty. They were interested in spreading the power. But in spreading the power, we now have 152 subcommittees, each one with its own staff, each one trying to make its chairman look good. And it's just hard as hell to put the pieces together and put the legislation through....

I go to all their caucuses. The freshman caucus. The sophomore caucus. The junior caucus. The black caucus. The Jewish caucus. The Mexican caucus. The Northeast caucus. The Middle American caucus. The steel caucus. The women's caucus. (Broder 1980, 36)

O'Neill's point about 152 subcommittees is a focal point of the large-scale expansion of the power that the Watergate babies seized on arriving in the Capitol. The committee structure, hardly changed in its essence since the early nineteenth century, has been taken apart and reassembled in different form and number.

His count differs in small respects both from my own and from those in that essential resource for those who could count things congressional, Ornstein, Mann, and Malbin's *Vital Statistics on Congress, 1989–1990*. The distinctions among substantive and select committees and subcommittees are more arcane than ever.

The central point is that (1) at the high-water mark in 1979–80 there were (by my count from the *Congressional Staff Directory*) twenty-eight House committees where there had been nineteen and (2) subcommittees sprouted wildly, even on Rules and on Ways and Means, which operated, traditionally and deliberately, with no subcommittees. The objective, of course, was chairmanships and staff. The formula was C + S = P, where C is the chairmanship of a committee or subcommittee, S is its staff, and P is power.

There is an additional major source of power in the House. Burdett Loomis in *The New American Politician* (1988) offers a useful definition of "power committees," whose influence is pervasive as well as profound. Mere membership on one of these important bodies places a congressman in the power structure of Congress. These are the committees on Appropriations, House Administration, Rules, Ways and Means, and starting in the Ninety-fourth Congress with the Watergate class of 1975, Budget. Their impact is not due to prestige in the sense of classy stature à la Foreign Affairs, perhaps, but to clout—their control over what happens to House members and their legislation, their personal staffs, their committee assignments and staffs, and their influence on their peers.

Table 13.3 reveals the course of expanding power in the House from the Eighty-fourth Congress to the Ninety-fourth, when the Watergate babies arrived, and (in the Ninety-eighth) the modest phasing back of some of the overeager growth of 1975–80.

Observe that in the 101st Congress more than half of the majority members chair a committee or a subcommittee, and 61 percent sit on the power committees. There is some overlapping, as the power committee chairmen

Table 13.3
Proliferating Power in the House: Growth of Chairmanships and "Power Committee" Posts

Cong.	Years	Majority Members Chairing Committees & Subcommittees		Positions on Power Comms.	
		No.	%	No.	%
84	1955–56	63	27.2	92	39.6
90	1967–68	111	44.9	95	38.3
92	1971–72	120	47.0	95	37.2
94	1975–76	142	49.1	133	54.0
96	1979–80	144	52.2	131	47.0
98	1983–84	124	46.4	136	50.0
100	1987–88	128	49.6	141	54.0
101	1989–90	134	51.0	162	61.0

Note: Power Committees are Appropriations, House Administration, Rules, Ways and Means, plus Budget, added in 94th Congress.
Sources: Ornstein, Mann, and Malbin 1989, Loomis 1988, *Congressional Directory* 1989[4]

appear in both categories, but manifestly *every member* of the House majority can count him- or herself one of the leadership.

In addition to congressional leadership, there is party leadership to consider. Loomis, who is a political scientist and a former congressional intern in the House, points out that Democratic Party leadership positions in that body expanded along with everything else after the arrival of the Watergate class.[5] In the Ninety-second Congress the House majority leadership consisted of the Speaker, the floor leader, the whip, the chairman of the Democratic Caucus, and twenty-one deputy and zone whips.

The same officers were in place in the 100th Congress—except that the number of deputy and zone whips had grown from twenty-one to eighty. Moreover, in addition to the Democratic Caucus a new Democratic Steering and Policy Committee had been established with thirty-one places for other leaders.

Twenty-two people made up the party's House leadership in 1971–72. In 1987–88 98 people filled 114 leadership roles. The party of Jefferson, for whom that government was best which governed least, may itself be governed not wisely but too well.

WHEN EVERYBODY'S A LEADER

Since when everyone leads there is no leader, this makes no sense whatever as an organizing principle. But in the post-Watergate Congress, no imperative is stronger than reelection. For reelection purposes, being able to claim a leadership role is the very essence of sense. It provides staff help as well as the public relations advantage of being able to flaunt the trappings of leadership, in addition to all the other assets of incumbency.

Table 13.4
House and Senate Office Staff per Member, 1947–87

Cong.	Year	House Total	Average Member	Senate Total	Average Member
80	1947	1,440	3.5	590	6.1
85	1957	2,441	5.6	1,115	11.6
90	1967	4,055	9.3	1,749	17.5
95	1977	6,942	15.9	3,554	35.5
100	1987	7,584	17.4	4,075	40.8

Source: Ornstein, Mann, and Malbin 1989, 132, Table 5-2.

The staff assistance available is very great indeed. First there is the member's own staff in his or her congressional office. In the House of the 100th Congress this averaged seventeen people; in the Senate, nearly forty-one (see Table 13.4). Numbers never retreat in congressional affairs, but in the case of office help a really massive surge in growth came in the Watergate babies' second term (Ninety-fifth Congress).

Nearly all House offices have an administrative assistant, one or two legislative assistants, a press secretary (though not all are named that candidly, for example, communications director), a personal secretary, a receptionist, and in most cases a computer specialist or "systems manager." Senate press secretaries generally have an aide or two of their own.

But that is not all. Back home in the district, the average congressman has a *district* office staff of nearly seven people; for senators in their state offices, the number is twelve, in both cases usually including caseworkers for constituent problems.

Members of either chamber who chair committees or subcommittees have a substantial claim on committee staff people for information, research, and general assistance. In the 100th Congress, House committee staff employees exceeded 2,000 and in the Senate twice as many. There is more. The support agencies of Congress cheerfully root out answers to the most difficult questions. One of these is a major resource for reference assistance, the Congressional Research Service (CRS) of the Library of Congress.

The enormous Government Accounting Office (GAO) does for numbers what the CRS does for general, social, political, and historical research. Other support agencies are the Office of Technology Assessment and the Congressional Budget Office. All of these bodies employ more than 6,200 people whose career is seeing that no congressman's or senator's question goes unanswered (Ornstein, Mann, and Malbin 1989, 132–39).

The Costs of Congressional Perks

It may seem that all this service costs money. Including the congressman's own salary of $125,000 (1991), the office of each House member is a substantial small business that, embracing salaries, fringe benefits, travel, and other covered expenses, but *excluding* postage, rents, and the value of CRS and other services, sets the taxpayers back by $922,000 per member per year (Ornstein, Mann, and Malbin 1989, 144). Telephone service including WATS lines, equipment, and maintenance, are "free"—that is, too difficult to apportion to each member, but not free to the taxpayer, whom they cost an aggregate far in excess of a half-billion dollars. Similarly "free" is travel service, radio-TV studio facilities, and live television coverage from the floor via C-SPAN—plus the "increasing professionalism and technological sophistication of legislators' offices," as Loomis puts it (1988, 139). In 1986 every senator but two and every representative but thirty-five used "computer systems of one kind or another, which cost [the taxpayer] more than $30 million annually to operate" (Loomis 1988, 139).

In the first year of the 100th Congress, its members used their franking privilege on 91,423,000 pieces of mail at a total cost to the taxpayer of approximately $495 million. In an election year volume rises sharply, and the cost can double.

All this helps explain the size of one year's legislative appropriation, which in 1988 exceeded $1.745 billion. Twenty years earlier, a decade before the Watergate class, the cost, *adjusted for inflation*, was about $95 million in 1988 dollars, or about 5 percent of 1988's cost (Loomis 1988; Ornstein, Mann, and Malbin 1989).

One of the congressional incumbent's advantages at campaign time may be more impressive than the others, although it is less visible and more difficult to measure. This is staff assistance in campaigning. Incumbents and staff people alike are reluctant to answer such questions. Ostensibly, and by law, congressional staff people do not campaign for their bosses. Most members profess to observe the formalities. Some do. Burdett Loomis quotes another political scientist's interview with an expert who was willing to speak "only on condition of anonymity," as contemporary journalists put it so often:

One California congressman's field representative flatly observed, "I'm never through campaigning—except for one evening every two years. Election night there's no campaign. We have a victory party, I drink a lot of champagne, and I go home and go to bed. Next morning I begin campaigning all over again." (Loomis 1988, 187)[6]

Congress has consistently exempted itself from employee relations regulations that it has imposed on the private sector and on the public sector outside the legislative branch. There are no unions to contend with, no overtime pay, and no maximum hours. Minimum-wage laws do not apply; there are no anti-discrimination regulations and no inhibitions to hiring and firing at will.[7] A congressman may stretch the budget as far as imagination allows and pay workers as little as eager applicants will accept.

Staff Jobs in Demand

Working for a congressman or, perhaps even better, a senator, is a perfect entry-level job for intelligent and ambitious young people seeking a career in government or public affairs. Congressional internships for bright students of law, political science, and public administration do not go begging. A few years spent at a visible legislator's right hand is widely and realistically viewed as a passport to advancement in other reaches of government as well as lobbying and the news media. For future careers in the law, public affairs, advocacy of consumer and special interests, there is no better foundation.

Still another advantage of incumbency is that the articulate, informed, accessible, and responsive member of Congress finds a ready forum in the news media. This is true for any member in the news outlets in the home district—to which reports, statements, and interviews may be sent by computer modem, fax, wire, or satellite direct from congressional studios. But for the incumbent with particular flair and an adept press secretary the job gives access to the really choice media—the national news and opinion elite: the reporters and columnists and op-ed pages of the *New York Times, Washington Post, Wall Street Journal, Los Angeles Times,* and the top public affairs programs of broadcast and cable television as well as radio.

Senate careers, governorships, and presidential candidacies are forged at this hearth, as are funding sources for future congressional campaigns. The widely recognized symbiotic relationship between reporters and politicians makes these exchanges mutually beneficial. Journalists need sources for stories—and for leads, leaks, confirmation or denial. Officeholders need the news media to preserve their incumbency.

Hardly ever does the challenger to an incumbent enjoy such a relationship with journalists, or even an opportunity to develop one. And the millions of dollars' worth of staff, equipment, research, and all the other services that fall to the incumbent as though by divine right must be bought by, or for, the challenger.

When the Watergate scandal led to the creation of the Federal Election Commission (FEC), which in turn ushered in the Political Action Committee as a new source for funding election campaigns, there was a fleeting apprehension among Democrats that, while they could count on labor and liberal "fat cats" to fund them, the really big money from corporate America would continue to flow to Republicans—as it had done since the days of Mark Hanna and before.

But whatever the personal preferences of bankers, industrialists, and other capitalists, the corporate PACs immediately discovered that access to the post-Watergate incumbent was not colored by partisan considerations. They found that a grateful yuppie Democrat was as accessible as his or her

Republican counterpart, and the money immediately flowed where the congressional votes were.

Every Cure a New Disease

In the apt phrase of Richard L. Berke in the *New York Times,* "Watergate reforms brought changes like public financing for presidential campaigns and limits on the amount an individual can give to a Congressional campaign.

"But every cure has become a new disease" ("An Edge for Incumbents: Loopholes That Pay Off," 1990).

Even for the devoted partisan fat cat with a PAC and a special-interest axe to grind, it proved both cheaper and more efficient to support incumbents than to spend large sums on the questionable prospect of ousting an incumbent for replacement by a challenger. In the new economics—political and corporate—incumbency was the thing.

Rich and regular financing by PACs has conditioned incumbents—give or take the occasional maverick—to pay careful attention to the concerns of the PACs. This has ceded to the corporate and other special-interest groups that create and fund the PACs a significant amount of control over the national agenda of the Congress of the United States.

Unseating an incumbent is an extremely costly venture and by no means assured of success, but it does work often enough to give pause to most incumbents. Success stories claimed, and indeed bragged of, by the lobbies of farmers, realtors, environmentalists, gun owners, advocates of handgun control, the homeless, civil rights, or secular protection from encroachments by religion and by foreign policy interests such as AIPAC make the agendas of such groups those of the Congress.

THE PROSPECT OF TERM LIMITATION

These events and discoveries, among others, have led to consideration of limiting congressional terms. The subject is crusted with irony. Its firmest supporters include many Republicans who see it as the only hope for vitiating Democratic control of both houses. A constitutional amendment limiting terms would return to Congress the gift it bestowed on the presidency with the Twenty-second Amendment. Its key provision is its first phrase: "No person shall be elected to the office of the President more than twice."

Franklin D. Roosevelt had been dead less than twenty-one months when the Eightieth Congress convened on January 3, 1947. This was the first Congress the Republicans had managed to control since the Seventy-second, which went out with Hoover in 1933. Immediately, the Eightieth thumbed its nose at FDR, who had died early in his fourth term. Wrapping themselves in the mantle of George Washington's refusal of a third term, so as to disguise any semblance of partisan rancor, the GOP leadership shepherded the joint resolution proposing the amendment through the House by February 6 and the Senate by March 12; the House accepted Senate amendments nine days later—a done deal in sixty days. It was ratified by February 1951—four years later. Only once since (as of 1991) have the Republicans controlled both House and Senate, in the Eighty-third Congress of 1953–55, and then thanks to the Eisenhower landslide of 1952.

Congressional incumbents, with a few exceptions, are extremely cool to the idea. Being invincible in all but the most extraordinary circumstances, they come to savor the power and attention; and even though their salaries are modest not lavish, their expenses are adequately met, and their retirement benefits beggar those of the private sector. After a few terms in Congress it is possible to retire on a pension larger than the member's actual salary.

Nevertheless, a considerable constituency has developed for a constitutional amendment to restrict congressional tenure to twelve years in both House and Senate, and in fact in the late 1980s an organization materialized to advance the idea—finding most of its support from Republicans out of office. Arguments for such an amendment are obvious in the extravagant incumbent advantages discussed above. A major argument against the notion is that it would greatly strengthen the existing congressional bureaucracy, which, as we have seen, outnumbers members of Congress by more than ten to one, and which already enjoys enormous power.

The unelected Congress, in the person of its administrative and legislative assistants (AAs and LAs), and especially its key committee staff people, already exert profound and often decisive influence on legislators, who may be preoccupied with thoughts about the next campaign. No matter how invincible congressmen may be, they all worry about the next election.

Two-Term Limit?

However, the proposed scheme of twelve-year limits on both House and Senate is a classic example of mindless egalitarianism. It completely ignores the distinction the Founding Fathers so carefully built into the Constitution, elaborated at the beginning of this chapter, of using the House as an instant messenger to the whole Congress to convey approval or disapproval of the state of the nation.

If an amendment is to be adopted—surely a debatable proposition but well worth debating—it would make much more sense to adopt a two-*term* limit for House and Senate, retaining the shorter term for the House of Representatives and making its entire membership vulnerable to voter displeasure.

It has been suggested that the states are empowered by Article I, Section

4 of the Constitution (in Clause 1) to regulate elections to Congress in such a manner that House terms would be effectively limited, an interesting idea that surely merits study.[8]

What makes the PAC and its money essential to the congressional incumbent is that it evades the restrictions the FEC imposes on individual contributions. And invincible or not, the incumbent who does not mount a competitive campaign squanders his advantage and will be quickly snowed under by a well-financed and aggressive challenger.

"Strong challenges do not emerge randomly; their occurrence varies with the prospects of victory." This observation by a political scientist, Gary C. Jacobson, predicts an aggressive campaign by a strong and well-financed challenger to any incumbent not ready to campaign vigorously to reap the benefits of incumbency ("Strategic Politicians and the Dynamics of U.S. House Elections 1946–86," 1989).

A principal reason why PACs are biased in favor of the incumbent is that the status quo works, protects the interests of the PAC, and supplies the needed access to the legislative process and influence on its agenda. It works because the congressional seat—given all its panoply of benefits—is exceedingly valuable to the occupant. This value immediately vanishes if the incumbent knows that in any case he or she will be out of office in four years (or possible two). Such a seat will be sought by candidates willing to disrupt personal life for a few years as a matter of civic responsibility, but not seeking a new, permanent career—precisely as the Founders intended.

Devaluing the Seat

Devaluing the seat would appear to be an effective approach to curbing the power and changing the nature of PACs as they exist. Whether an amendment should permanently bar running again at a later date is another question. It is one the Founders examined when they reflected on their brief experience with a three-years-out-of-six stipulation in the last years of the Continental Congress.

The countervailing argument, that debarring experienced congressmen from further service deprives the public of wisdom and judgment, is appealing. This would have been an impressive argument in the early years of the republic. Early congressmen were, in the main, an impressive lot. I examined the turnover and tenure of the first twenty Congresses and discovered that in every one of the first several Congresses a number of the members elected to the House would resign to take a judgeship, because of election to the Senate or as governor, or because of appointment to some Cabinet or diplomatic post. Turnover was almost constant.

Moreover, there was substantial and evidently bitter competition for House seats. Hardly one of the early Congresses did not see a contested election, with the frequent result of ousting the man who had already been seated. Sometimes a single seat would turn over two or three times in the two-year span of a Congress. But, as reflected in Table 13.1, there was not much precedent for extremely long tenure.

For all the talk here and elsewhere about congressional invincibility, the new Achilles does have a vulnerable tendon. As many illustrations in previous chapters make clear, if money is piled high enough and zeal burns hot enough, almost any king of Capitol Hill can be brought to earth. And great scandals or sea changes in public attitudes still have the potential to usher in massive changes in the composition of the House. But relatively ordinary comings and goings of popular discontent that the House was designed to reflect (and the Senate to be insulated against) are another matter. Between 1874 and 1954, forty Congresses were elected, and thirteen times party control was reversed in the House. But it hasn't happened since (as of 1991).

An electorate knowing that a change must be made will consider alternatives; an electorate knowing that going out to vote against an invincible incumbent will not defeat him or her has no such motivation. The sorry prospect of more of the same no matter what one does gives life to the old joke of the political pollster:

Q: Which do you think does the greater damage to American politics: ignorance, or apathy?

A: I don't know, and I don't care.[9]

14

Media Power and the Perception of Politics

For the populace at large, once out of school, the only source of day-to-day knowledge about politics, politicians, and political mischief is the news media.

American journalism's address to government and politics has gone through some remarkably different stages. Its roots were ardently and often rabidly partisan. Its vocabulary has ranged from gutter to pulpit. At various times it has been the perpetrator, and not just the reporter, of smears and slanders. Its attitudes toward presidents and other leaders, ebbing and flowing with partisan tides, have varied from contemptuous hostility to worshipful attention to the adversarial relationship with politicians and with government itself that any modern observer will recognize.

DEVELOPMENT OF JOURNALISTIC STANDARDS

For all the polemics of the early days, gradually a concern for accuracy arose among nineteenth-century reporters, stimulated in part by the demands of reporting the Civil War. Later in the century a new concern emerged: objectivity—reporting without letting the reporter's biases interfere.

The Associated Press (AP), the first American press association, or wire service, contributed to the adoption of objectivity as a standard. It was founded as a cooperative of several newspapers in 1848 to enable member papers to get dependable reports from other cities without having to station reporters there. As its number of subscribers grew, so did the range of their editorial and political views. AP had to supply accurate and acceptable copy to editors and publishers whose political outlooks were virtually at war with one another, so polemics and partisan bias had to be avoided.

Individual papers continued to use their own correspondents where they had them, or wherever the publisher's economic or political interests required one. Objective reporting from "the wires" coexisted with often biased and sometimes virulently biased reporting for many decades—which still persists here and there. But many of the leading newspapers and the better reporters were already pursuing objectivity on their own.

Soon the rush of new technology, scientific knowledge, and economic theory made much of what journalism had to cover incomprehensible to its readers, and its reporters. The better papers began to hire reporters with new levels of education and training. "The Front Page" was overtaken by the knowledge explosion.

The New Media: Radio and Television

Pittsburgh's pioneering radio station KDKA opened the era of broadcast political coverage in 1920 by transmitting Harding's election-eve speech and the next night reporting the returns that elected Ohio's Senator Harding over Ohio's Governor Cox. KDKA's tiny audience consisted of experimentally minded tinkerers listening through earphones.

Even then, primitive as it was, radio news of political events brought a sense of immediacy to the listener, which grew as the medium advanced rapidly through the next three decades. And radio gave a substantial advantage to political speakers who knew, intuitively or by training, how to use it effectively. The first major beneficiary of this fact was Franklin D. Roosevelt, who set a standard for radio rhetoric that was not eclipsed before television took over.

But for all radio's immediacy, listeners had to imagine the scene or news event being described. Not so with television. Very early in the TV era Marshall McLuhan called it the cool medium because it freed the viewer from the need to do anything but sit and watch.

McLuhan also quickly saw that modern communication, symbolized by television, was creating the Global Village. This first came true in U.S. politics as television news began to preempt the authority of the older news media, newspapers as well as radio. Network TV news created a national political audience. Kennedy was the first major American politician to use the new medium effectively. He was Roosevelt's heir in this respect, and his instant ease with it was unmatched until Reagan.

Presidents and the Press

For lengthy intervals during the century between the presidencies of Andrew Johnson and Lyndon Johnson, the attitude of reporters toward presidents was serious and attentive, although mere candidates were fair game. The authority and privacy of the president himself were almost uniformly respected. President Cleveland was insistent about his personal privacy; he also was the first to come under some regular scrutiny by the press. By the end of his second administration in 1897, reporters had begun watching the White House to spot and interview presidential visitors as they were leaving.

Even so, Cleveland was able to command privacy thoroughly enough to completely hide his secret cancer surgery aboard a friend's yacht in the summer of 1893. Surgeons cut away his cancerous left upper jaw, he recuperated for a few days, and the yacht landed the president at his summer retreat on Buzzards Bay. A week later a prosthesis was fitted, and nobody knew. It is inconceivable that such secrecy about a major health problem could be maintained by any modern president.

Teddy Roosevelt set up a press room in the White House. He was a public relations natural before the term was coined. His youth, vitality, and candor were admired and enjoyed by reporters, and this affection outlasted his presidential tenure. During his campaigning for William Howard Taft in 1908, a biographer notes that heroic stories of Roosevelt's labors for Taft were spread by "the faithful worshipers who adored him" and promptly "were published by similarly adoring newspaper correspondents" (Pringle 1939, 1:359).

Within a few years press agents began to take root in various Washington agencies, including the White House. Wilson established press conferences on a regular basis. Harding continued them and coined the term "White House spokesman," to which reporters were to attribute statements he read to them. This practice of not quoting the president directly became the norm for a generation.

Hoover engaged a press secretary to serve as a continuing liaison with the journalists. The advent of *Time* in the early 1920s, and network radio at about the same time, expanded both reporting about government and the Washington press establishment itself. In the heady early days of the New Deal, Franklin D. Roosevelt held two press conferences a week, but as World War II approached the frequency was cut to weekly.

Dwight Eisenhower was greatly aided by an extremely competent and reliable press secretary—really the first star in the job, James C. Hagerty. By this time candor had advanced substantially in the administration as well as the news media, and for the first time complete medical information about a president's health crisis, Eisenhower's heart attack, was immediately given out.

The combination of John F. Kennedy's youth, charm, and sophistication enabled him to convert most of the press corps into a sort of guerrilla PR force. He was the first president since Theodore Roosevelt to win so devoted a following. He was confident and quick enough on his feet to initiate live televised press conferences—a boon for the media but scarcely for his immediate successors.

Although Lyndon Johnson tried to manipulate the media as he did everyone else, his personality and vanity got in the way. Erik Barnouw, in *Tube of Plenty*, relates LBJ's challenge to one reporter who asked him an awkward question: "Why do you ask me, the leader of the Western world, a chicken-shit question like that?" (Barnouw 1975, 387–88). Highly proficient press secretaries, and he had several, could not save him from himself at such moments.

The presidential press secretariat had so swollen by then that under Richard Nixon it was a sizable department first headed by a longtime aide and veteran journalist, Herbert G. Klein, as director of communications. The press secretary role went to a low-level flack who had been a PR person for Disneyland, Ron Ziegler—who took his orders not from Klein but from his former ad agency boss, H. R. Haldeman, Nixon's chief of staff.

Ziegler parcelled out information exactly as he was ordered, and as reporters discovered that what they were getting was often false, the Watergate fictions poisoned the White House well for the Washington press corps. Ford, candid by nature, held press conferences about every six weeks, but the media mistrusted him because of the office and in spite of his known personal honesty and that of his press secretary, a veteran journalist, Jerry ter Horst.

The presidency of Ronald Reagan demonstrated that a president can control his own access to the press, and especially the broadcast media, without the transparent manipulativeness of Johnson or the deviousness of Nixon. But the slick effectiveness of the trained actor as president did nothing to win the trust and affection of the Washington media, whose heart had belonged only to Teddy Roosevelt and Jack Kennedy. It may be that the relation of president to press has been institutionalized—and poisoned—in such a way that the old norms and forms will no longer work.

CRITICAL CHANGES IN ATTITUDE

Apart from unabashedly radical or reactionary pamphleteers and other polemicists, journalists through much of U.S. history have treated government and political leaders with respect and not infrequently with deference. They were participants in the status quo and, knowingly or not, its defenders. Political reporters came to enjoy some prominence and prosperity as the American press outgrew its rowdy and wholly partisan origins.

This situation began the first of several very substantial changes in the aftermath of World War I. Michael Schudson, among many others, offers an explanation:

Journalists, like others, lost faith in verities a democratic market society had taken for granted. Their experience of propaganda during the war and public relations thereafter convinced them that the world they reported was one that interested parties had constructed for them to report. In such a world, naive empiricism could not last. (Schudson 1978, 6)

Here naive empiricism means accepting an objective recital of what the reporter saw, without interpretation. It is noteworthy that this statement could be paraphrased to account for the attitude changes—later versions of the same attitude change, really—that resulted from both Vietnam and Watergate, which are addressed below.

Some thirty years after World War I another wave of disillusionment hit the American news media. It was another major spur to a growing demand for interpretative reporting to supplement and explain beyond merely getting the facts straight.

The Effects of McCarthyism

Although the substance of the brief and turbulent era of McCarthyism is treated in Chapter 9, we are concerned here with its effect on the news media. From the moment in 1949 when Wisconsin Senator Joseph R. McCarthy claimed he had a list of 205 Communists that had infiltrated the State Department, he commanded media attention wherever he went.

Except for a reactionary minority (and many of them were cynical about McCarthy, too), most political reporters sensed that his figures were out of thin air and noticed that he never produced credible evidence. However, the sanctity of reportorial objectivity forced them to report what this increasingly important and notorious senator proclaimed.

In a later book, Douglass Cater, Washington editor of the *Reporter* magazine throughout the McCarthy era, quoted one of the senator's favorite targets, Truman's Secretary of State Dean Acheson. Addressing the American Society of Newspaper Editors, Acheson said, "I and my associates are only the intended victims of this mad and vicious operation. But you, unhappily, by reason of your calling, are participants. And your position is far more serious than mine" (Cater 1959).

Acheson's charge to the editors was true, and print and broadcast journalists realized it bitterly. Many of them have written pensively about it then and later. James Russell Wiggins, then executive editor of the *Washington Post*, acknowledged shortly after the censure vote that the press (here also embracing the broadcast media) had given McCarthy not only his platform and his power but also his ultimate defeat. "The press made him," he said, "but it's the press that brought him down" (Conversation with the author in 1956). With McCarthy's defeat, objectivity died as a sine qua non for journalism, and interpretative reporting emerged as the standard.

For the first time in so major and complicated a political crisis, television played a significant role in the exposure of McCarthy, particularly in long-format special programming, which is the only way commercial TV can provide interpretative reporting. Edward R. Murrow presented an hour-long documentary on his CBS News program "See It Now" that demonstrated in America's homes McCarthy's deceptions, distortions, evasions, and his sneering bullying of witnesses.

This experience engaged the uncommitted in a growing national backlash against the Wisconsin demagog. Televised hearings of a fight McCarthy picked with the army (and finally lost) went on for thirty-six days in 1954. They showed McCarthy in live action, not in carefully selected and edited film clips, and their effect was devastating. As Wiggins said, it brought him down.

Effects of the Vietnam War

By the time the small war in Vietnam grew big enough to notice, it was a nightly fixture on the evening news. The earliest U.S. involvement, including some fateful manipulations, began under President Eisenhower. John Kennedy took over and turned up the voltage considerably. But after Kennedy's murder it became Lyndon Johnson's war.

Up to this time, and for a year or two of the Johnson presidency, there had been little television coverage of the war. Erik Barnouw in his history of television demonstrates that network television was long a force for conformity with the view of Vietnam shared by the Johnson administration, the U.S. political establishment generally, and the military-industrial complex. He also observes that "No President before Lyndon Johnson had worked so hard to cajole, control, and neutralize the news media" (1975, 387).

International news coverage—coupled with highly effective propaganda by North Vietnam and its allies, and its U.S. supporters and growing numbers of other anti-war Americans—helped escalate U.S. interest, and with it news coverage. Vietnam became the first Living Room War. Now far from a force for conformity, television news helped bring down the administration.

(It was in a sense a dress rehearsal for what it would do to more malevolent powers in Eastern Europe twenty years later, in a new fulfillment of Marshall McLuhan's vision of the Global Village. The dazzling disintegration of Stalin's empire demonstrated what McLuhan knew very well: the impossibility of excluding disruptive truth when every household has a radio receiver and every person has some access to television.)

Leaving apart any questions of the validity of this view, for millions of U.S. citizens believed the war was justified, most journalists, like a very large plurality of other Americans, came to see in the Vietnam experience a bad war dishonestly mounted. Although no war has been fought without censorship and deception, the Vietnam conflict left most Americans convinced that its prosecution relied on a tissue of deliberate deceptions of the U.S. public by the whole administration of Lyndon Johnson and then Richard Nixon.

The resulting popular mistrust of government augmented the bitter aftertaste of the youth revolt and the civil rights revolution of the 1960s. The whole added up to mass cynicism in the American citizenry and pushed journalists hard in the direction of the adversarial stance toward government, regardless of party, that became the rule, and the new norm.

MEDIA INFLUENCE ON THE ELECTORATE

For practical purposes, the sources of news accessible to the general U.S. public are quite limited. The circulation gains of the most successful newspapers lag far behind population growth. Combined news magazine circulation amounts to about 3.2 percent of the population. With the exception of the Cable News Network and C-SPAN, no combination of television networks and local outlets devotes more than a few hours a day—counting actual newscasts and morning and evening shows that are news- and feature-oriented, such as NBC's "Today" and ABC's "Nightline." And yet, as will be seen below, it is network and local TV news coverage that informs the majority of Americans.

The Influence of the Media Elite

Although some of its members deny it, there is an elite of political journalists that profoundly influences the news of government and politics as it is received by most of the U.S. population. These are the most influential columnists, commentators, anchormen and women, editors and editorial writers, television news producers, and reporters of America's most prestigious newspapers, magazines of news and opinion, and major television networks.

Except for the on-camera television personalities, most of this elite would not be recognized in person by more than a handful of the people whose lives, or at least whose perception and understanding of the world, its members do so much to shape. The bylines of the print journalists of this select group are household words—but only in that minority of households where newspapers and opinion magazines are read and interest in public affairs is substantial.

However their importance goes far beyond the numbers of their readers, for the journalists of this elite regularly or very frequently see and are influenced by one another's work. There is a validating element in concerted attention to a particular story by the "heavy hitters" of the press corps. In continuing stories, the print media thus exert a strong influence on television news decisions about what to cover.

Timothy Crouse in *The Boys on the Bus* (1973) described (hilariously) the ways in which correspondents influenced each other on the 1972 campaign trail. Fifteen years later David Broder cautioned that the pack journalism Crouse sent up has changed somewhat, in good part because of the steady increase of television coverage of the critical phase of campaigns (Broder 1987). In video journalism each reporter is accompanied by technicians and a large impedimenta of sound and camera equipment. It is something like sending the whole Boy Scout troop to help the old lady across the street.

But the mutual influence reporters have on one another that Crouse (and many others) noted is real and does continue. Robert L. Denton and Gary C. Woodward observe that the influence of the most prestigious media is especially strong: "For this reason it is dangerous to underestimate the importance of the print media—especially the so-called 'prestige press' (*The New York Times, Washington Post, Newsweek, The Wall Street Journal*), and the smaller national political journals" (Denton and Woodward 1985, 169).

By virtue of their readership within the media elite, the impact of these prestigious publications is far out of proportion to their actual circulation. The *New York Times* and *Washington Post* together have a little less than the *Wall Street Journal's* circulation, which is 2 million. The circulation of the largest of the high-prestige magazines ranges from the *New Yorker's* 594,000 to the *Washington Monthly's* less than 50,000, with *Atlantic, Harper's, Mother Jones, National Review, New Republic* and *Progressive*, in that order, in between but all on the low end. Their combined circulation is only about 1.6 million.

The circulations of the three most influential newspapers and the eight prestige magazines aggregate a million less than *Time* magazine alone. It and its rivals *Newsweek* and *U.S. News & World Report* sell about 8 million copies combined. There is an enormous overlap of all these publications among their readers, but the grand total of their combined circulations is less than 4 percent of the U.S. population.

It is difficult to imagine an influential journalist in any medium who does not read or scan several, perhaps five or six or more of these papers and journals routinely—although the news magazines are more checklists than primary resources for the political press corps.

These lists omit several even smaller journals of political thought and opinion, which also have influence out of all proportion to their tiny circulations. In addition, most of the media elite follow television political and public affairs special programming as events and their interests dictate.

The Dominance of Television. But even the news magazines reach only a minor fraction (about one-thirty-eighth) of the U.S. electorate with news and opinion about politics. Television dominates the field. For thirty years to 1989 the Roper Organization conducted surveys for the Television Information Office (TIO) tracking people's primary sources of news. Newspapers started with a 6-point lead, but since 1963 TV has dominated the field (see Table 14.1). In 1988, 65 percent of respondents said television was their primary source versus 42 percent for newspapers.

Table 14.1
Primary News Sources in Percent by Year

	1959	1963	1968	1976	1988
Newspapers	58	54	50	49	42
Television	52	54	60	64	65
Radio	34	30	26	20	14
Magazines	8	7	8	7	4

Source: National Association of Broadcasters; some respondents named 2 or more media.

Respondents in the 1988 survey found TV nearly twice as credible as newspapers (49 percent to 26 percent, with radio at 7 percent and magazines at 5 percent). Only for information about local candidates did people rely more on newspapers than on TV (40 percent to 36 percent). To find out about state and national candidates respondents went right back to relying on the tube over print: U.S. House, 42 percent to 34 percent; governors and senators, 50 percent to 31 percent; and president and vice president, 70 percent to 20 percent.

In 1988 presidential campaign coverage, respondents saw TV news as generally fair to both Bush (54 percent) and Dukakis (54 percent). Was either candidate treated unfairly by television news? Dukakis 23 percent and Bush 13 percent. Was either favored? Bush 21 percent and Dukakis 9 percent.

The key question of the Roper interviewers asked respondents from which sources "you get most of your news about what's going on in the world today—from the newspapers or radio or television or magazines or talking to people or where?" A similar query in election year surveys since the 1950s conducted by the Survey Research Center brought similar answers. It is a devastating rejoinder to those who, believing that print can inform more reliably and effectively, rely on the print media to make up for the deficiencies of television news.

The News Hole

Modern print journalism places a premium on skillful writing—writing that informs, is easy to read, and that will keep the reader following the story through the "news hole." The news hole is a faintly cynical expression in the newspaper business meaning the proportion of each edition that is available to news and features and anything but advertising and comics, TV schedules, editorial and op-ed pages, etc. Proportions vary from paper to paper, but in a thriving metropolitan daily on a day with no special advertising sections the news hole may account for some 45 percent of total space. On heavy ad days it is a great deal less. This should not alarm the critic. News is the name of the game, but ads pay the piper. What goes into the news hole, as rather tartly put in the title of a book by a former *New York Times* editor, is *All the News That Fits* (Dinsmore 1969).

Though the term is less common, television has a news hole, too. Network-affiliated stations typically supply a two-hour morning show, which includes newscasts and often extensive special news coverage including sports and cultural topics. There is an obligatory half-hour (or hour) of network evening news, plus up to four or five hours weekly of special news programming.[1]

Many of the major figures in television news are dismayed that so many Americans depend on their medium for *all* their news. A thirty-minute national news show on a commercial network may deliver about twenty-five minutes of news, read at a speed no greater than about 150 words per minute. This means a theoretical maximum of 3,750 words even if read without a pause. That is, the entire text of a half-hour television news program would occupy less than a single inside page (where headlines are smaller than on page 1) in a full-size newspaper.

In *The People Machine*, Robert MacNeil addressed the same point.

Richard Salant [then president of CBS News] once had the text of a typical [Walter] Cronkite show set in type and dropped into the front page of the *New York Times*. It occupied barely six of the eight columns. On a sample week studied for this book, the three networks' programs each averaged a few hundred words more than the front pages of the *New York Times* and the *Washington Post*.[2] What the television viewer is getting essentially is a headline service. (MacNeil 1968)

What's more, as competition from TV and from TV-style newspapers like *U.S.A. Today* intensifies, standard newspapers devote more and more space to photographs—both more pictures and bigger pictures.

The Warp of Brevity. Moreover, the need for brevity rules out complete coverage of campaign news. Thomas W. Benson, professor of Speech Communication at Pennsylvania State University, referring to a TV newsman's complaint that candidates fragment real issues, comments that

political speeches are *reported* as fragments. One seldom hears, in television news reports of campaigns, anything like a whole argument. Instead, one hears a report of a promise, a slogan, or an accusation ... or as brief appeals to views or interests of voters (as when a candidate is shown defending social security in a retirement community).

Blaming Candidates for Media Sins

Benson goes on to analyze another familiar warp that video reporting introduces.

Television news formulas constrain correspondents to describe campaign rhetoric as a series of disjointed and dubiously motivated fragments, and then to complain about fragmentation and motivation. This fragmentation and reduction are more than mere gatekeeping:[3] the reshaping of candidates' talk through the dramatic fictions of television news change our political information and the context within which we can come to understand it. We do not simply hear a *part* of the objective world....

Reporters' continual references to hidden motivations bear a similar relation to television film's inability to record what the reporter thinks we ought to know.... The reporter tells us that what we have seen and heard did happen ... but that it is not the truth.... [W]hat might be reported as "we are not showing you the whole truth" becomes "they are not telling you the truth." (Benson 1983, 112)

Doctoring Spin. There are other illustrations of this phenomenon of the media criticizing the candidate for the sins of the media. Reporters are highly critical of campaign staff people functioning as "spin doctors" after a debate between candidates, collaring influential TV and print journalists immediately after the confrontation to assert confidently that their candidate clearly won and supplying what they hope are persuasive reasons. Yet campaign organizations began this practice to defend their candidates against what they saw as cynical, hypercritical, and unsupported assertions by journalists—instant assessments written in the minutes after the debate for tomorrow morning's paper or the network's post-debate special or morning news. The spin doctor was invented to undo the damage done by reporters in putting a tricky spin on a debate story in the first place.

William Adams cited the *Washington Post's* outstanding coverage *of* campaign coverage in the 1980 election. The paper ran two series of pungent critiques of spin in the overnight analysis of confrontations at the conventions and later in the campaign, by Tom Shales and Robert Kaiser, respectively. One of Kaiser's pieces dealt with the instant analyses of the sole Carter-Reagan debate of the campaign at the end of October. He observed dryly and accurately, "On the basis of our scant national experience with this art form [the presidential debate], instant analysis of it is usually worthless" (Adams 1983, 5).

Sound Bites and Photo Ops: Origins. Journalists also are sharp critics of campaign use of the "photo opportunities" campaign managers carefully stage to create a scene that will be irresistible to TV news producers and newspaper photo editors, and the crafting of punchy "sound bites" that will be fresh and sharp enough to guarantee that the media will use them. Yet both practices are as defensive as the spin doctor. News producers and newspaper photo editors inevitably pounce on any embarrassing or unflattering audio flubs, video shots, or still photos of candidates that may add spice to their coverage.

Denton and Woodward note that the antics of Billy Carter during his brother's 1980 campaign for reelection attracted enough media attention and coverage to generate reporters' questions of President Carter that he was obliged to answer even though they were wholly irrelevant to Jimmy Carter's conduct of the presidency. The fact is that Billy's buffoonery was a recurring sound-bite-*cum*-photo-op that the media discovered, nursed, and kept in reserve for whenever things were dull; it also had the added benefit, for the government-bashing media, of being potentially embarrassing and actively denigrating for the president (Denton and Woodward 1985).

In self-defense, the campaign organizations began prefabricating any dramatic and favorable camera setups their public relations people could dream up. Similarly the sound bite: limit access to the candidate on the campaign trail and provide a good, pungent comment that will make the news on its own with minimal danger of some open-microphone gaffe.

TV as Augmenting Print Coverage. If the brevity of its news reports makes television an inadequate sole source for all of a voter's news of politics, it nevertheless can add an extremely useful dimension to coverage by the print media. The political scientists Michael J. Robinson and Margaret Sheehan point out that "Old-style print and new-style video do provide meaningfully different versions of the same campaign—even of the same event.... [T]elevision is more *reactive*, more *thematic*, more *personal*, more *political*, more *critical*, more *analytical*, and more *mediating* in campaign coverage than is print news" (Robinson and Sheehan 1983, 26). This last observation, however, cannot be extended to "think pieces" in which the best print reporters analyze campaigns and issues.

As many studies have demonstrated, the most politically interested and informed television watchers also read newspapers. But the least informed and least interested do not. However, it is precisely the *least* politically interested that are the largest contributors to non-voting, the most reliant on television news, and a principal target of television advertising in the campaign. Campaign media experts recognize that the ten-second, highly symbolic spots they need to penetrate the consciousness of the uninterested citizen will not persuade and well may offend the political sophisticate. But they also recognize a need to galvanize and persuade the uninterested, as does any nonpolitical TV advertiser.

MEDIA BIASES: CONSERVATISM, LIBERALISM, SECULARISM

Most journalists believe, and argue, that they are advocates of neither left nor right. Some support for this notion can be adduced from the fact that they are sharply accused of bias by both flanks. See, for example, from the left, Todd Gitlin's *The Whole World Is Watching: Mass Media in the Making and Unmaking of the New Left* (1980), and, from the right, Edith Efron's *The News Twisters* (1971). There is an important distinction to be made, and it is often overlooked, between the political views of reporters and those of the owners of their papers, stations, and networks. In addition, whatever the merits of the bias argument in modern times, in the middle years of journalism in the United States the press, as noted earlier in this chapter, was indeed oriented toward the status quo.

Critics on the left tend to view the media as part of the apparatus of what they see as the reactionary oligarchy or conspiracy that manipulates and controls the society and maintains the status quo. To this point, Denton and Woodward (1985), cite, in addition to Gitlin, Lance Bennett's *News: The Politics of Illusion* (1983). Gitlin and others argue that whatever adversarial stance toward authority the media may believe they take, the fact is their bias does uphold the status quo and opposes voices of protest, as witness media treatment of Students for a Democratic Society (SDS) in the 1960s and its radical positions and pronouncements.

Liberalism in the Media

Considerably more criticism comes from the right. Those who see the media elite as generally liberal often identify it with a larger Washington elite of legislators, lobbyists, journalists, academics, et al. They speak of an "inside the Beltway" mentality—and crowd—that dominate social and political thought in the nation's capital. It is just this larger elite, augmented by smaller elites in America's larger cities and academic centers, that constitutes the natural audience for the pundits, largely of the press but also the news stars of television. These molders of opinion are political news junkies, who read several newspapers a day and several opinion magazines and journals weekly and monthly.

A good deal of research has been published on the political orientation of working journalists, who have generally been found to hold political views more liberal than their bosses, the owners. These studies go back to Leo Rosten (1937), who found Democrats among Washington reporters outnumbered Republicans about two to one, though most acknowledged that they trimmed their writing to accord with their publishers' opposite preferences.

Twenty-five years later, William L. Rivers, a former journalist and journalism professor, re-covered the same ground and recorded a three-to-one Democratic margin in the press corps; but only 7 percent said publishers' views influenced their reporting ("The Correspondents After 25 Years," 1962). Stephen Hess studied the field again after nearly twenty years more and, asking slightly different questions, found a 42 percent to 19 percent division between liberals and conservatives. Nearly half denied any bias in the press corps, but of the majority who did see bias 96 percent identified it as liberal (Hess 1981).

The most discussed recent research along these lines is probably *The Media Elite: America's New Power Brokers* by S. Robert Lichter, Stanley Rothman, and Linda S. Lichter (1986). It is part of a larger study on social and political leadership under the joint sponsorship of research centers at

Smith College and Columbia and George Washington universities. The media study was based on 1979–80 interviews of 238 journalists randomly selected from within the news staffs of the *New York Times*, the *Washington Post*, the *Wall Street Journal*, the three major national news magazines, the three commercial TV networks, and the Public Broadcasting System. It found a distinctly liberal cast in large majorities of the respondents and reflected their support for liberal versus conservative presidential candidates by majorities ranging from 94 percent for Johnson over Goldwater to down to 81 percent for Carter over Ford. By their own perception the respondents were liberal (54 percent, versus 17 percent conservative).

Herbert J. Gans, a professor of sociology at Columbia University and author of *Deciding What's News*, faults the Lichter-Rothman methodology on several counts, but he acknowledges that working reporters "are, on the whole, more liberal than their superiors and their colleagues in the business departments, as well as their sponsors and advertisers" (Gans 1980, 167–71).

Journalists too—including some at the top of the media elite—have sharply challenged the Lichter-Rothman study. David Broder quotes his boss, Ben Bradlee, executive editor of the *Washington Post*: "Not one of the twenty-five persons, reporters and editors, who could probably be described by anyone who knew anything about the *Washington Post* as the paper's elite, in terms of decision making and opinion making, was interviewed. And that bothers me" (Broder 1987, 328).

This is a heavy criticism indeed, and if any of the respondents at the *Post* considered themselves among the paper's elite they should worry about job security. However, the fundamental point of the Lichter-Rothman study— a 54 to 17 liberal-conservative split—closely reflects, and even understates, the comparable finding in a joint study conducted by the *Washington Post* itself with Harvard University, reported in the *Post* in 1976. The *Post*-Harvard survey found that Washington reporters divided themselves 59 to 17 on the liberal-conservative question ("Media Leaders Want Less Influence," 1976).

This is hardly implausible, given the generally liberal orientation of most American university faculties and student bodies, the universe from which most journalists now emerge. Liberalism in the academy has been remarked by scholars difficult to impeach. Richard Hofstadter in his classic defense of intellectuals and liberalism, *Anti-Intellectualism in American Life*, observes that "At least from the Progressive era onward, the political commitment of the majority of the intellectual leadership in the United States has been to causes that might be variously described as liberal (in the American use of that word), progressive, or radical" (Hofstadter 1962, 39).

Everett Carl Ladd, Jr., and Seymour Martin Lipset a decade later document this in a monograph for the American Enterprise Institute, *Academics, Politics, and the 1972 Election*, in which they review many scholarly studies of voting patterns and other political behavior in American academia. As they put it, "There is now an impressive body of empirical data demonstrating that the politics of American academics, for at least the last half century, have been disproportionately left of center" (Ladd and Lipset 1973).

Liberal orientation, however, does not mean putting a liberal spin on everything one writes. It has to do not with falsifying but with seeing, understanding, and hearing. This is not an important question with regard to opinion columns, but it is for reporting news. Professional standards are extremely important to seasoned journalists, including editors, whose responsibilities include keeping biased reporting out of the paper.

Furthermore, liberal orientation should not be confused with radicalism. Hofstadter, Ladd, Lipset, and virtually all of the scholars who have studied the question attest that the liberalism of academicians finds expression in humane and social issues and not in advocacy of revolution or overturning capitalism. Members of both the academic and the media elites are themselves capitalists, generously rewarded by the well-paid standards of only a generation earlier. Not surprisingly, the news "names" of television—commercial and public—lead this parade.

Secularism

While denying liberal political bias in the media, David Broder does concede a *secular* (that is, anti-religious) bias in the media. Referring to the Lichter-Rothman finding that half of the journalists in their sample had no religious affiliation, 8 percent attend church or synagogue weekly, and 86 percent seldom or never attended religious services, he writes, "I think that tilts our coverage."

Broder cited James M. Wall, a Methodist minister, Democratic politician, and editor of *Christian Century* magazine, who described the media bias he had perceived against religion. He quoted Wall's concern at "the implications of a religious tradition's being so out of sync with the prevailing public consciousness." Broder wrote,

But equally, I think, journalists need to consider if we are, as Wall contends, "hostile to any genuine religious witness." I am not suggesting that we must "get religion." But we certainly should not let the secularism that pervades the journalistic culture keep us from dealing intelligently and sensitively—without cynicism—with the many leaders and citizens in this nation who draw strength and motivation from their religious beliefs. (Broder 1987, 334–35)

Video Power and Limitations

Once television arrived on the scene, it did not take long to dominate political news coverage.

A curiosity in 1948, a pioneer in 1952, TV in 1956 played as big a part in 40 million U.S. homes as once the press did in bringing to people the faces, thoughts, arguments of political antagonists. The press was forced to a new level of communication. Still important, its role was nonetheless changed. It leaned more and more towards featuring "news *behind* the news" and "news you can't get on TV." ("TV and Press in Politics," 1957, p. 135)

Moreover, beyond audience domination, in every respect television seems to generate power and wealth, and this attribute troubles some of the most successful of TV journalists. Lichter, Rothman, and Lichter quote Stephen Hess to wrap up their "Group Portrait" chapter in *The Media Elite*: " 'Being described as an elite disturbs many reporters. But, of course, they are.' "

The team goes on in its own words: "Yesterday's ragtag muckrackers, who tirelessly championed the little guy against powerful insiders, have become insiders themselves. . . . But now, leading journalists are courted by politicians, studied by scholars, and known to millions through their bylines and televised images" (Lichter, Rothman, and Lichter 1986).

These media analysts are obviously embracing both print and electronic media in this portrait. But because of the enormous reach of television, the size of its audience, and the enormous sums paid its news stars, their portrait is at least accurate and well may be understated.

Limitations Imposed by the Video Imperative. Television news is vulnerable to the introduction of certain kinds of distortion that are intrinsic to the medium, at least as it has evolved. One of these is what might be called the visual (or video) imperative. Interesting footage, action, dynamism, contrast, conflict—these are what make the viewer stay tuned. They have much more to do with drama or other entertainment, even slapstick, than with news per se. But they are mandatory for television news in most circumstances.

Therefore, the news producer, whose judgment selects the precise segments of videotape footage to be shown, must cut and juxtapose scenes and images primarily for dramatic effect. He or she starts with many times as much footage as would fill the ten or fifteen seconds of air time the story will get. The same basic process governs the selection of the "live feed" from a mobile unit somewhere in the field that is coming in to the control room by radio, telephone line, or satellite relay. The producer controls the mix and sequence of live and videotaped material.

It is usually necessary to delete substance and minimize context to supply the dramatic instant for the screen. The inevitable result of such exigency is to shorten the story enough to trivialize it or to change its nature so it becomes a micro-commentary, a gloss, on the larger story that television has no time to show. Kathleen Hall Jamieson addressed this problem in *Eloquence in an Electronic Age.*

When thoughtful and observant newspaper columnists like David Broder analyze political discourse, Jamieson observes, they are playing a critical role in the classical understanding of the communication of political ideas, that of the opinion leaders of the community. They translate the rhetoric of the politician for the understanding of the general public. "But unlike broadcast reports," she writes, "these print reports are synopsizing not the effect of the speech or its strategic intent but its content" (Jamieson 1988, 249–50).

The effect of what the TV reporter interprets as its intent can be stated in a jiffy. To translate the content would take more time than is available—due, of course, to circumstances beyond our control. The feel of actuality the viewer gets from seeing and hearing the action may be completely convincing, but the missing ingredients that would fill out the whole truth are what Hollywood legend knows as the face on the cutting-room floor.

Noting that journalists actually constitute "a new class of orators," Lloyd Bitzer comments that perhaps they, "rather than the preachers and politicians, have become the dominant speakers in our political life. Whether the orators of news have an art of inquiry and communication adequate to their mission is a question of large importance" (Bitzer 1981, 244).

15

Further Perspectives on Reform

What is to be done about all the political mischief, all the ills and evils, so many of them grown from seeds of reform, that mar and beset politics in the United States?

The fundamental genius of the American polity is a spirit of compromise between ideological purity and zeal on one hand and freedom of thought and action on the other. This is reflected in the history and the content of the U.S. Constitution. Since its very inception in the hot Philadelphia summer of 1787, reformers have tried to make its prohibitions more stringent, and other reformers have tried to make its freedoms more broad.

FIRST REFORMER: THE SERPENT

Although it is not usually couched in these terms, the Judeo-Christian tradition teaches us (in Genesis 3) that the first reformer was the serpent in the Garden of Eden, who persuaded Eve that he had a better idea. So to get knowledge, the First Man, and his First Lady, ate the forbidden fruit. They discovered, and covered, their nakedness and got thrown out of paradise.

Not all subsequent efforts at reform have been so disastrous, but few have brought results as benign as their motivations. Once paradise is lost, one reformer's good is another's evil; and when zeal and fury run high on both sides, the resulting polarization has repeatedly sabotaged working arrangements that may be less than heavenly but still useful. In the United States, the real victim often has been tripartite government and its checks and balances. In such times the trickery, deceit, and bloodthirsty spirit appropriate to the campaigns of war permeate the campaigns of politics.

Still, corruption continues to flourish and the need for reform persists, as does the human urge to reform. But it always needs to be undertaken with careful study and great restraint.

Political reform can be examined from several different perspectives. One of these has to do with the perceptions of the observer. A good deal of attention has been paid in these pages to political polarization, for when a rival party or candidate is seen as a polar opposite rather than just a rival, the atmosphere is poisoned for any useful exchange. Ordinary political contests are matches between conflicting points of view and different judgments about public policy, but very rarely about good versus evil or loyalty versus treason.

Good and evil can have a place in political discourse, but more fruitfully in terms of the evil that good men and women do unwittingly and with the best intentions. Unfortunately, however, this is a concept with which the theologian or philosopher is far more comfortable than the politician. The temptation is great to see political conflict as cosmic warfare between good and evil. It rarely is that simple. "We stand at Armageddon, and we battle for the Lord," cried Theodore Roosevelt to his Progressive nominating convention in 1912. The convention nominated Roosevelt, but the voters elected Wilson.

The perception that the present age is an evil time, that the former era was a golden age, is another political troublemaker; so is its variant of a golden tomorrow, when we will have reformed away all the wicked practices of the present. These idle dreams distract our attention from the political realities: real needs and possibilities and real differences.

STANDARDS FOR POLITICAL DISCOURSE

Case after case of campaign mischief reviewed in the preceding chapters demonstrates that truth and relevance are the hallmarks of useful and honest campaign argument. Truth in the usage of this book is both larger and more important than fact, for facts isolated from the context that gives them meaning can have the effect of falsehood. Relevance is as critical as truth, for a perfectly true argument that has no bearing or scant bearing on the office being sought or the issue being decided is nothing better than clutter and diversion.

Appropriate standards for political discourse include the accurate identification and acknowledgment of the priorities that participants bring to the discussion. This implies some measure of explicitness in labeling, of truth in packaging. Though we demand it at the supermarket, we ban it from political discourse.

We live in an age of euphemism gone wild, far beyond the modest aspirations of Dr. Bowdler. He, poor fellow, wanted only to clean up fairy stories and the like to spare the sensibilities of little children. We may not refer to crippled or retarded or demented people except as handicapped. St.

Luke's "poor, the maimed, the halt, and the blind" now are more fashionably styled: persons below the poverty line, those with job-related disabilities, and the motor- and visually impaired. We may speak, see, or hear no evil—in a day when the merry shouts of children at play routinely use language that would have sent Dr. Bowdler begging for haven in a lunatic asylum.

When Mao Zedong named the People's Republic of China it was neither the people's nor a republic. Not all American lobbying and political action organizations are more accurately named. American Civil Liberties Union, Handgun Control, National Rifle Association—forthright enough. But Common Cause, People for the American Way, Public Citizen—grand titles hardly more genuinely descriptive than that Lebanese Shi'i militia, the Party of God.

Grandiose and inexplicit organization names appearing in the news as advocates or adversaries of this or that candidate or public policy proposal place an extra burden on the news media for meaningful identification of the interests of the organization in the matter at hand. When the media fail to supply such identification, as very often happens, the burden falls on the viewer or reader, for whom the only options are chance knowledge, inconvenient research, a meaningless blur—or being deceived.

This is particularly unfortunate, because often such groups—even those descriptively named—come at particular legislative or other political questions with the narrow focus of single-issue groups, such as those urging and those opposing abortion, busing, gun control, nuclear power, banning pesticides, allowing school prayer, etc. Single-issue advocacy groups have a real Balkanizing effect on American politics, nudging it toward a European style of splinter parties and coalitions. These groups have proliferated. They also, be it remembered, are exercising their constitutional right of free speech.

For all the reality of free speech in the United States, political discourse is restricted by a double standard; indeed, it has been since colonial times. For generations orthodox Protestants were entirely free to criticize any or all other identifiable groups, specifically including Catholics, Quakers, the unreligious, Jews, the savage redskin, the infidel Mussulman, the heathen Chinese, and, of course, blacks. But the God-fearing Protestants were safe against the public sneers and slurs of the others. Gradually, these taboos have shifted every which way.

Intricate pecking orders wax and wane with the irregular heartbeat of these special standards. Jews may criticize Christians but not the reverse. Blacks may criticize whites but not the reverse. It is bad form for blacks to criticize Jews but not quite as outré as for Christian whites to do so. Roman Catholics, once the easy target of Protestant japes and jokes, acquired immunity with the rise of liberal good will—only to lose much of it when liberals polarized against their church's opposition to abortion.

Unspoken Communication

Political messages, openly expressed and avowed, can be evaluated on the basis of their words and their authorship. Unspoken or unavowed messages are a more difficult matter. Whispering campaigns and unsigned campaign fliers may be constitutionally protected anonymity, like the Ku Klux Klan hiding behind its masks and sheets, but they are as cowardly.

The nefarious "gentlemen's agreements" that kept Catholics and Jews out of country clubs and blacks out of certain neighborhoods were not written and signed or openly declared, for they were a business too dirty for a gentleman to avow in public. Everybody knew that the public works bond deals John Mitchell rigged together were necessary. So nobody rubbed his nose in the fact that they contravened and even mocked the word and spirit of state constitutions and municipal charters.

Similar unspoken understandings pervaded Nixon's Committee to Reelect the President. No one had to tell Gordon Liddy or Howard Hunt what to do. Like a bloodhound with a whiff of the subject's hat, off they went, knowing by instinct and training what was expected of them, with no need for shouted commands.

Indeed, the ancient political tradition, "Don't write, send word," was so universal that one wonders how Matt Quay's Colonel Dudley could have been so careless as to write and post his Blocks of Five letter with its detailed instructions for fraud. How could James Blaine put his Mulligan Letters on paper, exposing himself as a liar and bribe-taker?

Probably arrogance is the answer. As Dudley and Blaine learned the hard way, in the dirty tricks department, some messages are too important for words. Thus we see that non-verbal communication, much talked of by modern social scientists, is one of the oldest staples of political mischief, going back to the original sly wink and conspiratorial nod.

Realistic Expectations

Skepticism about the probity of the political animal and its ecosystem helps fuel the fires of political reform. More importantly, perhaps, it helps set realistic expectations for reform. Uncritical approval of the most enthusiastic dreams of the most enthusiastic dreamers is at least as dangerous as uncritical approval of the system they would reform. Coming down with an urge to perfect the system? The best prescription may be: take two teaspoonfuls with a grain of salt and call me in the morning.

Skeptical examination of everything about politics is a necessary part of rational observation of and participation in that calling. And this applies with special force to political reportage and commentary in the news media. The media tendency toward a sense of superior knowledge and wisdom,

Table 15.1
Voting in Presidential Elections, 1932–88 (% of Voting Age Population, Plus % of Registered Voters from 1968)

Year	Major Candidates	% Voting Age	% Registered
1932	FDR, Hoover	52.4	N/A
1936	FDR, Landon	56.0	N/A
1940	FDR, Willkie	58.9	N/A
1944	FDR, Dewey	56.0	N/A
1948	Truman, Dewey	51.1	N/A
1952	Ike, Stevenson	61.6	N/A
1956	Ike, Stevenson	59.3	N/A
1960	JFK, Nixon	62.8	N/A
1964	Johnson, Goldwater	61.9	N/A
1968	Nixon, Humphrey	60.9	91.2
1972	Nixon, McGovern	55.2	87.1
1976	Carter, Ford	53.5	88.6
1980	Reagan, Carter	54.0	88.7
1984	Reagan, Mondale	53.1	87.7
1988	Bush, Dukakis	50.1	86.2

Notes: 1948: Thurmond and Henry Wallace led third-party efforts; 1968: George Wallace third party; 1972: total vote as percentage of voting age diluted when eighteen-year-olds became eligible with Twenty-sixth Amendment (though few voted then or since). Before 1968 percentage of registered voters is not uniformly available. Pre-1960s figures are distorted by such vote-inhibiting factors as poll tax and extra-legal prevention of black voting.

Sources: Federal Election Commission, Commission for the Study of the American Electorate, Bureau of the Census.

toward cynicism about politics and politicians, and toward trivializing both, treated at some length in Chapter 14, merits reemphasis here.

Many scholars and journalists mourn the low participation of American voters compared with those in other nations. This, too, calls for a somewhat skeptical hearing. In the time of ironclad Communist hegemony over the USSR and Eastern Europe, voting for single-candidate lists may have been meaningless, but it was mandatory. U.S. voting participation surges when concern, interest, and a sense of ability to affect the outcome run high in the electorate.

Moreover, voting participation must be measured two ways: against the total population of voting age and against registered voters, who by registering have demonstrated interest in voting. People of voting age who have not registered include some who do hope or intend to vote but also virtually the entire population of the uninterested and uninformed.

Table 15.1 reveals that only in a few elections have as many as 60 percent of voting-age Americans actually voted, but that never since around 1968, when reasonably accurate registration figures began to be available, have fewer than 86 percent of registered voters actually voted.

Some skepticism is also useful when one looks toward public education to improve public understanding of and participation in politics. The trend established during the 1950s and 1960s in primary and especially secondary education in the United States was to focus more on the problems of American democracy than its origins and evolution. Succeeding trends in history and humanities education have given the electorate a cohort with memories so empty that they would be astonished—if they could be brought to read it—at this modest review of campaign practices of the past two centuries.

There are some excellent high school government and American history texts in print, as well as more that are distinguished mainly for outdated trendiness. But the finest texts in existence are useless at the hands of teachers who must be disciplinarians or monitors first and of students who cannot or will not read them.

THE TARGETS OF REFORM

Every hotly contested U.S. election has brought calls for reform, and this was as true at the end of the eighteenth century as it is in the waning twentieth. In our time, however, there may be more reformers and fewer defenders of genuine political warfare than in the golden age of political mischief. No longer is there a John James Ingalls to set us straight with his famous snort, "The purification of politics is an iridescent dream!"

Up to that point, one can sympathize with Ingalls. The situation modern reformers find so deplorable came on the wings of two centuries of reform. Enough already. Let the system work. It does work. It is not tidy, but the Constitution, which gives Americans freedoms that are the envy of the world, does not promise a tidy system.

But the spellbinding Kansas senator did not leave it at that. He was talking to a reporter for the *New York World*, and he went on to state a theme that may not have been urged by any modern political figure since Stalin or Mao—perhaps excepting some of the principals in Nixon's 1972 Committee to Re-elect the President.

"Government is force," Ingalls went on to proclaim (in that 1890 interview). "Politics is a battle for supremacy. Parties are the armies. The Decalogue and the Golden Rule have no place in a political campaign. The object is success. To defeat the antagonist and expel the party in power is the purpose" (Williams 1972, 119).

Democracy versus the Republic

The reforms brought by those highly intelligent, well-motivated, conspicuously honest political leaders Robert La Follette and Hiram Johnson have been discussed at some length elsewhere in this book and need no further treatment here except to note again that they were protecting the people from politics and politicians. They were seeking to wrest away from the *demagogos* control over the *politeia*, so they could restore control to the *demos*, the people.

In other words, dissatisfied with the corruption of the representatives elected to manage the American republic, they sought—successfully in their states—to bypass the representatives and restore control directly to the people. Through initiative and referendum the people could make the laws they wanted when their legislators did not; through recall they could turn the rascals out without waiting for the next election; and by mandating nonpartisan local elections they could preserve whole local governments from the depredations of politicians. Down with the republic, up with democracy.

This, except for a handful of radicals among them, the Founding Fathers, whose Constitution guaranteed (at Article IV, Section 4) a republican form of government to every state, would have considered subversion.

Under the judicial doctrine of *stare decisis* (let [previous] decisions stand), no one at this late date is going to undermine the work of the Progressive reformers, for public consent has indeed let stand a body of decisions upholding their reforms. But orthodox politicians have always rankled especially under California's rich diet of constitutional populism, and they keep trying to temper it, even as contemporary reformers seek to extend it. As late as 1986 voters adopted a state constitutional amendment prohibiting any political party endorsement of nonpartisan candidates for local office. The ban was promptly challenged in Federal Court as restricting free speech. A full Ninth Circuit Court of Appeals found for the pols (8–3, in 1990) and reversed a three-judge panel's approval of the amendment ("Law," 1990).

Protecting the Voter

As the outrageous theft and purchase of votes discussed in Chapter 11 make clear, reform has been particularly necessary in the procedures of the polling place, including registration, voting, and counting. In the main, efforts to clean up this aspect of electoral politics have been successful, but even here each new reform has introduced complexities that called for new corrective measures. Voter registration was introduced to counter such abuses as Colonel Dudley's voting floaters in the notorious Blocks of Five. Promptly, onerous registration requirements became a means of discouraging would-be voters. Every innovation in guarding the probity of the count seems to inspire further innovations in the technology of cheating. But the process of reform, however flawed, must continue, if only running in order to stay in place.

Qualifying the Candidate

Efforts to define and control the eligibility of candidates for public office began in the Constitutional Convention, when it was stipulated that a president must be native-born and at least thirty-five years old and that senators and representatives must be, respectively, at least thirty and twenty-five. Many states have placed maximum limits of one or two terms on their governors.

The U.S. Constitution required a decennial census for the express purpose of adjusting congressional district boundaries to keep their populations approximately equal. This was a farsighted measure intended to prevent the kind of problem the British House of Commons was just beginning to recognize in the rotten borough, an electoral district that might lose so much population that a mere dozen citizens in one district would have as much representation as thousands of voters in another.

However, the U.S. process of census and reapportionment instantly opened the door to more cynical reformers. The third census, of 1810, gave the Massachusetts legislature and Governor Elbridge Gerry the opportunity to so redraw state senate districts as to concentrate most of the Federalist vote in a few districts, thus creating more districts that were safe for Democratic-Republicans. Thus the Gerrymander.

That much criticized creation, named because cartoonists thought its map to resemble a salamander, may have brought Gerry more opprobrium than he deserved. That particular district occupied the northeast corner of the state, and Gerry simply padded it a bit to west and south, and cut a rectangle out of the middle of its Atlantic coastline for a new district.[1] For all his effort, the district went Federalist after just one election anyway.

Far more serpentine and imaginative districts have been carved in most states in later years. The California congressman Philip Burton (who served from 1964 until his death in 1983) is generally acknowledged the master of this art. He was an instinctive redistricting wizard, whose brilliant cartography after the 1980 census gained five Democratic seats in California's U.S. House delegation while the Republicans were losing three and the state was gaining two new seats—all this while Republican voter registration was increasing and that of the Democrats declining.

Efforts at reform of redistricting have focused mainly on the courts, which have not proved much of a match for determined legislators of the controlling party in the state at hand.

REFORMING THE CAMPAIGN

Efforts to reform the financing of U.S. elections have received longer and more sustained attention than any other aspect of the election campaign itself. The effect of these efforts has been spotty at best. The reader interested in pursuing finance reform beyond the passing attention it receives here is referred to the work of the Citizens' Research Foundation, which is described briefly in Chapter 11.

The Federal Election Commission

Campaign costs and concern about them have grown in tandem in the twentieth century, and in 1971 Congress made one of its sporadic efforts at control and reform. The Federal Election Campaign Act of that year set limits on contributions and spending and provided for partial public funding of presidential campaigns. Post-Watergate amendments in 1974 created a Federal Election Commission (FEC) to oversee and enforce the limits. These amendments created new opportunities for contributions from business and other organizations through political action committees or PACs—which proliferated instantly.

A later Supreme Court decision enabled individuals or groups to spend political money on advertising or otherwise to support or oppose candidates without the candidate's approval regardless of FEC limitations.[2] This gave new freedom of action to such ideological groups as the liberal National Committee for an Effective Congress, the conservative Committee for the Survival of a Free Congress, and the AFL-CIO's Committee on Political Education (COPE)—or anybody else.

It also supplied a new stimulus to the action PACs like the National Conservative Political Action Committee (NCPAC), to the powerful pro-Israel lobby, American Israel Public Affairs Committee (AIPAC—itself not a conventional PAC), and to scores of single-issue groups that may have a campaign presence from time to time. These latter include Handgun Control and the lobbying arm of the National Rifle Association, proponents and opponents of abortion rights, and the Sierra Club among other environmental organizations.

But while these developments were empowering or strengthening the private interest groups, their unintended by-product was to further weaken the political parties as primary agencies for the collection and disbursement of campaign money. Public concern continues, as does congressional tinkering with possible revisions and reforms.

Access to the Voter

Modern campaigns beyond the purely local level, and indeed many local campaigns in large cities, involve television advertising as their most costly single element. The question of free television is always offered as at least a partial solution. Designation of certain public TV channels as election channels is proposed from time to time. By most reform schemes spot announcements would be forbidden on free television. Matching government funds would not be usable for spots under some schemes.

Commercial broadcasters respond that such ideas are nothing but piracy. However, while cable television operators own the wires carrying their programs to the viewer, broadcasters do not own the airwaves. The United States is all but unique in licensing private enterprisers to operate the radio and television industries. The worldwide norm is for state ownership and operation of broadcast facilities. Any effort to legislate free broadcast time for election campaigns would involve a bloody fight, including constitutional questions of ex post facto legislation, among others.

Defining the Forum. Most modern presidential campaign reform proposals would mandate debates between the major party candidates. In order to avoid cluttering the airwaves with insistent minor and splinter party hopefuls, these schemes would repeal Section 315 of the Federal Communications Act, which requires equal time for *all* candidates, consequential or not—itself an illustration of reform gone awry.

Proposals stipulating a series of debates, and not just one or two, predominate. The broadcast-oriented Markle Foundation sponsored a commission of scholars, journalists, and former U.S. senators that in 1990 recommended a mandatory series of four debates for presidential candidates. The League of Women Voters, which pioneered the implementation of modern presidential debates, and many other thoughtful advocates press this cause.

Candidate "debates" have indeed drawn large TV audiences, although none has employed an actual debate format. But with or without an interlocutory panel of journalists, any face-to-face confrontation between candidates does offer the possibility of smoking out ideas, challenges, responses, and conceivably an occasional thoughtful reflection; it also may give some glimmer of how a candidate fares under fire. This is all to the good.

But real debate or pseudo-debate, the audience is likely to consist of two groups: politically oriented and informed citizens, who do not rely on TV for news but come to this program to witness some kind of political debate, and TV news regulars, who tune in to see some kind of conflict erupt. The rest of the usual television audience—the great majority—will be watching ball games or sitcom reruns on another channel.

The Danger: Policing Thought and Speech

It is beyond controverting that the noise, verbal clutter, bombastic nonsense, and ever-increasing expense of modern campaigning are found highly offensive and even sinister by many millions of thoughtful Americans. But nearly every effort to regulate conduct or spending in a campaign setting runs afoul of the First Amendment or comes perilously close to doing so. My conclusion after watching election campaigns closely for thirty-five years is that most regulation holds more perils for a free society than letting the maladies of unbridled spending and dirty campaigning run their course.

These maladies do dissipate their energy and their poisons with the passage of time. Red scares come and red scares go, whether the prime agitator is some anti-Jeffersonian pamphleteer, Woodrow Wilson's attorney general, Joe McCarthy, or a newcomer. Tense race relations are exacerbated for electioneering purposes on occasion whether the century is the eighteenth, nineteenth, or twentieth, and assuredly that will hold true in the twenty-first. Great bombast and effulgence over nothing of consequence will irritate the purists from time to time tomorrow as yesterday and the day before. A large part of every reform proposal is driven by the taste of the critic rather than considerations of truth and relevance.

THE QUESTION OF FAIR CAMPAIGN PRACTICES

Only infrequently have efforts been mounted to move the public at large and outside the academy to employ rhetorical analysis (or rhetorical criticism, or critical analysis) on political speech, especially that of election campaigns. This sort of criticism has gone on for a good many years in the academic discipline usually styled speech communication and sporadically within the discipline of political science, in the 1930s and 1940s, and notably, perhaps, since the 1970s.

The Institute of Propaganda Analysis

Some of the great names of twentieth-century political science, including Charles E. Merriam and Harold Lasswell, pioneered in the public, critical analysis of wartime propaganda, and this eventuated on the eve of World War II in an Institute of Propaganda Analysis (IPA), which conducted research and began to develop a substantial outreach to news media, colleges, and the public schools, especially high schools. The IPA identified (and named) such propaganda devices as the bandwagon appeal, card-stacking, glittering generalities, and several others. Its work was too successful, for by the time it was well-launched the United States was in World War II, and the prospect of widespread citizen analysis of U.S. propaganda hit too close to home. At the instance of several of the institute's own scholar-board-member-patriots, including a Marine Corps officer named Paul Douglas who would later represent Illinois in the U.S. Senate, it disbanded.

As senator, about a decade later, Douglas played an indirect role in initiating another such effort, this one focused specifically on the propaganda of electioneering. That was the Fair Campaign Practices Committee, established in 1954, an experiment that brought a number of generally beneficial results before its effective demise in 1978.

Ever since, occasional calls have been heard for a reconstitution of that effort. Anyone contemplating such an attempt would do well to look at the actual history of the organization, what it did and did not do, and what happened to it and why, for misinformation about it is widespread.

Origins of the Fair Campaign Practices Committee

The mean-spirited and intemperate congressional campaigns of 1950, discussed in Chapter 9 and elsewhere, led to an interesting experiment. That period was the heyday of McCarthyism, and the most reckless charges were everywhere. Protesting a "nightmare of immersion in billingsgate," the *New York Times* editorialized:

So complete is the character assassination in some cases that those who reach public office will have lost the confidence of the voters who put them there. The most serious result of all, perhaps, is that if this sort of thing continues, it will become increasingly difficult to get decent men and women to stand for public office because of the unjustified abuse suffered en route....

When almost everyone is calling everybody else a liar and a thief, the result becomes a standoff. There is, then, no black and white of reputation in the public mind, only a muddy gray. ("Campaign Morals," 1950)

The Eighty-second Congress, which was chosen in that election, created a special subcommittee, headed by Senator Paul Douglas of Illinois, to study ethics in government. Testifying before it, Senator William Benton of Connecticut reinforced the somber apprehensions of the editorial writers and suggested a possible remedy: "a non-partisan continuing commission of distinguished private citizens" to study campaign conduct, report the facts, and recommend standards of responsibility for election campaigns (U.S. Senate [Establishment of a Commission on Ethics in Government], 1951, 40–41).

Meanwhile, the Senate elections subcommittee, headed by Senator Guy Gillette of Iowa, was investigating specific complaints of unfairness in the 1950 campaigns. Benton offered similar recommendations to it. The subcommittee adopted his proposal and called for "a continuing committee of eminent members of both parties, working jointly for higher and cleaner standards of campaigning," and suggested that such an effort could do "as much as the enactment of laws to rid this nation of abuses which are reaching alarming proportions" (U.S. Senate Hearings [Maryland] 1951).

The Douglas ethics subcommittee agreed, and pointed a direction for a continuing committee: "Progress depends also upon critical listeners who ask for evidence, are skeptical about unsupported assertions, and realize that name-calling, 'smears,' appeals to bigotry, and emotionalism generally are prima facie evidence that the speaker has frequently nothing more substantial with which to support his position."

Meanwhile, Senator Gillette and some of his associates, notably his own administrative assistant, Stewart E. McClure, drew up a model code of fair campaign practices.

CODE OF FAIR CAMPAIGN PRACTICES

There are basic principles of decency, honest and fair play which every candidate for public office in the United States has a moral obligation to observe and uphold, in order that, after vigorously contested but fairly conducted campaigns, our citizens may exercise their constitutional right to a free and untrammeled choice and the will of the people may be fully and clearly expressed on the issues before the country. Therefore:

I shall conduct my campaign in the best American tradition, discussing the issues as I see them, presenting my record and policies with sincerity and frankness, and criticizing without fear or favor the record and policies of my opponent and his party which merit such criticism.

I shall defend and uphold the right of every qualified American voter to full and equal participation in the electoral process.

I shall condemn the use of personal vilification, character defamation, whispering campaigns, libel, slander, or scurrilous attacks on any candidate or his personal or family life.

I shall condemn the use of campaign material of any sort which misrepresents, distorts, or otherwise falsifies the facts regarding any candidate, as well as the use of malicious or unfounded accusations against any candidate which aim at creating or exploiting doubts, without justification, as to his loyalty and patriotism.

I shall condemn any appeal to prejudice based on race, creed, or national origin.

I shall condemn any dishonest or unethical practice which tends to corrupt or undermine our American system of free elections or which hampers or prevents the full and free expression of the will of the voters.

I shall immediately and publicly repudiate the support of any individual or group which resorts to the methods and tactics which I condemn.

I, the undersigned, candidate for election to public office in the United States of America, hereby endorse, subscribe to, and solemnly pledge myself to conduct my campaigns in accordance with the above principles and practices, so help me God.

As a result of the controversy over a Minnesota campaign in 1958, which is described in Chapter 10, the penultimate paragraph of the code was revised by the Fair Campaign Practices Committee to read: "I shall immediately and publicly repudiate support deriving from any individual or group which resorts, on behalf of my candidacy or in opposition to that of my opponent, to the methods and tactics which I condemn."

A Committee Comes Together. Shortly before the 1954 congressional elections, a group of "eminent members of both parties" in fact came together to constitute the Fair Campaign Practices Committee, under the leadership of Anna Lord Strauss, then recently president of the League of Women Voters of the United States, and the publisher Harry Louis Selden, both of New York. Their colleagues included political moderates of both parties, among them the publishers Gardner Cowles (*Look* magazine), Palmer Hoyt (*Denver Post*), Barry Bingham (*Louisville Times* and *Courier-Journal*), and Charles P. Taft of Cincinnati.

They adopted the Code of Fair Campaign Practices and called a press conference at which that document was endorsed by the chairmen of the Republican and Democratic national committees, respectively Leonard W. Hall and Stephen A. Mitchell. The fledgling committee also mailed off copies of the code to every candidate for Congress, asking each to pledge publicly to abide by it and to return a signed copy to the committee.

The press conference was enlivened by a dispute between the two party leaders as to whose partisans would be most apt to disregard the code, and the entire effort was greeted with sardonic editorials and cartoons that acknowledged the need for improvement but voiced much skepticism about the effectiveness of the available instrument. The Fair Campaign Practices Committee subsided with election day but reemerged at the beginning of 1956 on a more permanent basis.

Behind the Scenes at the Founding. Such organizations, of course, do not simply rise out of the mist after a bolt of lightning. This one was created, informally but actually, by the National Committee for an Effective Congress (NCEC), a pre-FEC PAC for moderate liberals that grew originally out of the early-1940s American League for a Free Palestine. The story of the NCEC itself is the subject of Harry M. Scoble's *Ideology and Electoral Action* (1967). Although he does not refer to the earlier proposals of the Douglas and Gillette subcommittees, Scoble describes briefly the NCEC's role in establishing the Fair Campaign Practices Committee.

In anticipation of Senator Joseph McCarthy's announced intent to pose himself as the central issue of the 1954 midterm election, the Fair Campaign Practices Committee was created. This bipartisan committee was designed to be a counterforce against the campaign tactics of McCarthy or others who violated "the rules of the game" (that is to audit, analyze, and report on campaign tactics and so to crystallize public opinion in voting). George Agree claims to have been, and probably was, "50 per cent responsible" for encouraging the formation of the FCPC. (Scoble 1967, 51)

George Agree was executive secretary of the NCEC, which was based in New York. With the general approval and authorization of the organization's real motive force and éminence grise, Maurice Rosenblatt, in Washington, Agree did much of the telephone and legwork necessary to organize the Fair Campaign Practices Committee and get it off the ground in time for the 1954 campaign. A great deal also was done by Rosenblatt's cohort in founding NCEC, Harry Louis Selden, who became vice chairman and a selfless supporter and advocate of the FCPC. (I did not know it until Harry Scoble told me of his NCEC research in 1965, but all these men had worked together for years in the American League for a Free Palestine.)

Agree and I had become acquainted in the 1952 presidential campaign, where we were both active in Volunteers for Stevenson. I was a Republican moderate (and former Wisconsinite) who had been alienated from my hereditary party by its reluctance to discipline the Wisconsin wild man, Joseph McCarthy. (I registered as an independent during my decade on the committee staff, and a few years after I left it in 1966, I reverted to my original Republican orientation.)

I was offered the executive directorship of the FCPC while it was still on the drawing board, but after considerable reflection I demurred because I did not want to derail a promising public relations career for a low-paying job without fringe benefits or visible future. A young man named John Shields was hired for the duration of the 1954 campaign.

By 1956 one of my PR clients had gone to prison for fraud and another to Brazil to avoid that fate, and I had been beaten in a campaign for a local office in Armonk, New York, in which I was astonished to find myself the object of whispers that I was a Communist, among other lies. When the FCPC was resurrected in 1956, my perspective was entirely different, and I became the executive director of what was to be an ongoing, year-round, and scrupulously non-partisan organization based in New York.

Charles P. Taft, a lawyer and lay leader in the Episcopal Church, son of a president and chief justice, brother of the "Mister Republican" of that day, Senator Robert A. Taft, succeeded Anna Lord Strauss as chairman. With year-round activity it became possible to study weaknesses in the original concept and composition of the committee. One of these was political balance, in that there were moderate and liberal Democrats and Republicans, but no real conservatives of either stripe. There also were no veteran political operatives. I addressed this problem carefully and in time recruited, among others, Jim Farley and Leonard Hall, both conservative former chairmen of, respectively, the Democratic and Republican national committees.

Recasting the Code: A Standard, Not a Pledge

Eventually the code was abandoned as a pledge and was advanced purely as a reasonable standard by which candidates and voters, and the news media, might gauge campaign tactics. I began a biennial "State-by-State Study of Smear" after each election, a postmortem of the campaign with details of the year's crop of unfair campaigning, lacking only the names of the candidates and states, collected during the campaign from a national network of volunteers who were variously journalists, lawyers, party and other political staff people, and political scientists. This was introduced to find out where, when, and how unfair campaigns were being waged—and what made them succeed or fail. An experiment in teaching aids for high schools was begun, and this evolved into a series of pamphlets and news-letters, at first for schools and later for wider consumption.

Media attention, spotty and derisive at first, increased steadily, and committee reports and commentaries on the level of unfair campaigning and reminders of favorite tricks of distortion and deception were widely featured in print and on the air in the weeks approaching election day. Gradually the committee came to be recognized for what two national party chiefs, Democrat John Bailey and Republican William E. Miller, once agreed to call "its impartial and increasingly effective role as the conscience of American politics."

My decade as executive director of the committee was a unique opportunity to study, full-time, the conduct of American election campaigns in terms of political ethics. I came to know political pros and amateurs, bigots and zealots, demagogs and charlatans, idealists and pragmatists, radicals, moderates, conservatives and reactionaries—and a small number of smear artists whose mere appearance at an airport in September or October would galvanize the other party in that state into a frenzy of detective and defensive work.

I learned that unfair and dishonest campaigns are not a monopoly of Republicans or Democrats but of cynical or desperate human beings—and true believers, in Eric Hoffer's sense of fanatic (Hoffer 1951). I discovered that impartiality is surprisingly easy to come by, given only a genuine loyalty to the integrity of the political system. And I discovered fairly early that, usually, thoughtful and honest partisans, including political pros, despise smear and slander, whomever the target. Exceptions appear when temptations overwhelm scruples, a condition illustrated repeatedly in these pages.

I left the FCPC staff in 1966 as a result of a dispute with the man who had introduced me to it. I secured the approval of the committee's board for an unpaid leave in 1966 to teach for that spring semester at Hamilton College. When I mentioned this to George Agree, he considered it a serious mistake in an election year and intervened with board members to persuade them that I should not be away for that semester. I prevailed with the board but, concluding that this interference was both prejudicial and unacceptable, resigned, although I went on the FCPC board and executive committee.

I was succeeded as executive director by Sam Archibald, former administrative assistant to California's Democratic Congressman John E. Moss, and the operation was moved to Washington. It should be noted that this instance was the only such interference from anyone associated with the founding of the committee in my decade as its executive. The only other inside interference I experienced came from two board members whom I had recruited, Louis Nizer and Philip Stern, during the Bobby Kennedy affair related in Chapter 7.

By 1972 the Fair Campaign Practices Committee had been around for eighteen years and was participating in its tenth congressional and fifth presidential campaign, enjoying steadily increasing cooperation from the political parties and coverage and serious attention from the print and electronic news media. This was probably the peak of its influence and effectiveness. Consistently, the committee had proclaimed its goal of making a campaign issue of campaign tactics.

Its aim never was adjudication, but always to focus media (and thereby public) attention on fair and unfair campaign practices in the terms delineated in the code. With the active cooperation of the American Arbitration Association, an experimental procedure for arbitration of disputes over campaign tactics had been launched in the mid–1960s; it was used by candidates in thirteen House races in 1972.

High Point and Demise

At the congressional level, an interesting phenomenon had begun to occur. Candidates had noticed that advantageous media attention accrued to campaigners who were seen as victims of unfair attacks, and the incidence of complaints to the committee was rising sharply, numbering more in 1972 than in any election since 1960. But most of the new tide was minor, even trivial. It posed a curious problem for any such effort at reasoned reform: how to be taken seriously enough to have some impact without having the reform process so swamped by trivial complaints as to trivialize the reform process itself.

For all this outward success, financing the FCPC had always been an extremely difficult problem. It was supported entirely by voluntary, tax-deductible contributions from individuals, corporations, labor unions, and foundations, and the only reason it was able to continue its precarious existence as long as it did was the dedication of its small staff. In my 1980 smear roundup for the Independent News Alliance,[3] I wrote sadly,

The FCPC effectively is dead. (Its 'corporate shell' remains, subject to future resurrection, somewhat like a body in cryogenic storage.) After the 1978 election, the committee succumbed to financial malnutrition.

But one of the reasons it went under was the realization of its main objectives. There were three:

1. It sought to increase voter awareness and sensitivity to smear tactics, vicious personal innuendo, and deliberate distortion of an opponent's record.

2. It tried to stimulate fuller and more objective scrutiny of campaigns by the news media than was the rule in the early 1950s.

3. And, at the candidate level, it tried to make dirty campaigning a campaign issue.

Gradually, over the past 20 years, all three of these objectives have been realized, through the cooperation of the media and of politicians and the parties, the only real weapons the Fair Campaign Practices Committee ever had. ("Election '80: Dirty at the Top; Below That, Cleanest in Decades," 1980)

What Killed FCPC

The unending problem of financing the committee was complicated by two special considerations that rendered it particularly difficult. First, it never at any stage had a financial angel prepared to put up seed money and generous infusions of cash when necessary, and it lacked a visceral basis for popular fund appeals. It existed not to save maltreated orphans, abused laboratory animals, or the planet Earth but to encourage citizens to look beyond sensational charges to discern the reality behind them.

Occasional fund-raising consultants, some voluntary, some not, were disgusted at board and staff for resisting proposals to rig flamboyant fund-raising gimmicks that might cast the FCPC as the last bulwark against dictatorship or nuclear war. But the committee's role was essentially to enable voters to see through exactly that kind of fraudulently inflated rhetoric in the context of elections.

The second negative consideration was almost unceasing harassment by the Internal Revenue Commission (later Service). The Fair Campaign Practices Committee was regarded with suspicion and antagonism by many conservatives, and the commission itself harbored a bureaucracy with a large and dour component of them. From time to time throughout the life of the FCPC its staff would discover—early through leaks, later through the Freedom of Information Act—that some right-wing member of House or Senate had sicced the IRS on it.

The committee was granted a tentative tax exemption when it was established in 1954, but within a few months of its resuscitation in January 1956 the first of a twenty-one-year series of challenges and revocations arrived. Buried innocently within the charter of the FCPC was one of those generalities of legal boilerplate that included the phrase "and in any and all ways to" elevate, etc. Late in 1958, the committee was advised of the commission's intent to revoke its exemption in a five-page letter whose essence was the following paragraph:

An analysis of the information submitted discloses that your primary purpose is to elevate the standards of ethics and morality in election campaigns in "any and all ways." To propose to accomplish such purpose in "any and all ways" is not considered to be a declaration of an exclusively educational purpose within the meaning of section 501(c)(3). Furthermore, your primary activities do not appear to be educational *per se*, nor do they appear to fall within the generally accepted meaning of the term "educational," as, for example, the solicitation of pledges to your Code of Fair Campaign Practices; the dissemination of information to the press, radio, and other media; the giving of financial aid to other organizations, the character of which is not known; and the dissemination of information which may discredit a candidate for public office.[4]

Two Decades of IRS Harassment. It was 1977 before the IRS expressed satisfaction with the parade of answers, questions, explanations, and modifications of charter and procedure and restored—apparently unequivocally—the FCPC exemption, and a year later the patient was effectively dead of its chronic, pernicious, financial anemia. The struggle over exemption had proceeded through the administrations of Presidents Eisenhower, Kennedy, Johnson, Nixon, and Ford, with intercession from moderate and conservative members of both parties in both houses of Congress every step of the way.

The IRS letter revealed a petty and inflexible understanding of the scope of public education. The right to give money to other organizations was an utterly meaningless boilerplate provision easily dropped. The notion that FCPC intended to disseminate information that might discredit a candidate was pure misinterpretation.

The central and perennial sticking point for the IRS was inviting candidates to sign the code and treating it as a pledge. I came to feel that this practice, while useful, was not very important once the code became widely recognized as a reasonable standard, and I deemphasized it. Sam Archibald stressed it as a pledge more than I did. In time we had to scrap it.

The problem was that the IRS insisted that soliciting candidates to sign the code was intervention in their campaigns. Underlying this problem was section 501(c)(3) of the Internal Revenue Code, which defines the kinds of tax-exempt organizations to which contributions are tax-deductible. The section denies such exemption to any organization "which participates in, or intervenes in (including the publishing or distributing of statements), any political campaign on behalf of any candidate for public office."

The Missing Legislative History. Scholars and lawyers seeking to establish the intent of the Congress in this passage are out of luck, for there is no record of discussion or debate. Its only mention on the floor of either house appears in the *Congressional Record* for July 2, 1954 (p. 9604). A House-Senate conference committee was about to conclude a major revision of the Internal Revenue Code. The chief clerk of the Senate had just read the phrase quoted above, an amendment offered on the floor by the minority leader, Lyndon Johnson, who says of it:

I have discussed the matter with the chairman of the committee, the minority ranking member of the committee, and several other members of the committee, and I understand that the amendment is acceptable to them. I hope the chairman will take it to conference, and that it will be included in the final bill which Congress passes.

Mr. Millikin [chairman of the Senate Finance Committee]. Mr. President, I am willing to take the amendment to conference. I understand from the minority leader that the distinguished Senator from Georgia [Mr. George] feels the same way about it.

The Presiding Officer. The question is on agreeing to the amendment of the Senator from Texas [Mr. Johnson].
The amendment was agreed to.

501(c)(3): Backstage at the Creation. The invisible legislative history is this. Lyndon Johnson was seeking election to his second term in the Senate, where he already was minority leader. Back in Texas, he learned, pamphlets in the guise of "educational material" were attacking him. They were circulating under the auspices of a right-wing foundation that was tax-exempt. He discussed the problem informally with a number of colleagues, who agreed that tax-deductible charitable contributions should not be used to pay for campaign literature.

No one disagreed, and that principle never had a more enthusiastic advocate than the Fair Campaign Practices Committee. But it never had a more blindly zealous enforcer than the IRS bureaucrats who used it for nearly a generation to keep the FCPC off balance.

The committee was effectively dead at the end of the 1978 campaign. Sam Archibald left for a university faculty that promised regular and readily negotiable paychecks. Gallant volunteers maintained its files and, as long as possible, its information services. After consultations with Harry Selden, I went to Washington (from Chicago, where I was then living) to close the office. Then, at the suggestion of Evron Kirkpatrick, executive director of the American Political Science Association, I turned the files over to the political archive of Georgetown University.

Harry Selden, vice chairman and a founder, found a way to pay off— himself—the most outrageous debts and supported a mail address at the National Press Building for more than a decade, continuing long after his retirement from the Department of Health, Education, and Welfare. He and a volunteer executive in the person of the author of the code, Stewart McClure, by then retired from the Senate staff, continue to answer requests for copies of the code, information, and background. This is an act of generosity—on Selden's part over decades and costing him many thousands of dollars, and briefer but no less real on McClure's—that humbles me.

REESTABLISHING A FAIR CAMPAIGN PRACTICES COMMITTEE

Politicians, journalists, scholars, and reformers continue to inquire sporadically about resurrecting the FCPC. Anyone contemplating that prospect can learn important lessons from the fate of the original incarnation.

Money. The original Fair Campaign Practices Committee was founded without a source of seed money, a source committed to its being launched and supported for a period of years until it could become viable and develop its own financing mechanism. An entity of this kind enters the world without a natural constituency to keep it afloat until it can demonstrate its integrity and worth and become part of the establishment with enough momentum to sustain itself.

The best example of a precursor organization probably is the ill-fated Institute of Propaganda Analysis, whose demise came about for the extraneous reason of World War II. It was funded by the Filene Foundation. A few foundations, including Ford, helped modestly to maintain the FCPC, but only in its mid-career and at most to the tune of $20,000 over three years—and then only because it was thought useful "to keep a scholar in the field," as a Ford executive said.

A minimum of at least $150,000 annually (1990 dollars) for three to five years should be firmly committed as a precondition to any serious attempt to set up a new Fair Campaign Practices Committee.

Bipartisan Support. The absence of hard-headed conservative Republican support for the FCPC started it out under a handicap that it was never able to overcome completely. Its founders included Republicans whose conservatism was genuine enough but not conspicuous enough. To be a plausible objective interlocutor in the dialog of modern American political campaigns, solid, genuine, enthusiastic bipartisan support is a sine qua non.

Tax Exemption. The charter of any future Fair Campaign Practices Committee should be drawn up with the consultation and advice of the Director of Internal Revenue and his or her last living predecessor of the opposite political party, along with the chairman and ranking minority member of the congressional Joint Committee on Taxation. The zealots in the middle reaches of the IRS bureaucracy can best be fended off in advance and from above.

A charter should be drawn with a minimum of expansive, high-flown language, for every such benign phrase can be a booby trap. At several points in the history of the FCPC there was substantial interest on the part of members of both House and Senate in creating a congressional charter for the organization. But this would not guarantee tax exemption—could not do so legally. It should be considered as a possibility but not a necessity (or even necessarily desirable).

Staff. The first consideration in a staff head for a Fair Campaign Practices Committee should be some realistic experience of partisan electoral politics. At the same time, ardent partisanship or ardent commitment to a liberal or a conservative agenda should be an immediate disqualification. This position should under no circumstances be a first or second job for a young idealist or any job for a dedicated reformer. A well-worn and slightly jaded idealist might do.

The foregoing implies a certain maturity and some objectivity, and deliberately so. Experience in journalism or public relations would be useful, as also might be some background in campaign consultancy. For subordinate staff, neither idealism nor partisanship should be grounds for exclusion unless either is too passionately held. When picking staff for such an organization the model is a variation on Noah: two by two, one of each gender, or in this case, party.

Gender itself, or race, religion, or other distinctive attribute, is of no primary consideration whatever. However, such distinctions are a secondary consideration: the whole staff clearly should not be all of the same stripe— all male, all female, all black, all Catholic, Jewish, or agnostic, or all of any visible interest or ethnic group. A decent concern for variety of background, experience, and opinion would serve the organization well.

Location. Washington need not, and perhaps even *should* not, be the locus of a Fair Campaign Practices Committee. What goes on in Washington, and for candidates on the way to Washington, can in many respects be seen more clearly from outside the capital's famous Beltway.

Media Relations. During the existence of the original FCPC, journalists often sought to get the committee staff to declare that this or that campaign tactic was a smear. The committee's objective was to assemble verifiable, observable facts so that the media and the voter could draw their own informed conclusions. The FCPC never was authorized to make decisions for voters—or reporters. Often calls for the establishment of a new committee operate on the assumption that it did issue findings and make judgments. It did not. It served as a facilitator for the media and the electorate in arriving at their own judgments, and in any future incarnation it should do no more.

What Citizens Can Do

As politicians, journalists, scholars, and reformers often disbelieve, and perhaps more often forget, the American people are *not* fools, in the main. To paraphrase Lincoln's observation, all of them are vulnerable—some of the time—to an occasional con man, and some are always vulnerable. The rest are nearly as sensible as you and I. Eventually, the electorate tires of excess and will reward it with rejection. This goes even for the excesses of an invincible incumbent officeholder, an omniscient media, and any other excess of arrogance.

But because the citizens that make up the electorate do not live only for political news and opinions, it sometimes takes the voter a while to get up to speed on what's going on in the body politic. For that voter, an honest and neutral Fair Campaign Practices Committee, and its Code of Fair Campaign Practices, can be a useful yardstick for measuring campaign rhetoric.

A Revised Code

Absent such a committee and such a standard, I would offer the voter a condensed paraphrase of the original code, stripped to its essentials, bare of high-flown language, and augmented with additional points gleaned from years of wallowing in other people's deceit:

It is fair for any candidate to criticize an opponent's actual record.

Any new charge that is not germane to the office sought is mere static and an insult to the voter's intelligence.

Vilification, rumor campaigns, and attacks on any candidate's personal or family life are cowardly, dishonest, and unfair.

Distorting an opponent's record is dishonest and unfair. It is simply lying by another name. If it is true and relevant, it will be presented in context. That is, trust no vote or statement presented out of context.

Anybody who calls another candidate disloyal or a traitor without proof cannot be believed.

Race, religion, and ethnic background are irrelevant to public office in the United States.

Innuendo is a coward's way of lying.

Any charge made at the last minute is a lie, unless it is accompanied by proof— most unlikely—that it was only found out at the last minute.

An honest candidate will personally make any sensational charge against an opponent and will not rely on a surrogate.

An honest candidate will repudiate immediately and publicly anything on this list that irresponsilde supporters do *for* him or her or *against* the opposing candidate.

Regard every endorsement or attack on a candidate by any single-issue or special-interest group with suspicion. When in doubt call up the accused candidate's campaign office and ask for comment. Then use your judgment.

And good luck.

Notes

CHAPTER 1

1. Speech of Congressman Charles Ogle, reprinted in the *Log Cabin*, August 1, 1840.

CHAPTER 2

1. The films are in the archive of his son, Charles Benton of Public Media, Inc.

2. I am most grateful to Walter De Vries for putting me onto Quintus Cicero and his campaign manual.

3. I was one of the apprehensive observers in *Dirty Politics* (1966).

CHAPTER 3

1. James Thomson Callender, *The Prospect Before Us*, Part III, 58, and Preface, Part I, 179, quoted in Brodie 1974, 321.

2. Videotape copies of most of the significant political commercials of the television age are held by the Department of Political History at the Smithsonian Institution in Washington, D.C. Their curator is William L. (Larry) Bird and the department is headed by Keith Melder. Another important resource is the Political Commercial Archive at the University of Oklahoma, headed by Julian Kanter. The preeminent academic authority on political video is Kathleen Hall Jamieson, dean of the Annenberg School of Communication of the University of Pennsylvania.

Representative political video ads from the entire television era have been assembled on a series of videocassettes produced by the publishers of *Campaigns & Elections* magazine of Washington, D.C. These are held by sophisticated libraries and may be purchased from the publisher.

3. Jamieson, essay presented at her 1990 conference, "The Challenge of Creating an Informed Electorate," National Press Club, Washington, D.C., May 7, 1990.

4. In one of those frequent but unaccountable distortions that creep into scholarly recitals of campaign lore, Doyle Dane Bernbach's 1964 commercial showing the eastern seaboard being sawed off is described as being done with a power saw. In

the spot as it was aired, both visually and on the sound track, the sawing actually was done by a handsaw.

5. Ambiguities remain in the exploitation of the Willie Horton affair. The convict's name, race, and exploits were known to the Republican campaign manager, Lee Atwater, at the time of the focus group. Several "usually well-informed sources" among political reporters said he intended to "make a household word ["name," in some versions]" of Willie Horton. Atwater, shortly before he died of a cancerous brain tumor two years after the election, said he regretted the commercials and the focus on Horton. But this was Atwater in an obviously eschatological frame of mind, and the truth of the central elements—the paroled murderer, the rape and stabbing, the resonance of the affair in the electorate, and tensions between Atwater's campaign organization and "Americans for Bush" are uncontroverted.

Long after the campaign ended, "politically correct" critics continued to find fault with the ads, asserting that the Bush campaign called the killer-rapist "Willie Horton" in order, variously, to emphasize his race (compare such other Willies as Mays, Nelson, Sutton, Winkie, Wonka, et al.), and to diminish his human dignity (Germany's Brandt, California's Brown).

When Horton first came to public attention outside Massachusetts, he was identified as William Robert Horton in the *Washington Post* story of the Maryland shootout in which he was captured (April 8, 1987, p. D9). Subsequent stories in the *Boston Globe*, relying on prison records, consistently styled him William R. Horton, Jr., although an August 1, 1987, profile (p. 17) pointed out that Horton was "known as Willie." After the "Americans for Bush" ad appeared the following year, most of the media stuck with "Willie," although the more sober newspapers alternated the diminutive with the formal prison record styling of William R. Horton, Jr.

For his Maryland crimes Horton was sentenced to life in prison in that state, whose courts refused to return him to Massachusetts.

6. In a sample reel of his work. Joe Slade White Communications, New York City.

7. Remarks at League of Women Voters Education Fund symposium, "Positive Thinking About Negative Campaigning," Washington, D.C., May 11, 1990.

8. Produced by Ben Goddard, First Tuesday, then of Santa Monica, later Malibu, California, for Melcher's successful 1982 campaign. He was defeated fairly narrowly in 1988.

CHAPTER 4

1. My source for this oft-told tale is Sandburg (1939), and there are many others. Some modern revisionists assert that it did not happen. No committee minutes appear to survive, but abundant anecdotal evidence for the visit includes the account of "One member of the committee [who] told of what happened," as Sandburg (like several earlier sources) writes, and whom he quotes (1939, 200). The widespread suspicions of Mrs. Lincoln's loyalty, and the fact that three brothers of hers died in Confederate uniform, are uncontroverted.

CHAPTER 5

1. Jackson got shot at, too. He carried a bullet in him from a duel, and later an assassin fired two pistols at him point-blank; and both misfired (Remini 1988, 297)!

2. Conversation of author with Sam Archibald, November 1968.

3. One biographer suggests there were few others if any (Miller 1959).

4. Louis McLane, Delaware senator who became Jackson's secretary of the treasury (Remini 1988, 174).

5. As with all similar oral traditions, sources vary a trifle on the fidelity of Clay's paraphrase. The original line, in *Antony and Cleopatra* (Act 2, scene 2), is Enobarbus's description of Cleopatra and her infinite *variety*.

6. The *Washington Post* story was based on a *National Enquirer* article whose source was a former *Post* editor and friend of Mrs. Meyer, James Truitt. He confirmed the allegations when interviewed for the *Post* article.

7. "Alienist" began by alluding to his memories of "Mr. Greeley stumping the country for the Presidency and confident of his personal power with the people. I remember and, indeed, know well, the medical details of his final insanity and pathetic end."

8. "Alienist" showed an early distaste for negative campaigning.

9. Steffens's version was in response to a question from Bernard Baruch about the muckraker's trip with Bullitt: "I have been over into the future, and it works" (Steffens 1931).

10. The quotations from the Freud-Bullitt book are but a tiny sampling.

CHAPTER 6

1. Two were Roman Catholics, one a deist, and one was not known to have any religious affiliation. One was a minister; one was a lay preacher; three others had trained for the ministry; eleven had been educated by clergymen; and nine were deacons, elders, or vestrymen in their various churches.

2. The first two, relating to apportionment and congressional compensation, were rejected.

3. The Rev. Gerald E. Coughlin, the "radio priest" whose reactionary broadcasts were marked by anti-Semitic diatribes.

4. Hoover beat him badly, but almost no one noticed Smith's improvement over the even worse Democratic debacles of 1920 and 1924. The Democrat Cox, opposing Harding in 1920, polled only 35 percent of the two-party vote. In 1924, against the Republican Coolidge and the Progressive La Follette, the Democrat Davis slumped to 32 percent of the three-party vote. But Al Smith in 1928, for all the landslide of his Electoral College defeat, won significant gains for the Democrats by polling more than 39 percent of the popular vote.

5. Historians differ sharply on the truth or probability of the widely believed story that Jefferson fathered several children by Sally Hemings (whose name is sometimes spelled Heming). The leading proponent of the paternity school is Fawn M. Brodie of the University of California at Los Angeles, who assembled a most

cogent case in her Jefferson biography (Brodie 1974). After the president's death in 1826, but, N.B., not before, his descendants plausibly but not conclusively suggested that the dark lookalike had been sired by one of Jefferson's nephews Peter and Samuel Carr, both of whom lived at Monticello and reportedly confessed tearfully to continuing sexual relationships with Sally Hemings and her half-sister Betsey. This, the family said, accounted for the widely attested resemblance of the progeny to the president.

6. Chancellor was called on the carpet by his college's trustees, who fired him when he refused to disavow his tract.

7. See Betty Glad (1980), *Jimmy Carter: In Search of the Great White House.*

CHAPTER 7

1. Tuck is a brilliant spy and saboteur for mid-twentieth-century Democrats, whose exploits are addressed further in Chapter 10.

2. Who also copped the transcript of the story conference for the Democratic National Committee, which provided a copy to me.

3. In the U.S. Congress, tabling is *removing* a bill from consideration, putting it aside. In the British Parliament (as in other Commonwealth countries), to lay a bill upon the table is just the reverse: to take it up for consideration now.

4. Later Andrews became a reporter on the *Wall Street Journal* and a reporter and editor on the *New York Times.*

5. The Kennedy distortions and the bills involved are discussed in much more detail in *Dirty Politics* (Felknor 1966, 182–90. Additional relevant texts are included in appendixes. The Keating Senate speech on which Kennedy's surgeons did the most intricate reconstruction is there with the excerpts indicated. The original is also found at *Congressional Record*—Senate, September 23, 1963, pp. S17619–21.)

6. McGill, an old friend, obviously had not read the entire letter. Except for a "we" in a request for documentation and an "us" in receiving Keating's complaint, "I" was the only first-person pronoun in the letter.

7. Traditionally women, as verified by repeated polling, are more responsive than men to war-peace issues.

8. The House overwhelmingly adopted an Ethics Committee recommendation to reprimand Frank for the Gobie matter on July 26, 1990.

CHAPTER 8

1. The Republicans were swamped in 1964.

2. My source is correspondence and conversations with Riggs.

3. Butler served a lackluster two terms and retired voluntarily in 1962. He was something of a lackey to McCarthy during the latter's remaining few years. Stewart E. McClure, who was administrative assistant to Senator Guy Gillette in those days, remembers him during a roll call on some inconsequential bill McCarthy had introduced and then, for whatever reason, voted against. Another McCarthy ally, Herman Welker of Idaho, also voted Nay. Butler, who had voted Yea, rushed over to remonstrate with him: "But Herman, that was *Joe's* bill!" Butler was succeeded in the Senate by Tydings's stepson, Joseph D. Tydings, who won his nomination

after another bitter Democratic primary in which both sides generated more heat than light.

4. The journal presumably was dated at least five years earlier, since in 1839 Polk left Congress and the Speaker's chair to run successfully for governor of Tennessee.

CHAPTER 9

1. This was standard California practice until it was outlawed a decade later. Major candidates tried to get the nominations of both parties, and strenuous efforts were made to avoid partisan identification. Nixon angered many Democrats when he titled his first primary leaflet "As One Democrat to Another." The unofficial ground rules were a bit sophistic: it was proper to hide one's own party label, so people might think of a Republican as a Democrat; but it was morally wrong to come right out with a false statement about partisanship. Nixon's trick here was manifestly a false implication.

2. In fact, many House Democrats besides Marcantonio viewed Mrs. Douglas with distaste. One of these was John F. Kennedy, who during the 1950 Senate campaign handed Nixon a $1,000 contribution from his father, Joseph P. Kennedy.

3. Hall under interrogation by Senator Monroney. Note that Hall's point is a more restrained phrasing of Taft's (U.S. Senate Hearings [Ohio] 1951, 359).

4. The ACLU was founded in 1920 at the time of A. Mitchell Palmer's Great Red Scare, the Sacco-Vanzetti Case, manifold Negro lynchings, and industrial troops armed against union organizers. It defended absolute freedom of speech, religion, and association, and advocated no legislation. In the mid-1960s it began adopting legislative and other initiatives to redress economic inequities and in other ways radically broadened its goals beyond its original scope of defending civil liberties per se. These moves its founder, Roger Baldwin, thought badly mistaken: "Instead of supporting standards, we have played favorites with people who are disadvantaged. I understand it. I'm very sympathetic with it, but it destroys another principle. And they've chosen the wrong one." See William A. Donohue's *The Politics of the ACLU*, including its significant introduction by Aaron Wildavsky (Donohue 1985).

CHAPTER 10

1. The several strains of this event were confided to me (at the Fair Campaign Practices Committee) by various operatives and spies in both the Goldwater and Johnson camps.

2. Conversations of author with Roger Kent and other officials of the California Democratic State Central Committee, in 1962, 1963, and 1964, and documents filed with the Fair Campaign Practices Committee.

3. *Annual Report of the American Historical Association for the Year 1903*, Volume II. *Correspondence of the French Ministers to the United States, 1791–1797*. Adet's plan to swing the election to Jefferson was adumbrated as early as June, and subsequent reports to the French foreign minister accelerated in late October. See especially his letters at pp. 919–21, 954–59, 969–73, 982–83 (in French; notes in English).

4. Goland was sentenced to three months in a "jail-like institution" and 1,000 hours of community service by a judge who "said he meant to make Goland an example to deter others from such offenses" ("Goland Gets Jail Term for Illegal Campaign Gift," 1990).

5. Unsigned campaign literature in presidential or congressional elections was prohibited under the Criminal Code by 18 USC section 612. When the FEC was established this provision was repealed. A slightly different requirement, that whoever paid for the communication must be identified therein, was made part of Title 2 of the U.S. Code, which covers the Congress (at section 441d).

6. Later Robbie became the owner of the Miami Dolphins football team.

CHAPTER 11

1. Average family income was $573 a month and current-consumption expenditures $534; a theater ticket was worth from 25 cents to a dollar, and a congressman was paid $5,000 a year ($417 a month).

2. In his Blocks of Five letter, Col. Dudley went into meticulous detail in instructing his Hoosier agent. Material omitted from the excerpts on pages 157–58 included a warning against fraud from the other side:

Make our friends in each precinct wake up to the fact that only boodle, fraudulent votes, and false counting of returns can beat us in the State. Write each of our precinct correspondents, first, to find out who has Democratic boodle and steer the Democratic workers to them and make them pay big prices for their own men; second, scan the election officers closely, and make sure to have no men on the board whose loyalty to me is even questionable, and insist on Republicans watching every movement of the Democratic election officers; third, see that our workers know every Republican voter entitled to vote, and see that they do vote....

After the Blocks of Five instructions, Dudley turned to utilizing Republican volunteers for the psychological intimidation of greenhorn Democrats.

[F]ifth, make a personal appeal to the Republican business men to pledge themselves to devote the entire day, Nov. 6, to work at the polls, *i.e.*, to be present at the polls with tickets [Republican ballots]. They will be astonished to see how utterly dumfounded the naturalized Democratic voters will be, and how quickly they will disappear. The result will fully justify the sacrifice of time and comfort, and will be a source of satisfaction afterward to those who help in this way....

With a final exhortation to hard work and a reiterated promise of financial support, the colonel reminded his agent that, in effect, all this Republican fraud was a necessary weapon against the Democrats' demonstrated adeptness at fraud:

We will fight for a fair election here if necessary. The rebels and copperheads can't steal this election from us, as they did in 1884, without someone getting hurt. Let every Republican do his whole duty, and the country will pass into Republican hands never to leave it, I trust. ("The Political Campaign—Damaging Exposure of Republican Plots," 1888.)

3. Disdain notwithstanding, as Theodore H. White has observed, the speech's "success scored the mind of every realistic politician" (White 1975, 40).

4. Huey Long's use of National Guard troops in Louisiana, recounted earlier in this chapter, was not to intimidate but merely to prevent interference.

CHAPTER 12

1. Farrand 1966, 2:65.

2. The behavior of many of the Radicals dominating Congress was shabby and many of their claims were unconstitutional. For all that, Johnson confronted them straightforwardly, angrily, and in full light of day.

CHAPTER 13

1. In the First Congress the thirteen original states had a constitutionally apportioned sixty-five seats. The new states of Kentucky and Vermont were included in the first census, and Tennessee was admitted after the census and given one House seat. A seat was added for Ohio after the second census.

2. The nine-term veteran (Brown of Pennsylvania) went on to serve a thirteenth term, in the Fourteenth Congress. One of the four-term congressmen, Newton of Virginia, was elected to a sixteenth term in the Twenty-second Congress, although he was unseated by a challenger for most of the Twenty-first.

3. Harry S Truman, who as vice president succeeded President Roosevelt on his death in 1945, built his campaign for election to a full term of his own around his charge that the Eightieth, in which Richard Nixon was a freshman representative, was a "Do-Nothing Congress."

4. Committee chairs from Ornstein, Mann and Malbin, Table 4–6; Power Committees 84th–100th Congress from Loomis, 160; 101st Congress from *Congressional Directory* 1989.

5. Burdett Loomis is professor and chairman of political science at the University of Kansas.

6. Quoting John McCartney, "Congressional District Offices: Their Staff and Functions," paper presented at American Political Science Association, Washington, D.C., Aug. 31–Sept. 3, 1979, 48.

7. In 1991 the Senate, in a cosmetic gesture that may be extended superficially, granted limited access to the courts to some staff personnel.

8. Article I, Section 4 states, "The times, places and manner of holding elections for Senators and Representatives shall be prescribed in each State by the Legislature thereof; but the Congress may at any time by law make or alter such regulations." The suggestion was made by Stephen Glazier, a lawyer of New York and Washington, in the *Wall Street Journal*, June 19, 1990.

9. I am grateful to Herb Alexander for acquainting me with the "I don't know, and I don't care" joke.

CHAPTER 14

1. This does not include overnight news-oriented programs which on some networks compete with movies and revivalists for the small all-night audience.

2. Note that an actual front page contains the paper's large logotype, much white space, illustrations, and large headlines. It is by no means solidly packed with words.

3. Scholars identify "gatekeeping" as the role of media editors in deciding what stories get through the gate for attention by reporters.

CHAPTER 15

1. The squiggles that make the Gerrymander look absurd are the river forming the state line and the Atlantic coastline.

2. Buckley v. Valeo, 1976.

3. This was a biennial syndicated feature on the ethical level of the congressional and gubernatorial campaigns around the country, plus presidential campaigns in presidential years. I had begun it in 1964 for INA's predecessor, North American Newspaper Alliance.

4. Internal Revenue Commission to FCPC, December 4, 1958. The letter is in FCPC archives at Georgetown University.

Bibliography

BOOKS

Abbott, Lawrence F., ed. 1924. *The Letters of Archie Butt* [Taft's military aide]. Garden City, N.Y.: Doubleday, Page.

Abels, Jules. 1968. *The Degeneration of Our Presidential Election.* New York: Macmillan.

Adams, Charles Francis, ed. 1874–77. *Memoirs of John Quincy Adams.* 12 vols. Philadelphia: J. B. Lippincott Co.

Adams, John. 1961. *The Adams Papers: Diary and Autobiography of John Adams.* 4 vols. Edited by L. H. Butterfield. Cambridge, Mass.: Harvard University Press.

Adams, John, Abigail Adams, and Thomas Jefferson. 1959. *The Adams-Jefferson Letters.* 2 vols. Edited by Lester J. Cappon. Chapel Hill: University of North Carolina Press.

Adams, William C., ed. 1983. *Television Coverage of the 1980 Presidential Campaign.* Norwood, N.J.: Ablex.

Alexander, Herbert E. 1972. *Money in Politics.* Washington, D.C.: Public Affairs Press.

———. 1976, 1980, 1984. *Financing Politics: Money, Elections, and Political Reform.* 3d ed. Washington, D.C.: CQ Press.

———, ed. 1976. *Campaign Money: Reform and Reality in the States.* New York: Free Press.

American Council of Learned Societies. 1928–58. *Dictionary of American Biography.* 22 vols. New York: Charles Scribner's Sons.

American Historical Association (AHA). 1904. *Annual Report of the American Historical Association for the Year 1903. Seventh Report of the Historical Manuscript Commission. Correspondence of the French Ministers to the United States, 1791–1797.* 2 vols. Edited by Frederick J. Turner. Washington, D.C.: U.S. Government Printing Office.

Anderson, Totton J. 1969. "California: Enigmatic Eldorado of National Politics." In *Politics in the American West,* edited by Frank H. Jonas. Salt Lake City: University of Utah Press.

Barnouw, Erik. 1975. *Tube of Plenty: The Evolution of American Television.* New York: Oxford University Press.

Beer, Thomas. 1929. *Hanna*. New York: Alfred A. Knopf.

Bennett, Lance. 1983. *News: The Politics of Illusion*. New York: Longman.

Benson, Thomas W. 1983. "Implicit Communication Theory in Campaign Coverage." In *Television Coverage of the 1980 Presidential Campaign*, edited by William C. Adams. Norwood, N.J.: Ablex.

Bernstein, Carl, and Bob Woodward. 1974. *All the President's Men*. New York: Simon and Schuster.

Biographical Directory of the United States Congress 1774–1989: Bicentennial Edition. 1989. Washington, D.C.: U.S. Congress, Joint Committee on Printing, U.S. Government Printing Office.

Bitzer, Lloyd F. 1981. "Political Rhetoric." In *Handbook of Political Communication*, edited by Dan D. Nimmo and Keith R. Sanders. Beverly Hills and London: Sage Publications.

Boller, Paul F., Jr. 1984. *Presidential Campaigns*. New York: Oxford University Press.

Bowen, Catherine Drinker. 1966. *Miracle at Philadelphia: The Story of the Constitutional Convention May to September 1787*. Boston and Toronto: Little, Brown; Atlantic Monthly Press.

Bradford, M. E. 1982. *A Worthy Company*. Marlborough, N.H.: Plymouth Rock Foundation.

Bradlee, Benjamin C. 1975. *Conversations With Kennedy*. New York: Norton.

Brant, Irving. 1941–61. *James Madison*. 6 vols. Indianapolis: Bobbs-Merrill.

Broder, David S. 1972. *The Party's Over*. New York: Harper Colophon.

———. 1980. *Changing of the Guard*. New York: Simon and Schuster.

———. 1987. *Behind the Front Page: A Candid Look at How the News is Made*. New York: Simon and Schuster.

Brodie, Fawn M. 1974. *Thomas Jefferson: An Intimate History*. New York: Norton.

Brownson, Charles B., ed. 1959–90. *Congressional Staff Directory*. Mount Vernon, Va.: Congressional Staff Directory, Ltd.

Caro, Robert A. 1990. *Means of Ascent*. New York: Alfred A. Knopf.

Cash, W. J. 1941. *The Mind of the South*. New York: Alfred A. Knopf.

Cater, Douglass. 1959. *The Fourth Branch of Government*. Boston: Houghton Mifflin.

Chambers, Whittaker. 1952. *Witness*. New York: Random House.

Cicero, Quintus Tullius. 1853. "On Standing for the Consulship." In *The Treatises of M. T. Cicero*, ed. and trans. C. D. Youge. London: Henry G. Bohn.

Coyle, David Cushman. 1960. *Ordeal of the Presidency*. Washington, D.C.: Public Affairs Press.

Crouse, Timothy. 1973. *The Boys on the Bus*. New York: Random House.

DAB. 1928–58. *Dictionary of American Biography*. See American Council of Learned Societies, 1928–58.

Darrow, Clarence. 1970. "Realism in Literature and Art." In *The Land of Contrasts: 1880–1901*, edited by Neil Harris. New York: George Braziller.

Dean, John. 1976. *Blind Ambition*. New York: Simon and Schuster.

Denton, Robert E., Jr., and Gary C. Woodward. 1985. *Political Communication in America*. New York: Praeger Publishers.

Dictionary of American Biography, 1928–58. See American Council of Learned Societies, 1928–58.

Dinsmore, Herman H. 1969. *All the News That Fits*. New Rochelle, N.Y.: Arlington House.

Djilas, Milovan. 1957. *The New Class: An Analysis of the Communist System*. New York: Frederick A. Praeger, Inc.

Donohue, William A. 1985. *The Politics of the ACLU*. New Brunswick, N.J.: Transaction Books.

Dorman, Michael. 1979. *Dirty Politics from 1776 to Watergate*. New York: Delacorte Press.

Efron, Edith. 1971. *The News Twisters*. New York: Manor Books.

Elliott, Richard Smith. 1883, 1884. *Notes Taken in Sixty Years*. St. Louis: (by author) 1883. Boston: Cupples, Upham & Company, 1884.

Epstein, Edward Jay. 1973. *News from Nowhere: Television and the News*. New York: Vintage Books.

Exner, Judith, as told to Ovid Demaris. 1977. *My Story*. New York: Grove Press.

Farrand, Max, ed. 1911, 1937, 1966. *The Records of the Federal Convention of 1787*. Revised ed., 4 vols. New Haven: Yale University Press.

Felknor, Bruce L. 1966, 1975. *Dirty Politics*. New York: Norton, 1966; Westport, Conn.: Greenwood Press, 1975.

———. 1975. "Impeachment of a President." Special Report in *Britannica Book of the Year 1975*. Chicago: Encyclopaedia Britannica, Inc.

Findley, Paul. 1985. *They Dare to Speak Out: People and Institutions Confront Israel's Lobby*. Westport, Conn.: Lawrence Hill.

Flexner, James T. 1969. *Washington: The Indispensable Man*. Boston: Little, Brown.

Freud, Sigmund, and William C. Bullitt. 1967. *Thomas Woodrow Wilson, Twenty-eighth President of the United States: A Psychological Study*. Boston: Houghton Mifflin, and Cambridge: Riverside Press.

Friz, Richard. 1988. *Official Guide to Political Memorabilia*. New York: Random House.

Gans, Herbert J. 1980. *Deciding What's News*. New York: Vintage.

Gitlin, Todd. 1980. *The Whole World Is Watching: Mass Media in the Making and Unmaking of the New Left*. Berkeley: University of California Press.

Glad, Betty. 1980. *Jimmy Carter: In Search of the Great White House*. New York: Norton.

Graber, Doris A. 1989. *Mass Media and American Politics*. 3d ed. Washington, D.C.: CQ Press.

———. 1990. *Media Power and American Politics*. 2d ed. Washington, D.C.: CQ Press.

Greeley, Horace, ed. 1840–41. *The Log Cabin*. New York: (weekly).

Gresham, Matilda. 1919. *The Life of Walter Quintin Gresham*. 2 vols. New York: Rand McNally.

Gunderson, Robert Gray. 1957. *The Log Cabin Campaign*. Lexington: University of Kentucky Press.

Haldeman, H. R., with Joseph DiMona. 1978. *The Ends of Power*. New York: New York Times Books.

Haley, J. Evetts. 1964. *A Texan Looks at Lyndon*. Canyon, Tex.: Palo Duro Press.

Harris, Leon. 1975. *Upton Sinclair: American Rebel*. New York: Thomas Y. Crowell.

Heard, Alexander. 1960. *The Costs of Democracy*. Chapel Hill: University of North Carolina Press.

Herring, Pendleton. 1940, 1965. *The Politics of Democracy*. New York: Norton.

Hess, Stephen. 1981. *The Washington Reporters*. Washington, D.C.: Brookings Institution.

Hoffer, Eric. 1951, 1958. *The True Believer*. New York: Harper and Brothers, 1951; Mentor Books, 1958.

Hofstadter, Richard. 1962. *Anti-Intellectualism in American Life*. New York: Vintage Books.

———. 1963. "The Pseudo-Conservative Revolt—1955." In *The Radical Right*, edited by Daniel Bell. Garden City, N.Y.: Doubleday.

———. 1972. *The Idea of a Party System*. Berkeley: University of California Press.

Jamieson, Kathleen Hall. 1984. *Packaging the Presidency: A History and Criticism of Presidential Campaign Advertising*. New York: Oxford University Press.

———. 1988. *Eloquence in an Electronic Age: The Transformation of Political Speechmaking*. New York: Oxford University Press.

Jonas, Frank H. 1966. *The Story of a Political Hoax*. Salt Lake City: University of Utah Press.

———, ed. 1969. *Politics in the American West*. Salt Lake City: University of Utah Press.

———, ed. 1970. *Political Dynamiting*. Salt Lake City: University of Utah Press.

Jones, Stanley L. 1964. *The Presidential Election of 1896*. Madison: University of Wisconsin Press.

Josephson, Matthew. 1938. *The Politicos 1865–1896*. New York: Harcourt, Brace.

Kayden, Xandra, and Eddie Mahe, Jr. 1985. *The Party Goes On*. New York: Basic Books.

Kelley, Stanley, Jr. 1956. *Professional Public Relations and Political Power*. Baltimore: Johns Hopkins Press.

———. 1960. *Political Campaigning: Problems in Creating an Informed Electorate*. Washington, D.C.: Brookings Institution.

Kennedy, Stetson. 1946. *Southern Exposure*. New York: Doubleday.

Ladd, Everett Carl, Jr., and Seymour Martin Lipset. 1973. *Academics, Politics, and the 1972 Election*. Washington, D.C.: American Enterprise Institute.

Lasky, Victor. 1977. *It Didn't Start with Watergate*. New York: Dial Press.

Leech, Margaret. 1959. *In the Days of McKinley*. New York: Harper.

Lichter, S. Robert, Stanley Rothman, and Linda S. Lichter. 1986. *The Media Elite: America's New Power Brokers*. Bethesda, Md.: Adler & Adler.

Loomis, Burdett. 1988. *The New American Politician*. New York: Basic Books.

Lorant, Stefan. 1959. *The Life and Times of Theodore Roosevelt*. Garden City, N.Y.: Doubleday.

———. 1968. *The Glorious Burden: The American Presidency*. New York: Harper & Row.

McElroy, Neil. 1923. *Grover Cleveland: The Man and the Statesman*. New York: Harper and Brothers.

McGinniss, Joe. 1969, 1970. *The Selling of the President 1968*. New York: Trident Press, 1969; Pocket Books, 1970.

McMaster, John Bach. 1883–1913. *A History of the People of the United States,*

From the Revolution to the Civil War. 8 vols. New York: D. Appleton and Company.

MacNeil, Robert. 1968. *The People Machine.* New York: Harper & Row.

Mazo, Earl. 1959. *Richard Nixon.* New York: Harper.

Mencken, H. L. 1956. *A Carnival of Buncombe.* Baltimore: Johns Hopkins Press.

Meyer, Leland. 1932, 1967. *The Life and Times of Col. Richard M. Johnson of Kentucky.* Reprint, New York: AMS Press.

Michelson, Charles. 1947. *The Ghost Talks.* New York: G. P. Putnam's Sons.

Miller, John C. 1959. *Alexander Hamilton: Portrait in Paradox.* New York: Harper & Brothers.

Miller, Merle. 1973. *Plain Speaking: An Oral Biography of Harry S Truman.* New York: Berkley.

Miller, Robert Moats. 1958. *American Protestantism and Social Issues 1919–1939.* Chapel Hill: University of North Carolina Press.

Minnigerode, Meade. 1928. *Presidential Years 1787–1860.* New York: G. P. Putnam's Sons.

Minow, Newton, John Martin, and Lee Mitchell. 1973. *Presidential Television.* New York: Basic Books.

Mooney, Chase C. 1974. *William H. Crawford, 1772–1834.* Lexington: University of Kentucky Press.

Moore, Edmund A. 1956. *A Catholic Runs for President—The Campaign of 1928.* New York: Roland Press.

Morgan, Kay Summersby. 1976. *Past Forgetting: My Love Affair with Dwight D. Eisenhower.* New York: Simon and Schuster.

Morison, Samuel Eliot. 1965. *The Oxford History of the American People.* New York: Oxford.

Myers, Gustavus. 1943. *History of Bigotry in the United States.* New York: Random House.

Nevins, Allan. 1932. *Grover Cleveland: A Study in Courage.* New York: Dodd, Mead.

———, and Frank Weitenkampf. 1944. *A Century of Political Cartoons . . . 1800 to 1900.* New York: Charles Scribner's Sons.

Nimmo, Dan, and James E. Combs. 1980. *Subliminal Politics.* Englewood Cliffs, N.J.: Spectrum Books.

Nimmo, Dan D., and Keith R. Sanders, eds. 1981. *Handbook of Political Communication.* Beverly Hills and London: Sage Publications.

Nixon, Richard. 1978. *The Memoirs of Richard Nixon.* New York: Grossett & Dunlap.

———. 1990. *In the Arena: A Memoir of Victory, Defeat, and Renewal.* New York: Simon and Schuster.

O'Conner, Richard. 1970. *The First Hurrah.* New York: G. P. Putnam's Sons.

Official Congressional Directory. 1809– . Washington, D.C.: U.S. Government Printing Office.

O'Neill, Thomas P., Jr. 1987. *Man of the House.* New York: Random House.

Ornstein, Norman J., Thomas E. Mann, and Michael J. Malbin. 1989. *Vital Statistics on Congress, 1989–1990.* Washington, D.C.: Congressional Quarterly, Inc.

Peirce, Neal R., and Jerry Hagstrom. 1983. *The Book of America: Inside Fifty States Today.* New York: Norton.

Polsby, Nelson, and Aaron B. Wildavsky. 1964, 1968. *Presidential Elections*. 2d ed. New York: Charles Scribner's Sons.

Pringle, Henry F. 1921. *Theodore Roosevelt: A Biography*. New York: Harcourt Brace.

———. 1939. *The Life and Times of William Howard Taft*. 2 vols. New York: Farrar & Rinehart.

Reeves, Thomas C. 1982. *The Life and Times of Joe McCarthy*. New York: Stein and Day.

Remini, Robert V. 1988. *Life of Jackson*. New York: Harper & Row.

Richardson, James D., ed. 1911–14. *Messages and Papers of the Presidents*. Washington, D.C.: U.S. Congress, Joint Committee on Printing, 1897. Repaginated and indexed. New York: Bureau of National Literature.

Robinson, Michael J., and Margaret Sheehan. 1983. "Traditional Ink vs. Modern Video Versions of Campaign '80." In *Television Coverage of the 1980 Presidential Campaign*, edited by William C. Adams. Norwood, N.J.: Ablex.

Roosevelt, Theodore. 1952. *Letters of Theodore Roosevelt*. 8 vols. Edited by Elting E. Morison. Cambridge, Mass.: Harvard University Press.

Rosten, Leo. 1937. *The Washington Correspondents*. New York: Harcourt Brace.

Russell, Charles Edward. 1931. *Blaine of Maine: His Life and Times*. New York: Cosmopolitan Book Corp.

Russell, Francis. 1968. *The Shadow of Blooming Grove*. New York: McGraw-Hill.

Sabato, Larry J. 1981. *The Rise of Political Consultants*. New York: Basic Books.

Saloma, John S., III, and Fredrick H. Sontag. 1972. *Parties: The Real Opportunity for Effective Citizen Politics*. New York: Knopf.

Sandburg, Carl. 1926. *Abraham Lincoln: The Prairie Years*. 2 vols. New York: Harcourt, Brace.

———. 1939. *Abraham Lincoln: The War Years*. 4 vols. New York: Harcourt, Brace.

Scammon, Richard M., and Ben J. Wattenberg. 1970. *The Real Majority*. New York: Coward-McCann.

Schlesinger, Arthur M., Jr. 1960. *The Politics of Upheaval*. Boston: Houghton Mifflin.

Schouler, James. 1889–99. *History of the United States of America Under the Constitution*. 6 vols. New York: Dodd, Mead & Co.

Schudson, Michael. 1978. *Discovering the News: A Social History of American Newspapers*. New York: Basic Books.

Schwartz, Bernard, ed. 1971. *The Roots of the Bill of Rights*. 5 vols. New York: Chelsea House.

Scoble, Harry M. 1967. *Ideology and Electoral Action: A Comparative Case Study of the National Committee for an Effective Congress*. San Francisco: Chandler Publishing Company.

Sinclair, Upton. 1935. *I, Candidate for Governor, and How I Got Licked*. New York: Farrar & Rinehart.

Smith, Gene. 1964. *When the Cheering Stopped*. New York: William Morrow.

Smith, Page. 1962. *John Adams*. 2 vols. Garden City, N.Y.: Doubleday.

Snider, William D. 1985. *Helms & Hunt: The North Carolina Senate Race, 1984*. Chapel Hill: University of North Carolina Press.

Sorensen, Theodore C. 1965. *Kennedy*. New York: Harper and Row.

Steffens, Lincoln. 1931. *The Autobiography of Lincoln Steffens*. 2 vols. New York: Harcourt, Brace.

Stoddard, Henry Luther. 1946. *Horace Greeley: Printer, Editor, Crusader*. New York: G. P. Putnam's Sons.

Tivnan, Edward. 1987. *The Lobby: Jewish Political Power and American Foreign Policy*. New York: Simon and Schuster.

U.S. Bureau of the Census. 1960. *Historical Statistics of the United States, Colonial Times to 1957*. Washington, D.C.: U.S. Government Printing Office.

U.S. Congress (House). 1961. *Inaugural Addresses of the Presidents of the United States*. 87th Cong., 1st sess., H. Doc. 218.

Van Deusen, G. G. 1953. *Horace Greeley, 19th Century Crusader*. Philadelphia: University of Pennsylvania.

Wade, Wyn Craig. 1987. *Fiery Cross: The Ku Klux Klan in America*. New York: Simon and Schuster.

Werner, M. R. 1929. *Bryan*. New York: Harcourt, Brace.

White, Theodore H. 1961. *The Making of the President 1960*. New York: Atheneum.

———. 1965. *The Making of the President 1964*. New York: Atheneum.

———. 1969. *The Making of the President 1968*. New York: Atheneum.

———. 1973. *The Making of the President 1972*. New York: Atheneum.

———. 1975. *Breach of Faith: The Fall of Richard Nixon*. New York: Atheneum.

Wildavsky, Aaron. 1985. Foreword to *The Politics of the ACLU*, by William A. Donohue. New Brunswick, N.J.: Transaction Books.

Williams, Burton J. 1972. *Senator John James Ingalls: Kansas' Iridescent Politician*. Lawrence: University Press of Kansas.

Williams, T. Harry. 1970. *Huey Long and the Politics of Realism*. New York: Alfred A. Knopf.

Wilson, Edith Bolling. 1939. *My Memoir*. Indianapolis and New York: Bobbs-Merrill.

ARTICLES AND CONGRESSIONAL PROCEEDINGS

"American Campaign Consulting: Trends and Concerns." 1989. Walter De Vries, *PS: Political Science & Politics* 12 (March), pp. 21–22.

"Biden's Debate Finale: An Echo From Abroad." 1987. Maureen Dowd, *New York Times*, September 12, p. 1.

AP Dispatch No. 280. 1964. Syracuse, N.Y., September 20. Associated Press.

"Bryan's Mental Condition." 1896. "Alienist" (letter to the editor), *New York Times*, September 27, p. 12.

"Business Announcement." 1896. (Lead editorial) *New York Times*, August 19.

"Campaign Morals." 1950. (Editorial) *New York Times*, November 1, p. 34.

"Clearing the Air." 1919. William C. Bullitt (letter to Woodrow Wilson, reprinted), *The Nation*, May 31, p. 859.

"The Correspondents After 25 Years." 1962. William L. Rivers, *Columbia Journalism Review* 1 (Spring), p. 5.

"Dirty Campaigns 1978: '76's Record Low Equalled." 1978. Bruce L. Felknor, North American Newspaper Alliance, November 8.

"An Edge for Incumbents: Loopholes That Pay Off." 1990. Richard L. Berke, *New York Times*, March 20, p. 1.

"Election '80: Dirty at the Top; Below That, Cleanest in Decades." 1980. Bruce L. Felknor, Independent Newspaper Alliance, October 30.

"The Essential Quality." 1960. Marquis Childs, *New York Post*, March 28, p. 28.
"Films and Politics—Hollywood Masses the Full Power of Her Resources to Fight Sinclair." 1934. (Staff reporter) *New York Times*, November 4, sec. 9, p. 5.
"Free at Last, Free at Last." 1988. James Reston, *New York Times*, November 8, p. 27.
"Goldwater Awarded $75,000 in Damages in His Suit for Libel." 1968. Edward C. Burks, *New York Times*, May 25, p. 1.
"Goland Gets Jail Term For Illegal Campaign Gift." 1990. Kenneth Reich, *Los Angeles Times*, July 17, p. A3.
"Haddam Home of Hardings." 1920. *New York Times*, August 22, sec. 2, p. 1.
"In India, the Star of Video is the Candidate." 1991. Barbara Crossette, *New York Times*, April 30, p. A5.
"In the Nation: The Inflammatory Use of a National Chairman." 1944. Arthur Krock, *New York Times*, July 25, p. 18.
"Is Bryan Crazy?" 1896. (Editorial) *New York Times*, September 27, p. 12.
"Is Mr. Bryan a Mattoid." 1896. (News story) *New York Times*, September 29.
"JFK Had Affair With D.C. Artist, Smoked 'Grass,' Paper Alleges." 1976. Don Oberdorfer, *Washington Post*, February 23, p. A1.
"Keating Statements In Cuban Crisis Were Inaccurate, Kennedy Says." 1964. Joseph V. Ganley, *Syracuse Herald Journal*, October 20.
"Law." 1990. (Roundup article) *Wall Street Journal*, August 16, p. B5.
"McGovern Paid the Price for Rhetorical Excesses." 1972. Bruce L. Felknor, North American Newspaper Alliance, November 11/12.
"Media Leaders Want Less Influence." 1976. Barry Sussman *Washington Post*, September 29, p. A1.
Mencken, H. K. 1943. *Heathen Days—1890—1936*. New York: Alfred A. Knopf.
"Mr. Bryan as Revealed by His Speeches." 1896. Franklin Matthews, *Harper's Weekly*, 40 (September 26), pp. 947–50.
The Next in Order—Any Thing! Oh, Any Thing!" 1872 (cartoon). Thomas Nast, *Harper's Weekly*, September 14, p. 713 (front cover).
"1974 Campaign: Piety and Post-Watergate Moralizing." 1974. Bruce L. Felknor, NANA Release 11–8–74. New York: North American Newspaper Alliance, November 8.
"1960—When Johnson Told Dixie His Views." 1965. Peter Lisagor, *Chicago Daily News*, March 20, p. 17.
"The Peril of an Insane Administration." 1912. Allan McLane Hamilton, M.D., *New York Times*, May 12, sec. 6, p. 1.
"The Pillow Fight, With a Keg of Horseshoes in Reserve." 1958. (Editorial cartoon) Carey Orr, *Chicago Tribune*, September 6, p. 1.
"The Political Campaign—Damaging Exposure of Republican Plots." 1888. *New York Times*, October 31, p. 5.
"Pro-Israel Political Donor is Convicted of Trying to Sabotage Senate Campaign." 1990. John J. Fialka, *Wall Street Journal*, May 7, 1990, p. A16.
"Psychopathology and Politics." 1912. (Editorial) *New York Times*, May 12.
"The Reporter's Notes—Kennedy vs. Keating (con[tinued])." 1964. *The Reporter* (magazine), November 5, p. 12.
"Roosevelt as Analyzed by the New Psychology." 1912. Morton Prince, M.D., *New York Times*, March 24, sec. 6, p. 1.

"Sex Sold From Congressman's Apartment." 1989. Paul M. Rodriguez, *Washington Times*, August 25, p. 1.

"Stealing an Election." 1982. Sydney H. Schanberg, *New York Times*, October 23, p. 17.

"Strategic Politicians and the Dynamics of U.S. House Elections, 1946–86." 1989. Gary C. Jacobson, *American Political Science Review* 83:3 (September), pp. 773–93.

"Teetering Piles of 'Proof.' " 1964. Robert Sherrill, *Fair Comment* 1 (October).

"Topics of the Times." 1912. (Regular editorial page feature, this addressing Theodore Roosevelt's sanity) *New York Times*, March 23, p. 12.

"TV and Press in Politics." 1957. Bruce L. Felknor in Edmund Carpenter and Marshall McLuhan, eds., *Explorations* 7 (March).

"TV at Political Conventions." 1957. Robert F. Bradford in Edmund Carpenter and Marshall McLuhan, eds., *Explorations* 7 (March).

U.S. Congress. 1873– . *Congressional Record*. Washington, D.C.: U.S. Government Printing Office.

U.S. Senate Hearings. 1951. Maryland Senate Election of 1950. 82nd Cong., 1st sess. Subcommittee on Privileges and Elections, Committee on Rules and Administration.

———. 1951. Ohio Senate Election of 1951. 82nd Cong., 1st sess. Subcommittee on Privileges and Elections, Committee on Rules and Administration.

———. 1951. Establishment of a Commission on Ethics in Government. 82nd Cong., 1st sess. Subcommittee to Study Senate Concurrent Resolution 21 of the Committee on Labor and Public Welfare.

———. 1973. Presidential Campaign Activities of 1972. 93rd Cong., 1st sess. Select Committee on Presidential Campaign Activities of 1972. Book 7. Testimony of Harry Robbins Haldeman.

"We're Talking the Wrong Language to 'TV Babies.' " 1990. Robert W. Pittman, *New York Times*, January 24, p. A15.

"What Psychiatrists Have to Say About Goldwater." 1964. Warren Boroson, *Fact* (magazine), September-October, pp. 24–64.

POLITICAL TELEVISION ADS

Note: the entries in this section are arranged in the following order: producer's title (in most cases); date; party identification of sponsor or beneficiary; name of opposing candidate; office sought; formal sponsor; producer (where known); and an archive holding the film or videotape. "*C&E*" identifies ads in the three video cassettes of *Campaigns & Elections* magazine, which are listed below as Classics of Political Advertising (*C&E* 1), Power for Tomorrow (*C&E* 2), and Prime Time Politics (*C&E* 3).

Arm's Length TV. 1952 (Adlai Stevenson all but apologizing for using the medium.) Democrats vs. Eisenhower, President. Volunteers for Stevenson. (*C&E* 1)

Beard—"Castro." 1982. (Castro grateful for implied aid.) Republicans vs. Sasser,

U.S. Senate (Tennessee). (No citation) Nashville: Eric Ericson. (*C&E* 1, Smith-
    sonian)
Benton of Connecticut. 1950. (Pioneering campaign video.) Democrats vs. (Prescott)
    Bush, U.S. Senate (Connecticut). (*C&E* 3, private archive of Charles Benton)
Bombing the Bus. 1982. (Opposition to nuclear test ban treaty could lead to nuclear
    disaster.) Citizens for Common Sense in National Defense vs. Michel, U.S.
    House of Representatives (Illinois). Paid for by Citizens for Common Sense
    in National Defense. (Smithsonian)
Choice. 1964. ("Documentary" attributing riotous and lascivious public conduct to
    moral decadence of candidate.) Republicans vs. Johnson, President. Mothers
    for a Moral America. Raymond R. Morgan. N.B.: the film was repudiated
    by Goldwater and never broadcast. (Fair Campaign Practices Committee
    archive, Political Commercial Archive, University of Oklahoma)
Classics of Political Advertising. 1986. VCR cassette of campaign spots, narrated
    by former Senator Eugene McCarthy. Available from producer. Washington,
    D.C.: *Campaigns & Elections* magazine. (*C&E* 1)
Daisy. 1964. (Candidate likely to start nuclear war.) Democrats vs. Goldwater,
    President. Vote for President Johnson on November 3. New York: Doyle
    Dane Bernbach (*C&E* 1)
Death Squads. 1984. (Attacking candidate's friendship for Salvadorean rightist.)
    Democrats vs. Helms, U.S. Senate (North Carolina). Washington, D.C.: Ringe
    Media. (Smithsonian)
Eastern Seaboard. 1964. (Satirizing candidate's distaste for the effete East.) Dem-
    ocrats vs. Goldwater, President. Vote for President Johnson on November 3.
    New York: Doyle Dane Bernbach. (*C&E* 1; Smithsonian)
Fed Up. 1988. (Defense against distortions by opposing candidate.) Democrats vs.
    Bush, President. Paid for by Dukakis-Bentsen Committee, Inc. (Smithsonian)
Furlough from Truth. 1988. (Associating opposing candidate with furlough of es-
    caped rapist-murderer.) Democrats vs. Bush, President. Paid for by Dukakis-
    Bentsen Committee, Inc. (*C&E* 3; Smithsonian)
Hound Dogs. 1982. (Tracking down invisible candidate.) Republicans vs. Mc-
    Connell, U.S. Senate (Kentucky). Auth. by McConnell Sen. Comm. Pd. by
    Nat'l Rep. Sen. Comm. New York: Ailes Communications. (*C&E* 1; Smith-
    sonian)
Humphrey Laughing. 1968. (Candidate amused while surrounded by death and
    violence.) Republicans vs. Humphrey, President. (No citation) (*C&E* 3;
    Smithsonian)
Ike: Simple Answers. 1952. (Platitudinous homilies responding to simple queries.)
    Republicans vs. Stevenson, President. Citizens for Eisenhower. Rosser Reeves.
    (*C&E* 1)
Ike on Nixon. 1960. (Satirizing president's seeming dismissal of candidate's ability.)
    Democrats vs. Eisenhower, President. Citizens for Kennedy. (*C&E* 1; UCLA
    Film Archive)
In-Box. 1986. (Congressman absent while public business piles up.) Democrats vs.
    (a mythical) Borman, U.S. House of Representatives (a model spot for em-
    ulation and adaptation). Democratic Media Center, with introduction by
    Tony Coelho, chairman, Democratic Congressional Campaign Committee.
    Washington, D.C.: John Franzen Multimedia. (*C&E* 2; Smithsonian)

I Want To Live. 1982. (Opposition to nuclear test ban treaty could lead to nuclear disaster.) Democrats vs. Wilson, U.S. Senate (California). (Political Commercial Archive, University of Oklahoma)

JFK at Houston. 1960. (John Kennedy's address to Houston Ministerial Association answering apprehensions of Protestants about his Catholicism.) Democrats vs. Nixon, President. Citizens for Kennedy. (John F. Kennedy Library, Boston)

Lie Detector. 1980. (Stressing candidate's purported dishonesty.) Democrats vs. Pauken, U.S. House of Representatives (Texas). Paid for by Jim Mattox Finance Committee. Dallas: Mandate Campaign Media. (*C&E* 1; Smithsonian)

Nixon Weather Vane. 1968. (Classical theme emphasizing candidate's purported ambivalence on issues.) Democrats vs. Nixon, President. A pre-recorded political announcement paid for by Citizens for Humphrey-Muskie. New York: Doyle Dane Bernbach. (*C&E* 1; Smithsonian)

Packaging Bush and Quayle. 1988. (Political hacks in smoke-filled room try to make candidate look worthy.) Democrats vs. Bush and Quayle, President and Vice President. (Four spots ridiculing Bush and one Quayle.) Paid for by Dukakis-Bentsen Committee, Inc. (Smithsonian)

Prime Time Politics: New Directions in Political TV Advertising. 1989. VCR cassette of excerpts from significant campaign spots of broadcast history, plus a series of interviews with political consultants narrated by Ken Bodé, director of the DePauw University Center for Contemporary Media. Available from producer. Washington, D.C.: *Campaigns & Elections* magazine. (*C&E* 3)

Power for Tomorrow: Political Television Advertising Classics 1986. VCR cassette of 1986 campaign spots, narrated by former Senator Eugene McCarthy; political consultant Montague Kern. Unedited spots used in 1986 campaigns. Available from producer. Washington, D.C.: *Campaigns & Elections* magazine. (*C&E* 2)

Revolving Door. 1988. (Attributing weekend furlough of unnamed murderer to candidate.) Republicans vs. Dukakis, President. Paid for by Bush-Quayle 88. Milwaukee: Frankenberry, Laughlin & Constable. (*C&E* 3; Smithsonian)

Rifle. 1970. (Candidate shown handing AK–47 to Vietcong.) Roudebush vs. Hartke, U.S. Senate (Indiana). (Political Commercial Archive, University of Oklahoma)

Sasser Against Prayer. 1982. (Interpreting alleged Senate votes as anti-prayer bias.) Republicans vs. Sasser, U.S. Senate (Tennessee). Paid for by National Republican Senatorial Committee. (Smithsonian)

Strontium–90. 1964. (Imputing nuclear irresponsibility to candidate.) Democrats vs. Goldwater, President. Vote for President Johnson on November 3. New York: Doyle Dane Bernbach. (Smithsonian)

Talking Cow. 1982. (Homespun defense against attacks by Eastern politicians.) Democrats vs. Williams and (especially) NCPAC, U.S. Senate (Montana). Paid for by Melcher for Senate Committee. Phoenix (later Malibu, California): First Tuesday. (*C&E* 1; Smithsonian)

Too Liberal. 1982. (Describing senator as too liberal for state.) NCPAC vs. Melcher, U.S. Senate (Montana). National Conservative PAC. (Smithsonian)

Toyota Hall. 1984. (Revealing that Michigan candidate owns Japanese car despite auto industry depression.) Democrats vs. Loudsma, U.S. Senate (Michigan).

Paid for by Friends of Sen. Carl Levin, Ruth Broder, Treas. Washington, D.C.: J. Buckley & Associates. (*C&E* 1; Smithsonian)

Weekend Passes. 1988. (Naming Willie Horton as murderer who escaped on weekend furlough, subject of "Revolving Door," above.) National Security PAC vs. Dukakis, President. Political Message Paid by National Security PAC. Not Authorized by Any Candidate or Candidate's Committee. Washington, D.C.: Larry McCarthy. (*C&E* 3; Smithsonian)

Woods/Danforth. 1982. (Using candidate's own ads against him.) Democrats vs. Danforth, U.S. Senate (Missouri). Paid for by Woods for Senate Committee. New York: Joe Slade White Communications, Inc. (*C&E* 2; Smithsonian)

General Index

Acheson, Dean, 128, 201
ACLU. *See* American Civil Liberties Union
Adams, John, 15–16, 146; on caucus, 3–4; slurs against, 16; distaste for Alexander Hamilton, 31; on Hamilton's sexual appetite, 67; warns of foreign meddling in U.S. elections, 146
Adams, John Quincy, l50, 185; on excesses of 1840 campaign, 17–18; on political slurs as cause of voter alienation, 110
Adet, Pierre-Auguste (French ambassador), interferes in 1796 election, 145–46, 243 n.3 (Chap. 10)
Agree, George E., 228–29, 230
AIPAC (American Israel Public Affairs Committee): great influence on U.S. foreign policy, 148–50; claims credit for Findley defeat (1982), 149; on AIPAC power, 150. *See also* Goland, Michael R; Percy, Charles H.
Albany Register, and Madison and Jefferson as French, 146
Alexander, Herbert E.: authority on election finance, 156–57; on campaign advantages of wealth, 159
"Alienist," finds Bryan insane (1896), 75

Allen, O. K., governor as tool of Huey Long, 163
American Civil Liberties Union (ACLU): lightning rod for conservatives, 136; increase in activism after 1960, 243 n.4 (Chap. 9)
American Historical Association, Adet plot detailed, 146
American Israel Public Affairs Committee. *See* AIPAC
American League for a Free Palestine, and origins of NCEC, 228
American Medical Association, 74
American Psychiatric Association, 74
American Psychological Association, 74
American Republican Party (1844), 84
Americans for Bush (1988), Willie Horton ad sponsor, 40
Americans for Democratic Action (ADA), falsely depicted as pro-Communist, 112
Americans United. *See* POAU
Anderson, Earl, 152
Andrews, Frederick F. (FCPC researcher), and Kennedy-Keating Senate campaign (New York, 1964), 102, 105
Anti-black bias, of Ku Klux Klan, 86

Index of Mischief

For the reader's convenience, certain elements of political mischief are indexed separately, as follows: Invective and Accusations, Tactics, Special Media, and Techniques. A final section indexes the elections in which they occurred.

INVECTIVE AND ACCUSATIONS

About the Author

BRUCE L. FELKNOR is a well-known expert on election practices, the author of *Dirty Politics*, co-author of *Political Dynamiting*, and editor of *The U.S. Government: How and Why It Works*. He is the author of several other books and many articles on unfair electioneering. Felknor served as Executive Director of the Fair Campaign Practices Committee, Inc., from the mid–1950s to the 1960s and was Executive Editor for years of the *Encyclopaedia Britannica*.